Andrey Makarychev,
Alexandra Yatsyk (eds.)

BORIS NEMTSOV AND RUSSIAN POLITICS

Power and Resistance

With a foreword by Zhanna Nemtsova

ibidem-Verlag
Stuttgart

Bibliografische Information der Deutschen Nationalbibliothek
Die Deutsche Nationalbibliothek verzeichnet diese Publikation in der Deutschen Nationalbibliografie; detaillierte bibliografische Daten sind im Internet über http://dnb.d-nb.de abrufbar.

Bibliographic information published by the Deutsche Nationalbibliothek
Die Deutsche Nationalbibliothek lists this publication in the Deutsche Nationalbibliografie; detailed bibliographic data are available in the Internet at http://dnb.d-nb.de.

Cover picture: Vladimir Putin with Boris Nemtsov, leader of the Union of Right Forces parliamentary party. 04. July 2000. © Kremlin.ru via Wikimedia Commons. Licensed under CC by 4.0 (s. https://creativecommons.org/licenses/by/4.0/deed.en).

∞

Gedruckt auf alterungsbeständigem, säurefreien Papier
Printed on acid-free paper

ISSN: 1614-3515

ISBN-13: 978-3-8382-1122-0

© *ibidem*-Verlag
Stuttgart 2018

Alle Rechte vorbehalten

Das Werk einschließlich aller seiner Teile ist urheberrechtlich geschützt. Jede Verwertung außerhalb der engen Grenzen des Urheberrechtsgesetzes ist ohne Zustimmung des Verlages unzulässig und strafbar. Dies gilt insbesondere für Vervielfältigungen, Übersetzungen, Mikroverfilmungen und elektronische Speicherformen sowie die Einspeicherung und Verarbeitung in elektronischen Systemen.

All rights part of this publication may be reproduced, stored in or introduced into a retrieval system, or transmitted, in any form, or by any means (electronical, mechanical, photocopying, recording or otherwise) without the prior written permission of the publisher. Any person who does any unauthorized act in relation to this publication may be liable to criminal prosecution and civil claims for damages.

Printed in the EU

Soviet and Post-Soviet Politics and Society (SPPS) Vol. 181
ISSN 1614-3515

General Editor: Andreas Umland,
Institute for Euro-Atlantic Cooperation, Kyiv, umland@stanfordalumni.org

Commissioning Editor: Max Jakob Horstmann,
London, mjh@ibidem.eu

EDITORIAL COMMITTEE*

DOMESTIC & COMPARATIVE POLITICS
Prof. **Ellen Bos**, *Andrássy University of Budapest*
Dr. **Ingmar Bredies**, *FH Bund, Brühl*
Dr. **Andrey Kazantsev**, *MGIMO (U) MID RF, Moscow*
Prof. **Heiko Pleines**, *University of Bremen*
Prof. **Richard Sakwa**, *University of Kent at Canterbury*
Dr. **Sarah Whitmore**, *Oxford Brookes University*
Dr. **Harald Wydra**, *University of Cambridge*

SOCIETY, CLASS & ETHNICITY
Col. **David Glantz**, *"Journal of Slavic Military Studies"*
Dr. **Marlène Laruelle**, *George Washington University*
Dr. **Stephen Shulman**, *Southern Illinois University*
Prof. **Stefan Troebst**, *University of Leipzig*

POLITICAL ECONOMY & PUBLIC POLICY
Prof. em. **Marshall Goldman**, *Wellesley College, Mass.*
Dr. **Andreas Goldthau**, *Central European University*
Dr. **Robert Kravchuk**, *University of North Carolina*
Dr. **David Lane**, *University of Cambridge*
Dr. **Carol Leonard**, *Higher School of Economics, Moscow*
Dr. **Maria Popova**, *McGill University, Montreal*

FOREIGN POLICY & INTERNATIONAL AFFAIRS
Dr. **Peter Duncan**, *University College London*
Prof. **Andreas Heinemann-Grüder**, *University of Bonn*
Dr. **Taras Kuzio**, *Johns Hopkins University*
Prof. **Gerhard Mangott**, *University of Innsbruck*
Dr. **Diana Schmidt-Pfister**, *University of Konstanz*
Dr. **Lisbeth Tarlow**, *Harvard University, Cambridge*
Dr. **Christian Wipperfürth**, *N-Ost Network, Berlin*
Dr. **William Zimmerman**, *University of Michigan*

HISTORY, CULTURE & THOUGHT
Dr. **Catherine Andreyev**, *University of Oxford*
Prof. **Mark Bassin**, *Södertörn University*
Prof. **Karsten Brüggemann**, *Tallinn University*
Dr. **Alexander Etkind**, *University of Cambridge*
Dr. **Gasan Gusejnov**, *Moscow State University*
Prof. em. **Walter Laqueur**, *Georgetown University*
Prof. **Leonid Luks**, *Catholic University of Eichstaett*
Dr. **Olga Malinova**, *Russian Academy of Sciences*
Prof. **Andrei Rogatchevski**, *University of Tromsø*
Dr. **Mark Tauger**, *West Virginia University*

ADVISORY BOARD*

Prof. **Dominique Arel**, *University of Ottawa*
Prof. **Jörg Baberowski**, *Humboldt University of Berlin*
Prof. **Margarita Balmaceda**, *Seton Hall University*
Dr. **John Barber**, *University of Cambridge*
Prof. **Timm Beichelt**, *European University Viadrina*
Dr. **Katrin Boeckh**, *University of Munich*
Prof. em. **Archie Brown**, *University of Oxford*
Dr. **Vyacheslav Bryukhovetsky**, *Kyiv-Mohyla Academy*
Prof. **Timothy Colton**, *Harvard University, Cambridge*
Prof. **Paul D'Anieri**, *University of Florida*
Dr. **Heike Dörrenbächer**, *Friedrich Naumann Foundation*
Dr. **John Dunlop**, *Hoover Institution, Stanford, California*
Dr. **Sabine Fischer**, *SWP, Berlin*
Dr. **Geir Flikke**, *NUPI, Oslo*
Prof. **David Galbreath**, *University of Aberdeen*
Prof. **Alexander Galkin**, *Russian Academy of Sciences*
Prof. **Frank Golczewski**, *University of Hamburg*
Dr. **Nikolas Gvosdev**, *Naval War College, Newport, RI*
Prof. **Mark von Hagen**, *Arizona State University*
Dr. **Guido Hausmann**, *University of Munich*
Prof. **Dale Herspring**, *Kansas State University*
Dr. **Stefani Hoffman**, *Hebrew University of Jerusalem*
Prof. **Mikhail Ilyin**, *MGIMO (U) MID RF, Moscow*
Prof. **Vladimir Kantor**, *Higher School of Economics*
Dr. **Ivan Katchanovski**, *University of Ottawa*
Prof. em. **Andrzej Korbonski**, *University of California*
Dr. **Iris Kempe**, *"Caucasus Analytical Digest"*
Prof. **Herbert Küpper**, *Institut für Ostrecht Regensburg*
Dr. **Rainer Lindner**, *CEEER, Berlin*
Dr. **Vladimir Malakhov**, *Russian Academy of Sciences*

Dr. **Luke March**, *University of Edinburgh*
Prof. **Michael McFaul**, *Stanford University, Palo Alto*
Prof. **Birgit Menzel**, *University of Mainz-Germersheim*
Prof. **Valery Mikhailenko**, *The Urals State University*
Prof. **Emil Pain**, *Higher School of Economics, Moscow*
Dr. **Oleg Podvintsev**, *Russian Academy of Sciences*
Prof. **Olga Popova**, *St. Petersburg State University*
Dr. **Alex Pravda**, *University of Oxford*
Dr. **Erik van Ree**, *University of Amsterdam*
Dr. **Joachim Rogall**, *Robert Bosch Foundation Stuttgart*
Prof. **Peter Rutland**, *Wesleyan University, Middletown*
Prof. **Marat Salikov**, *The Urals State Law Academy*
Dr. **Gwendolyn Sasse**, *University of Oxford*
Prof. **Jutta Scherrer**, *EHESS, Paris*
Prof. **Robert Service**, *University of Oxford*
Mr. **James Sherr**, *RIIA Chatham House London*
Dr. **Oxana Shevel**, *Tufts University, Medford*
Prof. **Eberhard Schneider**, *University of Siegen*
Prof. **Olexander Shnyrkov**, *Shevchenko University, Kyiv*
Prof. **Hans-Henning Schröder**, *SWP, Berlin*
Prof. **Yuri Shapoval**, *Ukrainian Academy of Sciences*
Prof. **Viktor Shnirelman**, *Russian Academy of Sciences*
Prof. **Lisa Sundstrom**, *University of British Columbia*
Dr. **Philip Walters**, *"Religion, State and Society", Oxford*
Dr. **Zenon Wasyliw**, *Ithaca College, New York State*
Dr. **Lucan Way**, *University of Toronto*
Dr. **Markus Wehner**, *"Frankfurter Allgemeine Zeitung"*
Dr. **Andrew Wilson**, *University College London*
Dr. **Jan Zielonka**, *University of Oxford*
Prof. **Andrei Zorin**, *University of Oxford*

* While the Editorial Committee and Advisory Board support the General Editor in the choice and improvement of manuscripts for publication, responsibility for remaining errors and misinterpretations in the series' volumes lies with the books' authors.

Soviet and Post-Soviet Politics and Society (SPPS)
ISSN 1614-3515

Founded in 2004 and refereed since 2007, SPPS makes available affordable English-, German-, and Russian-language studies on the history of the countries of the former Soviet bloc from the late Tsarist period to today. It publishes between 5 and 20 volumes per year and focuses on issues in transitions to and from democracy such as economic crisis, identity formation, civil society development, and constitutional reform in CEE and the NIS. SPPS also aims to highlight so far understudied themes in East European studies such as right-wing radicalism, religious life, higher education, or human rights protection. The authors and titles of all previously published volumes are listed at the end of this book. For a full description of the series and reviews of its books, see www.ibidem-verlag.de/red/spps.

Editorial correspondence & manuscripts should be sent to: Dr. Andreas Umland, Institute for Euro-Atlantic Cooperation, vul. Volodymyrska 42, off. 21, UA-01030 Kyiv, Ukraine

Business correspondence & review copy requests should be sent to: *ibidem* Press, Leuschnerstr. 40, 30457 Hannover, Germany; tel.: +49 511 2622200; fax: +49 511 2622201; spps@ibidem.eu.

Authors, reviewers, referees, and editors for (as well as all other persons sympathetic to) SPPS are invited to join its networks at www.facebook.com/group.php?gid=52638198614
www.linkedin.com/groups?about=&gid=103012
www.xing.com/net/spps-ibidem-verlag/

Recent Volumes

172 *Maria Shagina*
Joining a Prestigious Club
Cooperation with Europarties and
Its Impact on Party Development in Georgia, Moldova, and Ukraine 2004–2015
With a foreword by Kataryna Wolczuk
ISBN 978-3-8382-1084-1

173 *Alexandra Cotofana, James M. Nyce (eds.)*
Religion and Magic in Socialist and
Post-Socialist Contexts II
Baltic, Eastern European, and Post-USSR Case Studies
With a foreword by Anita Stasulane
ISBN 978-3-8382-0990-6

174 *Barbara Kunz*
Kind Words, Cruise Missiles,
and Everything in Between
The Use of Power Resources in U.S. Policies towards Poland, Ukraine, and Belarus 1989–2008
With a foreword by William Hill
ISBN 978-3-8382-1065-0

175 *Eduard Klein*
Bildungskorruption in Russland und der Ukraine
Eine komparative Analyse der Performanz staatlicher Antikorruptionsmaßnahmen im Hochschulsektor am Beispiel universitärer Aufnahmeprüfungen
Mit einem Vorwort von Heiko Pleines
ISBN 978-3-8382-0995-1

177 *Anton Oleinik*
Building Ukraine from Within
A Sociological, Institutional, and Economic Analysis of a Nation-State in the Making
ISBN 978-3-8382-1150-3

178 *Peter Rollberg, Marlene Laruelle (eds.)*
Mass Media in the Post-Soviet World
Market Forces, State Actors, and Political Manipulation in the Informational Environment after Communism
ISBN 978-3-8382-1116-9

179 *Mikhail Minakov*
Development and Dystopia
Studies in Post-Soviet Ukraine and Eastern Europe
ISBN 978-3-8382-1112-1

180 *Aijan Sharshenova*
The European Union's Democracy Promotion in Central Asia
A Study of Political Interests, Influence, and Development in Kazakhstan and Kyrgyzstan in 2007–2013
With a foreword by Gordon Crawford
ISBN 978-3-8382-1151-0

Contents

Acknowledgements 7

Foreword 9
Zhanna Nemtsova

Introduction.
Boris Nemtsov: A Tragedy of Resistance 13
Andrey Makarychev and Alexandra Yatsyk

Nemtsov: A Variety of Perspectives 19
Vladimir V. Kara-Murza, David J. Kramer, Miguel V. Liñán,
Stefan Meister, Dmitry Mitin, Alla Kassianova, Yulia Kurnyshova

Russia as Alternative Model:
Authoritarianism and Corporatism Resurgent 41
Howard J. Wiarda

Boris Nemtsov
and the Reproduction of Regional Intelligentsia 61
Tomila Lankina

Governing Nizhny Novgorod:
Boris Nemtsov as a Regional Leader 87
Vladimir Gel'man and Sharon W. Rivera

Boris Nemtsov 1959–2015:
The Rise and Fall of a Provincial Democrat 111
Andre Mommen

**The Nemtsov Vote: Public Opinion and
Pro-Western Liberalism's Decline in Russia**......................143
Henry E. Hale

**Rocking the Sochi Olympic Narrative:
Boris Nemtsov and Putin's Sovereignty** 169
Andrey Makarychev and Alexandra Yatsyk

Nemtsov: "Ukraine's Success Gives Russia a Chance!"..189
Kateryna Smagliy

Appendix..207

Index..211

Notes on Contributors 215

Acknowledgements

We express our sincere gratitude to Robert Orttung under whose editorship some of the materials included in this volume have been originally published in a special issue of the *Demokratizatsiya* journal in early 2015. We are also thankful to the PONARS-Eurasia network, and in particular to our good colleagues Henry Hale and Cory Welt for organising a public panel at the Elliott School of International Studies, George Washington University, based on this special issue, in March 2015. We appreciate George Spencer Terry's assistance with language proof-reading and editing some texts of the book. Many thanks to Andreas Umland who encouraged us to invest our efforts in this edited volume, and the Johan Skytte Institute of Political Science at the University of Tartu for creating the best working atmosphere and helping with professional contacts that greatly facilitated our editorial work. Our special acknowledgement is to Zhanna Nemtsova, who has kindly shared her rememberances about her father.

Foreword

Zhanna Nemtsova

When asked about how his views and convictions evolved over his political career, my father, Boris Nemtsov, answered "Very little. I am a strong believer in the free market economy, freedom, and democracy." This core message embodies my father's political legacy. These words were not just beautiful in their content, but, in reality, these essential principles guided all of my father's actions and undertakings, no matter what position he held—either as a statesman or as an opposition politician.

In times of so-called economic stability, boosted by incredibly high oil prices, my father was widely regarded as a spent political force, completely disconnected with the Russian version of reality. Indeed, he did not bind himself to public opinion in order to win votes, but he instead strictly kept true to his values, which is quite a rare situation in Russian politics. He even started to criticize Putin early on when the majority of politicians did not notice any potential threats coming from the Russian President.

In his book *Confessions of a Rebel*, my father admits that liberal ideas are not as popular in times of prosperity. It was funny when a journalist approached him and asked, "Boris Efimovich, do you think Putin needs you?" my father then replied, "I don't care whether Putin needs me or not—our country needs me." This is one hundred per cent true. Our country especially needs leaders like my father in such difficult periods. A number of authors of the book unveil in their essays my father's crucial role in the transformation of the province of Nizhny Novgorod from a completely backward region, undergoing severe social and economic crises, to a democratic, dynamically developing island in the middle of a stagnating post-Soviet Russia.

My father's work as a governor of *Nizhegorodskaya Oblast* from 1991 to 1997 is often overlooked, as larger audiences know him as the most outspoken critic of Putin, since he had been in the opposition movement for more than a decade until the end of his days. In his role as governor, he managed to conduct a number of reforms, many of them in *Nizhegorodskaya Oblast*, pioneering small-scale privatization, truck privatization, and land reform. These exemplary reforms were expanded to a national level. Under his leadership, the province of Nizhny Novgorod entered into the top ten most attractive regions for investment.

Once again, we witnessed that Russia needed my father was when he was elected to the regional parliament of Yaroslavl region in 2013, an unprecedented and unexpected success for a politician of the so-called "roaring nineties." He was the only independent lawmaker in the parliament who managed to push through some of his own initiatives, including the reduction of expenses for local bureaucracy and the resignation of the corrupt Deputy Governor Alexander Senin, who oversaw healthcare, specifically the procurement of medicine. My father also fought the growth of tariffs, as this growth represented the direct results of corruption. Consequentially, the vast majority of people in the region of Yaroslavl supported my father's initiatives.

These examples display that Russia desperately needs honest and dedicated value-orientated liberal politicians, but smear campaigns inspired by the Kremlin strongly affected their attitudes towards my father.

His brutal murder on 27 February 2015 in front of the walls of the Kremlin — a symbolic place for the Russia psyche — has immediately made him a Russian liberal icon and a symbol of resistance for those who refuse to give up. Many Russians have already paid tribute to my father, when thousands took to streets in the March of

Grief. For more than two years, volunteers have continued to support the People's Memorial to my father on the Bolshoi Moskvoretsky Bridge—the site of the murder—despite the fact that the authorities keep trying to destroy it. In addition, the government has even decided to close the bridge for "renovation."

He did not enjoy praise or even constructive analysis of his work during his lifetime—especially in his last years—but at least he gets it now. I would like to thank all of the authors who contributed their essays to this book and hope that their works will provide deeper insight both into my father's political legacy and into Russia as a whole.

Introduction.
Boris Nemtsov:
A Tragedy of Resistance

Andrey Makarychev and Alexandra Yatsyk

In Russian politics, Boris Nemtsov is definitely one of the most tragic figures, and not only because he was shot dead at the age of 56 in close vicinity to the locus of Russia's power, the Kremlin. The "transparency of evil" in this specific case was shocking: Nemtsov's murder was filmed by a surveillance camera, which confirms the explicitly demonstrative and insolent character of the assassination.

This political tragedy has other dimensions too. Nemtsov was one of the few Russian politicians who—having behind him a decade-long history of public service in the 1990s—intentionally refused to integrate with the ruling elite, as many of his formerly liberal colleagues did. Among them are Sergey Kirienko (currently the deputy head of presidential administration), Anatoly Chubais (the head of Rosnano corporation), Nikita Belykh (the former governor of Kirov Oblast), Irina Khakamada (a business coach and author), and each of them has chosen to be part of the regime, presuming that their service can civilize and ennoble it. Unfortunately, even Nemtsov's death failed to become a consolidating factor for those who constituted the first generation of democratic leaders in post-Soviet Russia. Their hopes for improving the regime largely failed. Yet, so did Nemtsov's campaigning against Kremlin-sponsored corruption and nepotism; most of his compatriots ultimately turned a blind eye to the well-recorded wrongdoings of the Kremlin only because it managed to annex Crimea, support insurgents in eastern Ukraine, and intervene in Syria.

No less tragic was the likely origin of the deadly plot against Nemtsov, as its roots are being traced in Chechnya, where Russia waged two devastating wars that Nemtsov tried to stop years ago. In 1996, he campaigned for the end of hostilities and managed to collect one million signatures for that, challenging President Yeltsin's policy and risking his own political career. His contribution to the anti-war movement was essential, which makes the probable Chechen ties to his murder even more ominous.

Nemtsov's death illuminated the political core of the current regime that tolerates, if not incites, extra-legal actions against those it arbitrarily considers to be "foes," "traitors," or members of the "fifth column."[1] Yet, this is a tragedy of the whole country, where clandestine groups can physically punish dissenters, castigate opponents, and lynch "enemies."[2] This situation is even evident with a new wave of anti-corruption protests sparked—unexpectedly for many Russia observers—in March 2017, when mass-scale demonstrations, temporarily discontinued under the impact of the post-Crimea consolidation of the ruling regime, resumed with a new strength all across the country.

This edited volume incorporates our experiences of participating in and attending numerous several events dedicated to Boris Nemtsov, including the Nemtsov Forums in October 2016 and October 2017 in Berlin and the public discussion on Boris Nemtsov organized by the Open Estonia Foundation in Tallinn in September 2017. These events helped to integrate our analysis into a wider range of activities and discourses of people in Russia and the West who are committed not only to preserving Nemtsov's political legacy, but also are keen on actualizing his contribution to Russian politics as a core element of political struggles in an even more complicated and troublesome environment of today's Russia.

The death of Boris Nemtsov and its concomitant political symbolization as a major landmark in the evolution of contemporary Russia contributed to the emergence of two narratives whose roles

---

1   Andrey Makarychev. "Commemorating Boris Nemtsov," The University of Tartu blog, 3 March 2015, http://blog.ut.ee/commemorating-boris-nemtsov/ (as of 2 September 2017)
2   Aleksandr Baunov. "Ubiystvo Nemtsova: nevidimye proskriptsii i degradatsii rossiiskogo avtoritarizma," *Moscow Carnegie Center*, 28 February 2015, http://carnegie.ru/2015/02/28/убийство-немцова-невидимые-прос криппии-и-деградация-российского-авторитаризма/i33b   (as of   2 September 2017)

are crucial in understanding the genealogy of the Kremlin's rule. First, the ongoing debate on Nemtsov's political heritage gave a powerful impulse to reconceptualize the 1990s—the decade of Nemtsov's ascendance to the top of Russian political pyramid—as a time of hopes and "windows of opportunity" that have been gradually shrinking under Putin's presidency and ultimately almost totally vanished. In this sense, the retrospective look at in the early 1990s Russia from the viewpoint of the documentary film "Nemtsov," shot by Vladimir Kara-Murza, is mostly about new chances and possibilities that the fall of the Soviet Union opened to Russia, and almost unique opportunities for democratic forces to turn the country into a European democracy. This narrative drastically differs from the mainstream discourse widely propagated by the Moscow officialdom that prefers to interpret the 1990s as a decade of economic and moral decay, corruption, "wild capitalism" and dependence on the West, all of which are viewed as being detrimental to the Russian nation. Yet for the Nemtsov generation of young urban professionals, who are well-educated and who express their views rather than escape in a post-political world of technocracy and de-ideologization, the story of the post-Soviet Russia looks different from the Kremlin version. This might be a story of steadily curtailing democratic freedoms and human rights for the sake of hyper-centralization and reification of imperial instincts, rather than that one of a country "rising from its knees". With all its divisive potential, the attitude to the 1990s will remain a major political marker in Russia in the years to come.

Secondly, Nemtsov's murder and the ensuing events—from Putin's awkward remark, "It is far from certain that he should have been killed"[3] to the regular attempts of the Moscow municipal authorities to remove mountains of flowers from the place of assassination—reveal a lot about the political system in Russia. The mostly informal rules established by Putin's regime make the expression of basic signs of respect, compassion and condolence (such as giving an interview about Nemtsov or immortalizing his memory in a

---

3 "Sovsem ne fakt, chto vcheloveka nuzhno ubivat'," *Radio Svoboda*, 9 October 2016, https://www.svoboda.org/a/27989738.html (as of 2 September 2017)

plaque) acts of exceptional political courage. We do know that it is only a minority in Russia that is capable of these acts of courage, which makes them even more valuable.

At the intersection of these two narratives—re-signifying the years of Yeltsin's presidency and Nemtsov's governorship in Nizhny Novgorod as a decade of new openings, innovations, and experimentations, and exposing the Putin regime as deeply authoritarian and insecure—Boris Nemtsov himself features as a politician whose approaches are destined to remain relevant years after his death. His electoral appeal to young generation of Russians—analyzed in this volume by Henry Hale—becomes even more topical in light of new waves of protests that in 2017 brought to the streets the generation of those who have not seen any other model of leadership apart from Putinism. Nemtsov's vehement campaigning against Russia's support and encouragement of anti-government insurgents in Donbas—which is a central part of Katerina Smagliy's analysis in this book—remains critically important not only for Ukraine, but also for Russia and the whole Europe. In this sense, Nemtsov's voice today would definitely endorse those who support sanctions against the Kremlin, which remain one of the most effective tools the United States and the European Union can use to deter and contain Russia. Today Nemtsov would have strengthened those voices in Russia that view sport mega-events, including the upcoming 2018 FIFA World Cup, not as the manifestations of Russia's greatness, but as the evidence of misappropriation of public funds by the top government officials and connected to them corporations. This is examined in greater detail on the example of the Sochi Winter Olympics 2014 in the chapter by Andrey Makarychev and Alexandra Yatsyk.

Being fully cognizant of the predominantly politically driven and highly affective discourse on Boris Nemtsov, in this volume we tried to approach it from a more analytical perspective. It was our main challenge to start thinking and speaking about Nemtsov, applying vocabularies of comparative politics, sociology, and international relations. We tried to avoid politically biased appraisals of Nemtsov's life and career. Yet, in addition to academic chapters, this volume also includes colorful personal notes and reflections.

We wanted to present to the readers a palette of diverse assessments of Nemtsov's personality by people for whom he was one of the leading figures in their research on Russia's post-Soviet transformation (for example, see the chapter of Vladimir Gelman and Sharon Rivera). We also gave space to those — mostly Western — experts who had personal experiences of either living or travelling to Nizhny Novgorod, when it was governed by Nemtsov (Stefan Meister, Howard Wiarda, and Andre Mommen). The plurality of opinions collected in this volume corresponds with we hope Nemtsov's rich political legacy that will always be duly remembered.

Nemtsov: A Variety of Perspectives

Vladimir V. Kara-Murza, David J. Kramer, Miguel V. Liñán, Stefan Meister, Dmitry Mitin, Alla Kassianova, Yulia Kurnyshova

Boris Nemtsov: From Kremlin Heir to Dissident

Vladimir V. Kara-Murza

Throughout his political life, Boris Nemtsov was a maverick, a "white crow," as we say in Russian, always choosing principles over political expediency—as when he took on the Communist establishment in the last Soviet elections (and won); when, as governor, he shepherded his Nizhny Novgorod region onto the path of liberal and free market reforms; when, as deputy prime minister of Russia, he challenged the all-powerful "oligarchs" and the system of political nepotism they represented. But it was the rise to power of Vladimir Putin and the solidification of his authoritarian regime that proved Nemtsov to be almost unique among Russian politicians—including those who styled themselves as "democrats" but quickly adapted to new political realities, accepting lush positions in government and state corporations—in staying true to his beliefs, regardless of the risk.

Putin's arrival in the Kremlin in December 1999 coincided with Nemtsov's election to Parliament in what was (to date) the last genuinely competitive election for the Russian Duma. From the very start, Nemtsov was suspicious of the motives of the former KGB operative and, unlike other leaders of the liberal SPS party, did not back Putin in the 2000 presidential election, voting instead for Grigory Yavlinsky. In the Duma, Nemtsov quickly emerged as a leader of the parliamentary opposition, vocally challenging Putin's Kremlin on such issues as the reinstatement of the Soviet national anthem, the closure of independent television networks, heavy-handed tactics during the Nord Ost hostage crisis, and the politically motivated arrest of oil magnate Mikhail Khodorkovsky.

As parliamentary politics in Russia fell victim to the Kremlin's authoritarian consolidation, and as the heavily manipulated elections in 2003 and 2007 purged the State Duma of opposing and independent voices, Nemtsov found himself in a new role—that of a leading dissident in an increasingly repressive and intolerant system. He did not shun this role, accepting it as necessary for upholding his views and his aspirations for a democratic Russia against an emerging dictatorship. "I have decided… that I will continue this fight," Nemtsov told *Novaya Gazeta*. "They [the authorities] want to destroy my country, they are doing great damage to Russia, they are acting against Russia's interests. And we must have people in our country who are not afraid to tell the truth."[1] With the parliamentary and electoral route closed, and television off-limits to him because of a blacklist imposed by the Kremlin, Nemtsov used what avenues he could to deliver his message. He became a regular participant in street protests, frequently arrested and thrown in detention cells, once spending the Christmas holidays in near-torturous conditions in police detention after taking part in a peaceful rally in support of the freedom of assembly. A firm believer that political and civic enlightenment will, in the end, break down the barriers of dictatorship, he published reports detailing the corruption and abuse of power by the Putin regime and presenting facts suppressed by government propaganda.[2] A poll taken by the Levada Center in 2015 showed that 11 per cent of Russians (and 19 per cent of Muscovites) were aware of the substance of Nemtsov's expo-

---

[1] Elena Masiuk, "Boris Nemtsov: Oni ne smogut zastavit' menia zamolchat', prosto ne smogut," *Novaya Gazeta*, 2 March 2015, http://www.novayagazeta.ru/politics/67457.html (as of 1 September 2017)

[2] See, for example, the report "Putin. Results," http://www.putin-itogi.ru (as of 1 September 2017)

sés — a remarkably high figure given the pervasive media censorship.[3] Using his high profile and his influence in the Western political world, Nemtsov vigorously campaigned for the successful passage of the U.S. Magnitsky Act that imposed targeted sanctions on Kremlin-connected human rights abusers, introducing an important measure of accountability. In Russia's traditionally fragmented pro-democracy movement, Nemtsov managed to bring together a wide coalition, Solidarity, that would play a key organizing role in the winter protests of 2011–2012. During those rallies, which brought tens of thousands of people to the streets of Moscow after a rigged parliamentary election — Russia's largest pro-democracy protests since 1991 — Nemtsov's voice was one of the loudest. "They have proven that they are a party of crooks and thieves," he told the 100,000-strong crowd in Bolotnaya Square on 10 December 2011, echoing Aleksei Navalny's famous line. "We must prove that we are a proud and free nation."[4]

Nemtsov genuinely liked people, and they liked him in return. He could as easily communicate with high-ranking foreign dignitaries as with a pensioner *babushka* or a local market salesman. A former governor, parliamentary leader, and deputy prime minister, once an heir apparent to the Russian presidency, who had seen the heights of power and privilege, Nemtsov did not shy away from handing out leaflets in the streets and in metro stations, or personally canvassing voters in door-to-door meetings, as he did during his last election campaign in Yaroslavl in 2013. It was a campaign he won, despite the customary media blackout and administrative pressure: the list of the People's Freedom Party headed by Nemtsov passed the threshold required for representation in the Regional Duma, winning him his first legislative seat in a decade. With this comeback, it seemed the corner had been turned. Nemtsov, the sole opposition legislator in a 50-strong chamber, used his mandate to successfully challenge corrupt officials in Yaroslavl, forcing high-

---

3   "Boris Nemtsov," Levada Center, 18 March 2015, http://www.levada.ru/old/18-03-2015/boris-nemtsov.

4   Boris Nemtsov, *Speech on Bolotnaya Square*, 10 December 2011, https://www.youtube.com/watch?v=x74T19np_28 (as of 29 August 2017)

profile resignations and refuting the Russian proverb that "one on a battlefield is not a warrior." He was planning to run for the State Duma in Yaroslavl in 2016, and his chances of success—despite the absence of a level playing field—were not insignificant. The return of Boris Nemtsov to the Russian parliament was surely not a welcome prospect for the Kremlin.

The last year of Nemtsov's life was marked by opposition to the war the Kremlin had unleashed on Ukraine after mass protests there toppled a corrupt and authoritarian president, Viktor Yanukovych. This was an analogy too close to home for Vladimir Putin. Nemtsov was firm and persistent in his criticism of Putin's annexation of Crimea and his proxy war in the Donbas region. "The war against Ukraine is a crime," he wrote in August 2014. "It is not our war. It is Putin's war for his power and his money."[5] For his position, he was vilified by the Kremlin's propaganda machine and denounced as a "traitor." In September 2014, Nemtsov led a 50,000-strong Peace March through the streets of central Moscow. Another antiwar rally was planned for 1 March 2015; Nemtsov also began work on a new report—this time, on Putin's war against Ukraine. As always, he believed that the Russian people deserved to know the truth.

He also believed that, for all the repression and propaganda, Putin's regime would eventually succumb to the forces of history, and that Russia would return to a democratic path. "When people hear the truth, those 86 per cent [Putin's official poll numbers] will fall apart. This is why... we are not allowed on television," Nemtsov said in his last interview on Ekho Moskvy radio, hours before he was assassinated in front of the Kremlin. "Because once people realize that everything... is built on lies, this regime will crumble to dust."[6] Just as Boris Nemtsov believed, one day Russia will be free from authoritarian rule. And, although he has not lived

---

5 Boris Nemtsov, "*To soldiers of the Russian Armed Forces*," *Ekho Moskvy*, 29 August 2014, http://echo.msk.ru/blog/nemtsov_boris/1389578-echo/ (as of 29 August 2017)

6 Boris Nemtsov, "Vesennee vozrozhdenie: vernyotsya li oppozitsiya v politicheskoe pole?," Interview, Ekho Moskvy, 27 February 2015, http://echo.msk.ru/programs/year2015/1500184-echo (as of 29 August 2017)

to see that day, his contribution to Russian democracy will have been one of the most important.

Boris Nemtsov:
A True Russian Patriot

David J. Kramer

It is hard to believe that a year has gone by since Boris Nemtsov was shot and killed just yards from the Kremlin walls. Boris' assassination reminded us that Russian critics and opponents of the Putin regime face significant danger, whether they live and stay in Russia or emigrate to seemingly safer places overseas (see Alexander Litvinenko, poisoned in London in 2006). Boris chose to stay and fight for what he believed was right. He felt it his patriotic duty and responsibility to shine a light on the abuses and outrages of the Putin clique. And for that he paid the ultimate price.

Few people were as outspoken and courageous as Boris, a true Russian patriot who sought the best for his country. Boris believed that Russia had taken a seriously wrong turn under the reign of Vladimir Putin, and he regularly criticized the policies and authoritarianism that he felt were threatening his country's future. He sought to expose the corruption and wrongdoings of the Putin regime and issued regular reports, whether on the Sochi Olympics or Putin's palaces, revealing how rotten and kleptocratic the regime had become.

At the time of his murder, Boris was working on a report, *"Putin. War"*, on Russia's invasion of Ukraine. Thanks to a number of Boris' friends and colleagues who bravely filled the void, the report was released, albeit posthumously for Boris, to expose the involvement of Russian forces fighting in Ukraine, the extent of Russian casualties, the economic and financial costs of the war for Russia, and the role of forces sent by Chechen leader Ramzan Kadyrov. It is not clear whether Boris' plans to issue the report played a role in his murder, but the possibility certainly cannot be ruled out. Despite repeated warnings that he was risking the ire of the Kremlin, Boris was determined to do what he believed was right. It is heartening to see other Russian patriots determined to bring his unfinished work to fruition, a fitting tribute to Boris' tireless efforts.

One of the issues Boris believed in passionately was the Sergei Magnitsky Rule of Law and Accountability Act, which the U.S. Congress passed in 2012 and President Obama signed into law that December. On numerous occasions, Boris stressed that this legislation was not anti-Russian, but in fact was pro-Russian because it targeted individuals who engaged in gross human rights abuses, including the murder of the lawyer Sergei Magnitsky. There was no better spokesman than Boris to counter nefarious Kremlin propaganda painting the Magnitsky Act as anti-Russian. In the absence of justice inside Russia, Boris believed, the Magnitsky Act was the next best thing to providing some element of accountability. Because it targeted individuals, not the country, if people did not engage in human rights abuses, they had nothing to fear from being sanctioned through a visa ban and asset freeze.

Despite considerable risk back home, Boris became an active advocate for the legislation, meeting in Washington with Members of Congress and their staffs. Boris knew that going after a corrupt, abusive Russian official's ability to travel to the United States and his ill-gotten gains was risky to his own safety. But he believed it was the right thing to do, and no risk would dissuade him from pursuing justice.

Along with others, he and I on several occasions pushed publicly for the Magnitsky legislation, and it was clear to me that Boris' advocacy made a big difference. He had an excellent reputation among Senators and Representatives, and his cogent presentations convinced Members that voting for the Act was the best way to press for rule of law and accountability in his homeland.

Throughout the years, I appeared several times with Boris on panels and at meetings, including the rollout in Washington of his report, "*Winter Olympics in the Sub-Tropics: Corruption and Abuse in Sochi*," which detailed allegations of rampant corruption in preparation for the 2014 Sochi Winter Olympics. I last saw him in Sweden at an annual gathering on Visby Island in October 2014, four months before his murder. He was his usual ebullient self, with great insights into what was happening in his country and what should be done about it. He was an eternal optimist and believed that his struggle for human rights, rule of law, and a better life in Russia would pay off eventually.

On several occasions, Boris would raise with me cases of friends and colleagues who faced considerable danger and risk inside Russia and needed help. He was always looking out for others. I was at that time president of Freedom House, which had a program that could provide emergency assistance to such individuals. In retrospect, I wish Boris had availed himself of such emergency assistance, for had he done so—and had I pushed him to do so—he might still be alive today.

Some observers write off Boris, saying he had little support among average Russians. And yet doing the right thing when the government and its stooges in the media relentlessly attack you and the population seemingly ignores you makes Boris' struggle even more impressive.

Putin, whether he was directly behind the murder of Nemtsov or not, created the environment in Russia that condones, if not encourages, violence against anyone bold enough to speak out. Russian critics of the Kremlin are demonized, part of a "fifth column" or enemy of the state seeking to overthrow the government. Nationwide television, controlled by the Kremlin, paints a bull's eye on them. Thus, Putin, in my view, bears ultimate responsibility for Boris' assassination.

One of the most important ways to remember Boris is to demonstrate solidarity with Russian democracy and human rights activists who understand the threat posed by Putin's authoritarianism to their pursuit of a better future. Writing them off as insignificant, or writing off Russia as a hopeless country, would be a betrayal of the cause Boris fought for and, in the end, for which he sacrificed his life.

Boris Nemtsov and the Chechen-Russian conflict

Miguel V. Liñán

After the assassination of Boris Nemtsov, Ramzan Kadyrov was quick to offer the media his version of the facts—a rather unimaginative rendering based on some of the common beliefs churned out by the Kremlin's propaganda machine. Generally speaking, what Kadyrov was saying was that the crime could have been committed by the American and Ukrainian secret services, with the help of Chechen terrorists. With a confidence born of impunity, he did not provide a jot of evidence to support his accusation.

Following a pattern that has characterized other cases, such as the assassination of Anna Politkovskaya, it was not long before the Russian police, with the habitual cooperation of the state-run TV channels, exhibited several Chechens who were presumably the perpetrators of the crime. It should be remembered that these same TV channels have over recent years disseminated "information" inviting viewers to regard Nemtsov and other members of the opposition as fifth columnists in the pay of the West and, "therefore," as traitors to their country. This is the image—hegemonic in present-day Russia—that Kadyrov tacitly conjured up in his statements. The Chechen leader immediately put the assassination into context: this is what happens to those who work for the West; when they are no longer useful alive, their Western friends are capable of anything, even of making them disappear and using foul play to destabilize Russia.

As in the case of Politkovskaya, the murder suspects are from the North Caucasus, specifically Chechnya. It is a sad fact that, in such a broken society as contemporary Russia, it is simple to find someone willing to pull the trigger, and complicated to conclude criminal investigations affecting the murder of journalists, human rights advocates or politicians blowing the whistle on the corruption of the country's elite.

Nemtsov was one of them. His verbal clashes with Kadyrov, which in present-day Russia constitute an act of political courage, were conspicuous. At the beginning of the second Chechen campaign, which would turn out to be crucial to Vladimir Putin's success in the upcoming presidential elections, Nemtsov was among those who, against the grain and in a context in which ethnic hatred and the association of Chechens with terrorists was the norm, endorsed a different policy, now forgotten, whose aim was to avoid a war that seemed then like the only solution.

In fact, history frequently suffers from memory failure as regards unsuccessful initiatives, namely, those that are short-lived or regarded as having had little impact on future events. But at that time, at the onset of the Second Chechen War, to denounce, as Nemtsov did, the excesses of the Russian army and the situation of the Chechen refugees, in addition to calling for negotiations with Aslan Maskhadov, then president of Chechnya, was tantamount to defending an about-face in the official line of the Kremlin as regards the conflict.

Not all the proposals presented by Nemtsov, a member of the State Duma at the time, addressing Chechnya were sound, although among his good judgment was to have known how to distinguish between the stance of Shamil Basaev, organizer of terrorist attacks such as the seizure of Moscow's Dubrovka Theatre in 2002, and the Beslan school massacre in 2003, and that of Maskhadov, who strongly condemned both atrocities. Nemtsov was fully aware that the support of the so-called "moderate" Chechens (led by Maskhadov) in favor of a compromise could have isolated the followers of Basaev and thus facilitated a negotiated solution to the conflict. In fact, in the year 2000 Nemtsov personally conducted a series of talks with Chechen MPs (elected in 1997), which were not without significant symbolic value at a time when any contact with the Chechen authorities was interpreted by the Kremlin, and the media companies under its control, as an act of treason. In the same year, the Russian government had started to implement its policy geared to "Chechenizing" the conflict, choosing Akhmad Kadyrov, the father of the current Chechen president, to oversee the process in situ.

Since then, and until his assassination in February 2015, Nemtsov constantly railed against Kadyrov's authoritarianism and the corruption characterizing relations between Moscow and Grozny. Personally, I do not share Nemtsov's ideology. I am neither a "liberal" nor do I endorse the conventional (and reductionist, in my opinion) division that journalists and scholars make between "liberals" and "Putinists." This notwithstanding, in a context of conspiratorial silence and sycophancy towards those in power, the courage of politicians like Boris Nemtsov is nowadays essential so as to be able to look to the future in Russia with at least some degree of optimism.

The Legacy of Boris Nemtsov

Stefan Meister

When I studied international relations at Nizhny Novgorod State University in 1999/2000, Boris Nemtsov had already left the city, having been appointed first deputy premier minister of the Russian Federation. While he served as governor of Nizhny Novgorod between 1991 and 1997, the region became a "laboratory of reform." Beloved by international investors and Western politicians, his liberal reforms were often chaotic, but brought the region significant economic growth. I did internships in different departments of the regional administration during my year there and still met Nemtsov's slowly dying ghost almost everywhere. Many young and well educated Russians, who had been appointed during Nemtsov's two terms, were still there and tried to fight with the old bureaucrats, who had no interest in reforms, efficient structures or transparency.

But this young generation was leaving, with many going abroad. Nemtsov's laboratory was slowly killing off all the hopes of the young, well trained people with international experience. As a member of the team working with liberal economist Anatoly Chubais, he also had to resign his position in the government following the crash of the Russian stock market in August 1998. The experiment was over. Nemtsov became one of the leading opposition politicians in the Putin era. As a former deputy prime minister, he was part of the Russian elite. That was the reason why Nemtsov was able to say and do things which other opposition politicians were never able to do without being sanctioned by the regime. His protection (*krysha*) ended on 27 February 2015.

Nemtsov stood for the group of the sometimes naive young reformers of the 1990s who really wanted to change Russia for the better. Only a few of these people were successful after 2000, when Boris Yeltsin left office. Nemtsov was one of them and, despite the growing influence of the old Soviet security mentality, he never lost his optimism. Nemtsov represented the other Russia; he had been part of the power structures, but never stopped dreaming about a democratic Russia which lived according to the rule of law. He was a self-made man who managed to change the former closed city of Nizhny Novgorod and its region into a prominent testing ground for new ideas. At the same time, he represents the failure of post-Gorbachev Russia. He could change positions in the administration, but was not able to change his mentality.

His murder is the victory of the cynical Russia, which has been growing under Vladimir Putin. If Nemtsov, who was linked to Putin for some time, can be killed, no opposition figure is safe in today's Russia. There is no place anymore for optimists, for politicians who want to break with the Soviet legacy. You have the choice: Either you leave the country, go into internal exile, or you might lose your life. All this stand for the beginning of a new Russia which started with Putin's return in 2012. The current era has been completely cut off from the democratic achievements of Gorbachev's time and the 1990s, a period now defined as a tragic accident of history.

Boris Nemtsov and the Optimism of Early 1990s

Dmitry Mitin

I met Boris Nemtsov in spring 1992. With the ideological, administrative, and economic landscapes shifting at an accelerated pace, these were the days of dizzying change. Much of that transformation was driven by improvisation and gut feeling, rather than clear prescriptions and meticulous planning. Of course, Russia's institutional contours could not be rewritten de novo—despite the radical departure from the past, this was a redesign shaped by the path-dependent, sticky characteristics of the communist era. In the case of Nizhny Novgorod, the legacy of Soviet development most visibly manifested in unwieldy state-run manufacturing giants—highly militarized, but inadequately modern—that turned irrelevant in the emerging consumer-oriented economy. The manufacturing sector appeared unreformable, but its collapse would spell a devastating social dislocation.

The situation was not entirely bleak. The distortions and liabilities of the industrial sector seemed to be offset by the region's solid educational system, qualified work force, remarkable research and development institutions, and proximity to Moscow and foreign markets. To top it off, Nizhny was favorably ranked among other regions in terms of civil unrest and probability of ethnic conflict. It looked like the hazards of free market reform and political decentralization came with the opportunities for recovery and growth.

That spring, I observed Boris Nemtsov in action in a series of negotiations with potential foreign investors. As I recall, the delegation was fairly low-ranking, but the governor was right there for most of the day. He was hands-on, fully engaged, personally taking the visitors across several of Nizhny's scientific centers, and for hours fielding their questions about local industry. He was definitely going beyond the ceremonial meet-and-greet, one would expect of the top executive in a major region. Nizhny Novgorod had used to be cordoned off to foreigners, and now Boris Nemtsov was making up for the lack of publicity by showing off local R&D assets, playing up regional strengths, and promoting the area as a hub for innovation, trade, and diversified economic development.

Years later I wondered whether in that particular instance advocating for the region and building up investor confidence could have been delegated to someone else. Was the governor micromanaging the situation? It appears that such tasks—fairly routine in well-established governments—acquired the highest urgency in the context of Russia's administrative disarray, political uncertainty, and imminent economic collapse. Moving away from communism was no longer a sufficient objective; the period of deconstruction was coming to an end. It was up to the folks like Nemtsov to figure out by trial and error how to translate vague visions about post-communism into specific, implementable missions. His was a cohort of leaders tasked with operationalizing and administering post-Soviet state-building. Reassembling the broken pieces of public administration without the glue of ideology, mitigating economic contraction, and cushioning social dislocations became the top priorities. But there were no roadmaps for navigating such challenges; making sense of post-communist confusion had to be a process of hands-on experimentation.

Nineteen ninety-two was a turbulent year, but it did not yet feel traumatic. This was the time before the promise of massive foreign investments failed to materialize, prior to the fall of Russia's first republic, before economic collapse, the Chechen war, and broad disillusionment with democracy. These were the upbeat nineties—a period of hope and optimism. Governor Nemtsov was a perfect expression of this exciting moment in Russia's post-communist transition.

Boris Nemtsov and Los Alamos

Alla Kassianova

When Boris Nemtsov's name exploded in the news feeds and email subject lines in the early hours of the last day of the winter of 2015, the shock wave rolled through some unexpected communities. One such community that took the news very close to heart was that of Los Alamos, NM, the home to the Los Alamos National Laboratory (LANL). LANL is the birthplace of the US first atomic bomb and remains the principal nuclear weapons laboratory in the US Department of Energy (DOE) system.

From the communications on that tragic day and later conversations, it emerged that several senior nuclear weapons scientists from LANL, all of them now retired, and a former Los Alamos County Chairman happened to have personal encounters with Nemtsov. These encounters were, with exception of Mann, one-time and short, but memorable to each of them. Their recollections of the meetings come from email communications and, in Mann's case, a personal interview.

How did this connection come about?

It may not be widely known that Los Alamos, a city with its past and present inseparable from those of the laboratory that it houses, has a sister city, the only such connection in its history so far. Wildly improbable in the decades of the Cold War but only logical after its end, Los Alamos' one and only sister city is Sarov, the birthplace of the Soviet Atomic bomb and the home of the principal Russian federal nuclear center and nuclear weapons research institute, all-Russian Research Institute of Experimental Physics, RFNC-VNIIEF. The cooperation in science and nuclear materials and weapons safety that connected LANL and VNIIEF provided a strong foundation to the Sister City relationship. Established in 1994, this relationship was thriving throughout the 90s and all the way into the 2010s. It formally exists today with practically no interaction since 2014. As Governor in 1991–1997 of the Nizhny Novgorod Oblast, a larger administrative unit for the city of Sarov,

Nemtsov was present at the most vibrant time of contacts between the two laboratories and the two cities.

How do the Los Alamos people remember Nemtsov?

Scientists being scientists, conferences provided opportunity to meet Nemtsov. LANL Director at the time Siegfried Hecker met him in 1996 in Sarov at a conference celebrating the 50th anniversary of VNIIEF. Hecker had a brief conversation but remembers the occasion well. A senior LANL nuclear physicist James Toevs met Nemtsov at a different conference around the same time. Toevs, who led several US-Russian major cooperative projects, introduced himself during a break. Their conversation ranged from discussing the 1996 Operation Desert Strike in Iraq which Nemtsov quickly referred to as "Operation Monica" to a colorful sketch that described Nemtsov's approach to quality control: to check a newly built road, he would place a shot of vodka on the hood of his Volga car, invite the builder into the passenger seat, and drive a good stretch of the road. If the shot still held the vodka at the end of their drive, the quality check was passed.

Another LANL top physicist and organizer of the cooperative programs with the Russian nuclear weapons institutes Paul White remembers a shared transoceanic flight on board of DL 31 from Moscow to JFK. White was lucky enough to get upgraded, and Nemtsov was in the seat immediately behind. Their interaction took off with exchanging pleasantries about who they were, the reasons White had been in Russia, and recollections about Nizhny Novgorod during White's transits to and from Sarov. White remembers that Nemtsov's manner was open and friendly, and after their brief conversation, he spent most of the rest of the flight interacting with colleagues who came in a slow but steady stream from coach to discuss business.

Lawry Mann, who put in 10 years as Chairman, Vice Chairman and member of the Los Alamos County Council, met Nemtsov in Nizhny Novgorod and in Los Alamos. Their interaction is best described in Mann's own words during a recorded interview.

"I think he was 36 when we met him and he was a very successful governor of Nizhny Novgorod. He sent us down to the Volga river to watch the air show. They were practicing for the big show the next day, and the planes were flying upside down and straight up. It was just magnificent.

When we got back, he asked, "Well, what do you think about Russian planes compared to yours?" I said, "I don't know, I've never seen ours up that close." Then he started to tell us stories. He was very proud of the automobile, Volga. They had the longest manufacturing line in the world and he was also interested in what we've done in Levittown, a U.S. project that made single-family housing available that people could afford. He said he'd like to get his people out of the Soviet-style apartments into houses of their own. He talked about that quite a bit, and then he had us to lunch, where we had a really good borscht. He said to us, "I want you to know, I paid for this, it did not come out of state money or anything."

A photo from Mann's archive shows him in conversation with young and lanky Nemtsov next to the Russian flag in the Governor's office. His archive also preserves the April 2015 issue of Los Alamos Monitor, which puts this photo on its front page and says, "Los Alamos residents remember Boris Nemtsov".

Mann and LANL scientist Irv Lindemuth, both of whom were instrumental in starting the Sister Cities relationship, saw a similarity between Nemtsov and the Governor of New Mexico Garry Johnson. They started an initiative to make Nizhny Novgorod Oblast and New Mexico "Sister States." Nemtsov and Johnson governed the states where their nation's nuclear weapons were developed and both were young, up and coming politicians thought to be future presidential candidates. As a result of Mann's and Lindemuth's efforts, Nemtsov and Johnson communicated several times, but the U.S. Department of State interfered to stop the initiative when Nemtsov became the first Prime Minister in March 1997.

What does the Los Alamos connection signify?

Like other stories, it adds a few extra details to the human and political persona of Boris Nemtsov: open, approachable, interactive in English as easily as in Russian, enthusiastic about Russian-made products, organically democratic and with a broad interests horizon.

As a unique perspective, it illuminates a type of leadership that evoked respect and engagement of Los Alamos highly sophisticated and politically savvy science and community leaders, a commodity that both US and Russia need especially badly today.

Boris Nemtsov:
A Ukrainian Afterword

Yulia Kurnyshova

If Boris Nemtsov were alive, his place would likely be in Ukraine. Just like Mikhail Saakashvili, he could become a citizen and an office holder to try to implement some of his ideas in a country that served as an important reference point for him. This move would be possible, given that the situation in Russia has reached a point where political dissent is literally becoming life threatening. Nemtsov was aware of this danger and predicted a possible assassination attempt on himself only a few weeks before it happened.

His murder has not been able to overturn his own theory of the "Teflon Putin." In an interview ten years ago, Nemtsov pointed to the fact that nothing "sticks" to the Russian President—in spite of the multiple casualties in Chechnya, or mass-scale economic and social deprivation all across the country, his approval rating remains high. This disconnect was not a paradox for Nemtsov, who put the blame on Russian media propaganda, even more cunning and malicious than under Stalinism. In Ukraine, in his opinion, the overall situation was not even close to that. Corruption—yes, perhaps as deadly as in Russia—but, at the same time, the passion for freedom and non-violence. At least that is how he saw the Orange Revolution.

Nemtsov was the only Russian politician who stood together with Ukrainians in the frosty Maidan of 2004. Together with the then leaders—Viktor Yushchenko and Yulia Tymoshenko, in an orange scarf, full of enthusiasm. For some Ukrainian politicians, his engagement with this country was even too much. In 2005, Oleg Tyagnibok, then a little-known right-wing politician, proposed to the Verkhovna Rada a measure that would prevent Nemtsov from continuing to serve as an official adviser to the president, since this position would be tantamount to "interference in the internal affairs" of Ukraine. Ten years later, Nemtsov became a target for Russian senators who ganged up on him due to his participation—

along with the "Right Sector"—in the "Vyshivanka[7] March" in Odessa, protesting against Russia's intervention in Ukraine.

After years spent in direct contact with Ukraine, Nemtsov hardly idealized its leaders. During the Euromaidan, then President Viktor Yanukovych banned him from entering the country. As for the current leaders of Ukraine, Nemtsov thought that the most essential for them would be to make a choice—to work for the country's future, or for their electoral ratings.

His active position on Ukraine in the past year and a half elevated his dissent to a "mature opposition" to Putinism. The evolution of his views was heavily influenced by the understanding that after the annexation of Crimea and the outbreak of the war in Donbas, Putin's regime had crossed a red line. The liberal Nemtsov did not limit himself to mere liberal language. He not only led protests against the war in Ukraine, but also collected empirical material for an investigative report on Putin's crimes in Ukraine. His language was not politically correct or neutral, but filled with damning contempt, which was typical for late Nemtsov. What no one dared to say publicly, he did. Even here in Ukraine, no one has written about the war better than he did.

None of the Russian opposition figures supported Ukraine so consistently and vividly. Of course, there were Garry Kasparov and Valeria Novodvorskaya, but they paid comparatively less attention to Ukraine. Nemtsov had a clear take on the annexation of Crimea and considered it a crime. Some of his predictions were quick to come true. For example, reflecting on the reasons of the current conflict, he hypothesized that the Kremlin would eventually trade a ceasefire in Donbas for lifting economic and political sanctions against Russia. In this scenario the question of the legality of Crimea's inclusion into Russia would be removed from the agenda, and Western countries would recognize the peninsula as Russian territory, if not formally, then *de facto*. It is obvious that today the question of Crimea is practically withdrawn from the international negotiations, and the West periodically alludes to the possibility of lifting the sanctions.

---

7   Ukrainian national dress with ethnic embroidery.

Nemtsov was among the first critics of the Minsk agreements as inoperative, and called for Ukraine to wall off the breakaway regions in the Donbas: "The sooner Ukraine understands that the so-called "DNR" [The break-away Donetsk People's Republic] is its Gaza Strip, the better." As for Putin himself, his deeds, in Nemtsov's words, are worthy of "several Hague Tribunals." A year later, there are some modest hopes for establishing an international tribunal for one of the most audacious crimes of Putin's regime — the shooting down of the Malaysian airliner over eastern Ukraine. The rest — snipers at the Euromaidan, Ukrainian citizens kidnaped and thrown into jail by Moscow, thousands of war victims — are still waiting for punishment.

Russia as Alternative Model: Authoritarianism and Corporatism Resurgent

Howard J. Wiarda

Introduction

In the winter and spring of 1992, when I first went to Russia, it seemed as if "spring" was breaking out all over. We had the "Prague Spring," the "Polish Spring," the "Moscow Spring" and numerous other "Springs." Samuel Huntington had just published (1991) his celebratory *Third Wave*[1] of democratization and Francis Fukuyama was just publishing (1992) his wildly improbable, romantic, and idealistic path to universal democracy, *The End of History and the Last Man*.[2] In Latin America as well as Iberia, Greece, and parts of Asia, authoritarianism appeared to have been vanquished, giving rise to the overly hopeful "Transitions-to-Democracy" literature; in Eastern Europe and Russia, by some intellectual legerdemain and concepts-stretching, an effort was made to apply and then adapt the same "transitions" literature. In the metaphors used at the time, democracy was presented as "the only game in town," the "one model left standing." On the international front the U.S. government's National Endowment for Democracy (NED) was riding high politically and budgetarily as the agency that would bring democracy to the whole world.

At AEI (American Enterprise Institute for Public Policy Research) in the early-to-mid 1980s, I was in on all the planning and early conferences that gave rise to what was at first the "Democracy

---

[1] Samuel Huntington, *Third Wave* (Norman: University of Oklahoma Press, 1991).
[2] Francis Fukuyama, *The End of History and the Last Man* (New York: Macmillan, 1992).

Project" and then NED.³ However, as a comparative politics scholar, I was from the beginning skeptical of the universalist claims of the democracy "true believers." Democracy could not become institutionalized and consolidated that fast or that easily.⁴ In many parts of the world, neither the culture, the institutions, the level of development nor the social structure would be supportive of democracy. Hence in my writings, while certainly favoring a pro-democracy policy, I generally advanced a careful, go-slow, evolutionary approach that would allow for numerous compromises and half-way houses—"democracy with adjectives," as it was then called. The image I set forth was that of a trellis or lattice, with numerous and diverse routes to development and multiple cross-members allowing for horizontal shifts, stalled outcomes, and even room for reversals. That now appears to have been a more accurate picture than the one that predicted a single and unilinear path to democracy.

At least six factors seem to be at work here explaining these diverse outcomes:

1. History and culture in many areas (Russia, China, the Middle East) have proved to be more resistant to change and democratization than was earlier thought.
2. While it is relatively easy to alter institutions, underlying social structures, values, and developmental indicators are far harder to alter.
3. Countries like Russia, China, and Iran have either reasserted themselves as global powers and alternative models (the case of Russia and China) or have emerged as influential regional alternatives (Iran).

---

3 Howard J. Wiarda, *The Democratic Revolution in Latin America* (New York: Holmes and Meier, 1990) Chapter 6.
4 My early essay on this theme, "Can Democracy Be Exported?" first published as Occasional Paper #157 by the Woodrow Wilson International Center for Scholars and then reprinted in numerous collections, caused a large stir. The answer to the question posed, after some 30 pages, was a resounding "No!"

4. The Western Model of a liberal and democratic political order, a modern-mixed (state and private) economy, and free trade has lost, because of the global economic downturn, a great deal of its luster.
5. "The Rest" (Argentina, Brazil, India, Mexico, South Africa, Turkey, Venezuela, others), after the title of Fareed Zakaria's book,[5] have also risen to offer either variations on or alternatives to the previously dominant Western Model.
6. Not only has the Western Model of democracy proved less than universal but the Western system of international consensus, based on equilibrium, balance of power, and community of interests has begun to unravel as well.[6]

Although there are now diverse models "out there," far more so than appeared likely in 1991 — China, Japan, India, Iran, ISIS, Brazil, Mexico, South Africa, Turkey, etc., and the subject of my most recent book[7] — the one that commands our attention here is Russia. Russia under Vladimir Putin is variously described as autocratic, aggressive, authoritarian, nationalistic, dictatorial, and corporatist. While the autocratic, authoritarian, and xenophobic aspects of Putin's Russia have received considerable attention, the corporatist aspects, *the* focus of our attention here, have not. In addition, we wish to argue that the Putin Model of authoritarianism and corporatism has now become popular and even entrenched in such diverse countries as Belarus, Kazakhstan, China to some degree, Kyrgyzstan, Egypt, Syria, Turkey, Venezuela, and perhaps others. Moreover, isn't it interesting, as judged by Putin's recent visits, that these are precisely the countries to which a resurgent Russia has opted to extend its foreign policy!

---

5   Fareed Zakaria, *The Port-American World and the Rise of the Rest* (New York: Penguin, 2009).
6   See Henry Kissinger's recent and quite remarkable book, *World Order* (New York: Penguin, 2014), written at age 91. It should have been titled "The Absence of World Order."
7   Tentative title: *Comparative Global Systems*.

Russia in Early 1992

I first went to Russia in the late winter and spring of 1992. The Soviet Union had just collapsed, the Cold War was over, and Boris Yeltsin had just been elected president.

I went to Russia initially at the invitation of Andrei Makarychev and Nizhny Novgorod University.[8] He had read some of my writings on foreign policy and comparative politics; he wanted me to lecture at the University, participate in a conference organized around the themes of my writings, and assist in the creation of a new, non-Marxist department of political science at Nizhny Novgorod University.

Nizhny Novgorod was Russia's third-largest city, after Moscow and Saint Petersburg. Located about 250 miles east of Moscow, at the confluence of the Volga and Oka rivers, Nizhny had been, because of the concentration of Russia's military-industrial complex there (tanks, armed personal carriers, submarines, MIG fighter planes, nuclear and chemical weapons), a closed city. In early 1992 I was one of the first westerners to be allowed in. Boris Nemtsov had just recently been appointed governor.

I had a wonderful time during my visit to Nizhny. My hosts were wonderful, Russian hospitality (tables groaning with food and drinks that cost someone a month's pay) was on full display, and I saw and did a lot. We traveled by car and train all around the region, I visited all those arms factories mentioned above (this was before Nunn-Lugar when Russian was shipping everything it could down the Volga, across the Caspian, and hence to the world), and was warmly welcomed by the mayor of Arzamas 16, Russia's nuclear facility.

Meanwhile our efforts to bring Western-style political science and international relations to Russia's decrepit and old-school, Marxist-dominated universities was going forward. We put on academic conferences, met with deans and rectors, helped reform the

---

[8] For the full story see Howard J. Wiarda, *Adventures in Research: Volume III – A Global Traveler* (Lincoln, NE: iUniverse, 2006) Chapter 19.

curriculum, brought in new faculty, and introduced new international affairs courses and programs. Mrs. Dr. Iêda S. Wiarda, whose Ph.D. is in political science but whose recent career was as a Specialist at the Library of Congress, was also brought in to help upgrade Russian university libraries and introduce computers and digitized archival records for the first time. As part of this reform effort we also made arrangements for Russian scholars to come to the U.S. or Western Europe on fellowships from such institutions as the Woodrow Wilson International Center for Scholars, various Washington think tanks, presidential libraries, and American and European universities.

Not all of these efforts produced happy or beneficial results. Old-school Russian academics often resented the presence of Americans in their midst. At the academic conferences we put on, there were often physicists, novelists, chemists, philosophers and others who had no common basis of discussion or understanding. Nor was political science or any other social science accepted as a separate, autonomous discipline within the university. Local officials from the old regime, communist party functionaries, and what we would call "townies" often attended these conferences; on more than one occasion I was shoved aside and had the microphone ripped out of my hands by these officials who either objected to what I was saying, or to me personally as an American "interloper," or both.

Nevertheless, despite these occasional dust-ups, I can say that in general we were received warmly by the Russians who extended us traditional Russian hospitality, itself sometimes a bit overwhelming. The Russians we met were in the main eager to learn, eager to welcome visiting Americans and others, and open to new ideas and concepts in political science, other disciplines, and society generally. For at the time that we were there initially in the winter-spring of 1992, everything in Russia was grinding to a halt and/or falling apart: factories, the state farms, government, production, the Communist Party, agriculture, universities, the armed forces, transportation, almost all societal institutions. And Russia was eager to fill these voids, presumably with Western institutions based on democracy and capitalism.

During my visits to Russia, I tried to stay away as much as possible from Moscow and Saint Petersburg, Russia's two most Westernized cities, because they were not representative of the huge interior of Russia. Instead, I spent most of my time in Russia's interior cities, east of Moscow, up and down the Volga River, and toward the Ural Mountains. In contrast to my friend and Amherst, Massachusetts colleague Bill Taubman, who wrote the romantic and overly-optimistic *Moscow Spring*,[9] I found little cause for optimism "out there" in the vast Russian interior: no democracy, no capitalism, no emerging civil society. Rather, what I found were closed and dysfunctional factories, few jobs and no new investment, the collapse of the state farms because no one was paying their employees, government offices that were being ripped off by their own employees, a collapsing communist party but nothing there as yet to replace it, massive corruption, and everywhere breakdown, dysfunction, uncertainty, and anger. Russia was teetering on becoming — may have already become — a failed state.

At that time Robert Strauss, a well-known Texas lawyer, and Washington wheeler-dealer, had just been named as U.S. Ambassador to Russia. I knew Bob Strauss well, having worked for him as lead consultant to the 1980s Kissinger Commission on Central America of which he was a leading member. So at the end of my trip I made an appointment to see Strauss in Moscow to report on my experiences. But by then U.S. policy was so committed to the NED-democracy-free market agenda that it did not want to hear my message of breakdown, dysfunction, and the need to go slow, as contrasted with the "crash" program of economist (and adviser on Russia) Jeffrey Sachs.

I would argue that in Russia, and elsewhere, U.S. policy, as well as the reformist Russians themselves, went too far too fast. We should have slowed and tempered the pace of change, and been willing to accept compromises on both economic and political reform, until Russian institutions and civil society had had a chance to adapt, stabilize, and become consolidated. Perhaps we had no choice in the matter: after all, how can the United States of America

---

9   Bill Taubman, *Moscow Spring* (New York: Summit Books, 1990)

not stand for democracy, human rights, and free-market capitalism? But by pushing so hard and uncompromisingly for immediate change, U.S. policy helped undermine Russian traditional institutions that might have eased the transition to democracy. And in so doing, we contributed to the vacuum, the dysfunction, the breakdown, and the nationalistic distemper that paved the way later in the decade for Putin.

Encountering Boris Nemtsov

It was in this context of change and upheaval in the spring of 1992 that I first met Boris Nemtsov, the new governor of the Nizhny Novgorod *Oblast* or region. I both interviewed Nemtsov formally and ran into him socially at numerous openings, receptions, and political gatherings in Nizhny. Then in his thirties, Nemtsov had a reputation as a young reformer committed to a more liberal philosophy and to privatization. He had gathered around him a team of like-minded reformers from the Nizhny region. With a background in physics, Nemtsov had first gained prominence by opposing the building of a planned nuclear power plant in Nizhny; in the showdown with the old-line communists a few months before my trip to Russia in August, 1991, Nemtsov had sided with the pro-reform, pro-Yeltsin forces.

In office, Nemtsov soon gained a reputation, in Russia and abroad, as a liberal agent of change. He opened up Nizhny to political debate, encouraged the privatization of small shops and businesses, and gave his approval to the opening of a Nizhny Novgorod stock exchange. His liberalizing, privatizing efforts attracted the attention of prime ministers Margaret Thatcher, John Major, and Alain Juppe, as well as U.S. Speaker of the House Newt Gingrich, all of whom made pilgrimages to Nizhny. Later on, Nemtsov would become the *elected* governor of Nizhny; in 1997 he moved to Moscow after having been appointed first deputy prime minister by Yeltsin. I followed his career over the years and met with him on several of his visits to Washington.

I was not as taken with Nemtsov as were others at this time. Perhaps that is my training as a political scientist; maybe it was to do with the skepticism and cynicism imbued after too many years in Washington. I found Nemtsov bubbly, enthusiastic, and personable but also young and even boyish in his enthusiasms, inexperienced, naive, and overly romantic in his views of what could be accomplished in Russia at that time. Perhaps it was his physics background that led him to see too-simple and single-minded solutions to Russia's manifold and complex problems, without adequate focus on the means in Russia's chaotic and disintegrating economic and political system at that time to get there.

Actually, living in Nizhny at that time, I did not see much in the way of the touted privatizations of small businesses which was Nemtsov's claim to fame; in fact mostly what I saw was the state's harassment of small businesses. And the large military-industrial complex in the city was, when I was there, in complete chaos and freefall, as it sought to transition from state control to privatization. Nor were the relations with the old-time communists with whom Nemtsov initially shared power in Nizhny managed well; eventually these reactionary forces staged a comeback, replacing Nemtsov. Meanwhile, because of excessive borrowing, Nizhny had sunk deeper into debt, there were charges of corruption under Nemtsov, and the *Oblast* became more and more a political and financial dependency of Moscow.

I admire Boris Nemtsov because, whether in Nizhny or Moscow, he raised and carried the flame of Russian liberalism, freedom, and democracy. However it is not enough to lift up a glorious banner; eventually as a politician you also have to deliver and provide results. But you have to be realistic about it. You cannot in the process stray too far from Russian political culture and the realities of Russian power politics; you cannot as a driver of the bus get too far ahead of your passengers or take them in a direction they no longer want to go. Nemtsov was a beacon of reform but he was also, in Putin's Russia, a liberal voice crying in an increasingly authoritarian and autocratic wilderness. Eventually he succumbed to another Russia, one that was not peaceful, joyous, and democratic but aggressive, brutal, mean, ugly, nationalistic, and non- and anti-liberal, anti-Western, and anti-democratic.

Totalitarianism, Pluralism, Corporatism and Authoritarianism: Alternative Civil Society Models[10]

The liberalism that Yeltsin, Boris Nemtsov, and their followers advocated involved a belief in pluralism and democratic civil society. That included the belief not only in free speech but also the freedoms to assemble, organize, form associations, and petition.

Civil society and free associability are now closely associated with democracy and liberalism. James Madison and Alexis d' Tocqueville championed the free associability of American political life, and Madison's famous Federalist #10 elevates pluralism to near-constitutional status. Civil society and free associations are seen as bastions of liberty, protecting citizens from possible abuses by the state and at the same time serving as transmission belts to transmit citizen demands to government authorities.[11]

Civil society and democratic pluralism are now ubiquitous in our discussions of democracy, the sociology and political science literature, and foreign policy. Building and strengthening civil society are at the heart of our democracy-promotion efforts. In the last two-and-a-half decades the United States and its Western allies have sought to build civil society in Latin America, Eastern Europe, Russia, Asia, the Middle East, and Africa. The assumption is that a strong civil society is essential to a strong democracy which in turn tends to be more peaceful, stable, and pro-Western than other kinds of systems, all of which serve both the interests of humankind and U.S. foreign policy. Or, at least, those are the hopes.

Those assumptions and hopes are, in turn, based on a vast social science literature called "developmentalism" that posits that all societies, as they become more economically developed and socially modern, will also become more democratic. Democracy and pluralism are seen as the end products of a long process that leads

---

10 Some of these materials were previously included in David Horton-Smith (ed.), *Handbook on Volunteering and Non-Profit Associations* (New York: Palgrave, 2015).
11 Howard J. Wiarda, *Civil Society* (Boulder, CO: Westview Press, 2002).

from traditionalism and underdevelopment to democratic and socially-just modernity. Developmentalism as applied to the Third World was popular in academic and policy circles during the 1960s, then it went into a certain hiatus in the 1970s as authoritarianism reasserted itself, only to come roaring back in the 80s and 90s — see again the books of Huntington and Fukuyama — as, first, Latin America, then Eastern Europe, and now presumably Russia and others democratized. The developmentalist literature posited a singular and universalist path in which all societies regardless of history, culture, and other factors would ultimately look just like we do or approximately so. How comforting it is when your social science both lends legitimacy and proclaims as inevitable your foreign policy goals.

After increasing for two decades, the democracy indicators in recent years have shown either a flattening out or stagnation of the democracy curve or, in some cases, quite dramatic reversals. A new literature has begun to emerge on what has come to be called "the new authoritarianism" or "illiberal democracy."[12] Illiberal democracy in this literature refers to regimes that have some of the trappings of democracy — an opposition, parliament, regular elections — but which are otherwise "illiberal" — that is, they deny or make difficult such basic freedoms as speech, assembly, petition, and press. In some cases such regimes resort to opposition jailings, killings, repression, and torture.

All these features of the New Authoritarianism are worthy of condemnation and comment. However in my research and writing I have focused on one particular aspect of almost all authoritarian regimes: the corporatist organization of society. Corporatism as we use it here refers not to the modern social-democratic corporatism of an Austria, Germany, or Sweden in which business, labor, farmers, etc. are incorporated into the decision-making of the state as well as the implementation of social policy. Instead, corporatism is seen in an older sense as a way of controlling, regulating, and sometimes suppressing social groups or structuring them under state

---

12   Fareed Zakaria, "The Rise of the Illiberal Democracy," *Foreign Affairs*, 76, No. 6 (Nov.–Dec., 1997): 22–43

control. Corporatism is thus an integral part of the New Authoritarianism or of Illiberal Democracy. Historic examples include Franco's Spain, Salazar's Portugal, Pilsudski's Poland, Vargas' Brazil, and many others.[13]

In fact, throughout history, the *overwhelming majority* of societies have *not* been organized on a liberal, pluralist, free, democratic basis; democracy outside the West is a relatively recent and uncertain arrangement. In contrast, the vast majority of societies and governments in the world have been top-down, authoritarian, or totalitarian: kingships, sheikdoms, chiefdoms, *caudillos*, and various other forms. Corporatism often accompanied these authoritarian regimes. Even today the Freedom House and Polity measures of democracy in the world show that (1) democracy is not inevitable, (2) authoritarianism and corporatism may still be more strongly present than democracy, (3) there are, the World Values data shows, cultural as well as socioeconomic distinctions among the world's regions regarding the acceptance of democracy/authoritarianism, and (4) quite a number of countries (Ukraine, Turkey, Egypt, Russia, to name a few) may be regressing from earlier democracy to authoritarianism.

These results, on the ground, have forced social scientists to go back and reexamine their original assumptions. Is democracy really both inevitable and universal? Is pluralist civil society really as ubiquitous as thought and the inevitable outcome of the development process? What about other systems of national organization? How about the numerous mixed forms? What have been the policy consequences, often misdirected, of our focus so strongly on building a particularly Western form of democracy and civil society?

This work of re-conceptualizing began in the late-1960s, early 1970s. First, it involved a severe questioning and critique of the then prevailing literature on national development and modernization. Among other things it suggested that development and democracy in the Western model were neither universal nor inevitable, that the experience and sequential stages of today's developing nations

---

13 Howard J. Wiarda, *The Other Great "Ism": Corporatism and Comparative Politics* (New York: M.E. Sharpe, 1996).

were substantially different from the earlier European and North American developers, that "tradition" and "modernity" were misplaced bipolarities for most developing or transitional nations, and that there were cultural as well as regional differences in the approach to development. Second, the new literature suggested that there were many and varied routes to development, our trellis image and framework rather than just a single path.

This literature in turn grew out of some other bodies of research emerging from the growing dissatisfaction with developmentalism. One approach focused on the persistence of authoritarianism in the modern world, its flexibility and adaptability, its ability to hang onto power despite rising modernization, and particularly its distinction from earlier totalitarianism. Another body of literature began to focus on corporatism and patrimonialism, not as simply temporary and transitional features of modernizing regimes but as possibly permanent institutional forms, long-lasting, with features and dynamics all their own, *alternatives* to the prevailing development models and not just way-stations on the way to pluralism and democracy. A third trend among emerging nations, which began slightly later and came to fruition in the 1979 Iranian Revolution, was the rising sense that neither the Marxian nor the U.S.-favored route to development was appropriate in their own circumstances, that they would have to develop their own nationalistic, Islamic, Russian, East Asian, African, or Latin American model of development. Or, as that sage social scientist Frank Sinatra put it, "We'll do it *our* way."

The result in the 1970s, 1980s, and continuing to today was a deep and broad reconsideration in the academic literature (although not in policy, which remained committed to the developmentalist liberal and pluralist approach) of how we think about Third World development. Along with, and sometimes in substitution of, the older, socioeconomically-based division of the world's political systems into First World (developed countries), Second World (developed but Communist nations), and Third World (developing countries), now we had a classificatory scheme based on structure, institutions, and socio-political organization. This classification included four categories of regimes: pluralist regimes, totalitarian or authoritarian command regimes, corporatist regimes, and populist or neo-syndicalist regimes.

We need here to offer definitions of these four types of regimes:

1. *Pluralism* refers to a political system, generally a democracy, in which *all groups* are free to assemble, organize, and lobby within the system without the need for state licensing, regulation, or control. This is the kind of civil society that the U.S., the West, and the main international lending agencies have been advocating in recent decades.
2. *Totalitarianism* refers to a regime that exercises *total* (hence the term) control over *all* groups in society, as well as having a monopoly of political and economic power and controlling mass communication, education, propaganda, even private thought processes (brainwashing). There are few such "total" regimes—North Korea, Cuba, Vietnam—left in the world; Russia, China, and other formerly totalitarian regimes have in recent decades moved or evolved away from this model. Totalitarianism is to be distinguished from *authoritarianism* where the controls are less absolute, some areas of life (religion, family, and the economy) maintain a degree of autonomy, and the regime lacks the modern technology (hence this form occurs mainly in developing countries), the will, or the institutions necessary to impose totalitarian-like thought control. Historically there have always been many more authoritarian regime in the world than any other kinds; today there are nearly as many democratic-pluralist regimes as there are authoritarian ones.
3. *Corporatism* is the new or newly-rediscovered phenomenon. Often associated in the 1930s and 1940s with fascism, corporatism can in fact take a variety of other forms, including Christian-democratic, liberal, social-democratic, populist, and modern-progressive. Corporatism was (in the 1930s) and is often presented as a "third way" between totalitarianism of either the left or right variety and liberal-

pluralism. Under corporatism, the state licenses, grants monopolies to, and regulates civil society, associations, and interests groups; but neither totally controls them (totalitarianism) nor allows them complete autonomy (pluralism). Under corporatism and the New Authoritarianism, the state typically limits the number of interest groups, requires that they acquire state recognition before they can function (which also carries with it the power to withhold or deny recognition), and creates a system of officially-sanctioned interest associations favorable to the regime that then enjoy special favoritism. In the early literature, two types of corporatism were identified. These were (1) *state corporatism*, often associated with authoritarian regimes — e.g. Franco's Spain, Mubarak's Egypt, and a host of Latin American dictatorships — and (2) *societal corporatism* usually associated with modern welfare states — e.g. Austria or Sweden. In both these types, it is true, the state licenses, grants monopolies to, and regulates major corporate groups — for example, business associations, farmers' groups, trade unions — but the differences between these two types may be so great that they do not belong in the same "corporatist" category. Societal corporatism is liberal and democratic; state corporatism is authoritarian and often dictatorial. It is the state kind that we are now seeing in Russia and other countries.

4. The fourth type has been called "neo-syndicalism" or, as some prefer, "populism." In the early corporatist literature Italy, during the "hot summers" of the 1970s, seemed to be close to that stage. That is, a regime in which the state was relatively weak and power seemed to be passing directly to the streets in the form of revolutionary trade unions, students groups, red brigades, and others. More recently we might put such countries as Venezuela under Hugo Chávez or Bolivia under Evo Morales potentially in that category. That is, of regimes in which the older elites (Church, Army, oligarchy) have been vanquished and newer forms of neo-syndicalism in which direct, revolutionary action by newer

groups (workers, peasants, the indigenous) have been encouraged.

The New Authoritarianism concentrates power, may stifle opposition parties, often rules arbitrarily, employs nationalism and xenophobia, but employs violence sparingly. Its newest technique is to control the Internet. It usually maintains sufficient democratic facade (elections, parliament) to retain domestic and international legitimacy, but it regularly oversteps democratic bounds. And of course it controls and regulates socio-economic and political groups through newfound or resurrected corporatist controls.

The Resurgence of Corporatism

Russia is perhaps the prime example of the resurgence of authoritarianism and corporatist control mechanisms, but there are many others and the number is increasing.

In Russia a 2012 bill passed by the Duma or Parliament requires that organizations receiving money "or other aid from outside Russia" would have to register with the Justice Ministry as "acting as a foreign agent." Such groups would also have to undergo twice—yearly tax audits to check on the sources of their funds and also submit to monitoring by law enforcement officials. The law was aimed especially at Golos, a Russian organization that monitors elections, but it was also aimed at the myriad of Western non-governmental organizations (NGOs)—the National Endowment for Democracy (NED), the International Republican Institute (IRI), Amnesty International, the National Democratic Institute, the Moscow-Helsinki Group, and many others—that had established offices in Moscow in the 1990s and early 2000s.

The law imposed stringent requirements on human rights organizations, election monitors, and other politically-active organizations that receive foreign money. For example, since 1992, Russia had received almost $3 billion from the U.S. Agency for International Development (AID) for both social and economic development and, through NED, NDI, and IRI as dispersing agencies, for Russian human rights, NGO, and democracy-promotion groups.

All these groups would now come under strict surveillance from the government and leave them vulnerable to expulsion from the country. In some cases these groups had to open up their membership rolls to the state, register with the government, and show where their funds came from. Not able to function under these conditions, quite a number of NGOs were obliged to close down.

It was but a short step from requiring the registration and control over groups receiving foreign funds to requiring that all politically-active groups open their books and register with the state — full corporatism. Later legislation in 2015 extended these controls to prevent "undesirable" foreign groups from operating in the country. Such groups could be expelled or they could be denied the right to enter the country. Financial institutions would likewise be barred from processing money transactions for or from these "undesirables." How a group was designated a "foreign agent" or "undesirable" was particularly unclear, lost in the arbitrary control and repression labyrinth of the Russian state, although records showed that several dozen such groups had been closed down in recent years, forced to curtail their activities, or obliged to leave the country.

Most of the groups had been closely aligned with U.S. and European human rights, democracy promotion, and civil society groups. They also tended to back the democratic opposition, including Boris Nemtsov and his pro-democracy, anti-war campaign. As such, they were an irritant and more to Vladimir Putin's regime. Their ties to foreign, mainly U.S. anti-regime groups, even more so after the war and annexation of the Ukraine began, made them vulnerable to charges that they were "anti-Russian."

As Russian nationalism surged, as Putin's popularity ratings (over 80%) soared, and as anti-Americanism in Russia also grew, it became relatively easy for the regime to exploit these sentiments, clamp down on the opposition, and put in place anti-foreign and anti-democracy, anti-pluralism restrictions. In my own recent revisit to Russia, I found anti-Americanism there to be very intense and rising, and concluded that, in contrast to the early 1990s when I and other outside advisers were warmly received by the Russians, this was not a good time for foreign groups or their governments to be doing democracy promotion.

But Russia is not the only country where democracy has recently suffered reversals and where authoritarianism and corporatism are on the rise. In Belarus, Moldova, Egypt, Turkey, Hungary, Venezuela, Kazakhstan, Kyrgyzstan, Syria, Tajikistan, Cambodia, Bangladesh and others, democracy is under attack while "illiberal democracy" is on the rise. Authoritarianism is growing, and legislation much like Russia's is pending or has already been decreed in most of these countries providing for the registration of all groups receiving foreign funds and for the corporatization of socio-economic groups, especially those associated with opposition movements.

We cannot analyze in detail all these distinct countries; as an early pioneer in the analysis of corporatism, I'm now ready to leave this task to younger scholars. However, we do need to analyze this resurgent corporatism, its diverse forms, and how in this globalized world the corporatist formula can spread from one country to others with Internet speed. In Turkey, for example, President Recep Tayyip Erdogan has become increasingly intolerant, nationalistic, autocratic, and inclined to clamp down on opposition critics, especially those linked to or receiving funds from foreign organizations. In Egypt former presidents Hosni Mubarak and Mohamed Morsi and current president Abdel Fattahel-Sisi took steps against foreign-funded civil society groups and proposed legislation to restrict their activities, resulting recently in formal legal charges against some NGOs (including the directors of both NDI and IRI), a diplomatic crisis between Cairo and Washington, and a threatened curtailment of Egypt's over $1 billion aid package.

Hungary is a particularly interesting case for us, not least because Hungary is a member of both the EU and NATO and was thought to be safely in the democratic camp. But Prime Minister Victor Orban has sometimes grown impatient with the slow workings of Hungarian democracy, has tried to clamp down on the media and other public outlets of expression, and has taken steps to curb the opposition as well as foreign NGOs operating within his nation's borders. In doing so Orban, borrowing from Fareed Zakaria, has *proudly* called himself an "illiberal democrat," not exactly what Zakaria, who coined this term and was himself critical of the rising illiberal democracy tide, had in mind.

China is another fascinating case. It is fascinating for a large number of reasons but is of interest to us here especially because China is coming to corporatism from the left whereas most of the regimes mentioned so far have been right-wing regimes where authoritarianism and corporatism go hand-in-hand. But China is evolving away from Marxist-Leninist-Maoist totalitarianism and toward a somewhat looser, and more relaxed form of authoritarianism. And we know from David Shambaugh's research[14] that the Chinese leadership has been reading the literature on corporatism, seeing in a corporatist regime a way to regulate and control the perhaps inevitable pluralizing and democratizing pressures set loose by rapid economic development and massive social change. Through corporatism China hopes to prevent either democratization or the mass upheaval and instability that too-fast modernization frequently leaves in its wake. Hence China like the others discussed is drafting laws to restrict foreign funding (mainly from Hong Kong) of civil society groups and is also clamping down on independent organizations of women, students, workers, religious persons and others at the domestic level.[15]

Conclusion

The death of Boris Nemtsov is tragic. Many of us knew and liked him a lot, even while recognizing his limits as an opposition political leader and that his star was fading. He was a true liberal and a

---

14   David Sambaugh, *China's Communist Party* (Berkeley: University of California Press, 2012).
15   In 2013 the University of Hong Kong organized a path-breaking conference on "Corporatism and State-Society Relations in Asia." Some of the papers from that conference have been published individually and are available from UHK, but the book planned from the conference proceedings has not to my knowledge appeared.

true democrat trying to function in a Russian context where liberalism and democracy appeared to be on the wane.

But Nemtsov's death also provides us with an opportunity to reflect on Russian democracy or the lack thereof, and on this broader phenomenon not limited to Russia of rising illiberalism, authoritarianism, and corporatism in the modern world. In contrast to earlier decades, democracy's march, once seen as both inevitable and universal, has slowed, been stymied, and even reversed in quite a number of countries. The reasons for democracy's stagnation include a certain decline in the lustre of the Western democratic model, the remarkable persistence of traditional and often antidemocratic political cultures and social structures in non-Western societies, the disappointing inability of many new democracies to deliver real goods and services, the world economic decline beginning in 2008, and the rise of the other models ("the Rest") — Russia under Putin, China, East Asia, India, Iran, now ISIS — to challenge the historically prevailing Western and liberal-democratic one. It is striking that almost all the theorists who in the early-1990 wrote laudatory books often celebrating more than analyzing democracy, including Huntington, Fukuyama, and the present author, later wrote books retracting their earlier conclusions.

Latin America, most of Eastern and Central Europe, much of East Asia except for China and North Korea, India and South Asia, and quite likely much of Southeast Asia and parts of Subsaharan Africa ended up in the, mainly, liberal-democratic-pluralist camp. But not Russia, China, Central Asia, or the Islamic Middle East and North Africa (MENA). So what explains the differences: is it history, geography, resources, level of socioeconomic development, class structure, location, timing, political culture, institutions, or some combination of all of these? It turns out that all the great issues in the social sciences, instead of being resolved by the progressive, inevitable march of democracy, are still with us.

At this stage I see four main models "out there" in the now-globalized world of development studies, with totalitarianism of both the left and right varieties having for the most part disappeared. The first and still, in the main, most attractive and most widespread one is liberal-pluralist democracy as practiced in numerous variations in the countries/regions listed above. The second and now increasing in numbers and popularity, at least among party and regime elites, is corporatism and authoritarianism, alternatively viewed as either a transitional or a quasi-permanent regime. The third alternative is a populist or neo-syndicalist regime, sometimes popular if not often very effective in left-wing, revolutionary regimes, or regimes in which institutions and civil society have previously been weak or dysfunctional—Bolivia, Venezuela, others. And the fourth alternative, in Iran, the Middle East, some parts of Africa and perhaps elsewhere, involves the search for an indigenous or home-grown model, whether Islamic or other, alternative to the usually imported and often ill-fitting Western one. We may *wish* that the Western democratic model triumphs universally but we ought to be prepared, in Russia and elsewhere, if it does not.

Boris Nemtsov and the Reproduction of Regional Intelligentsia

Tomila Lankina

I first heard of Boris Nemtsov when I was a young Russian graduate student in America in the mid-1990s contemplating pursuing a PhD in Russian regional politics.[1] For a new, post-Kremlinologist, generation of political scientists, it was the phenomenon of leaders like Nemtsov that made the study of Russian provincial politics fascinating and exciting. In the post-Soviet hyper-federalist Russia of the early years of Boris Yeltsin's presidency, sub-national regions quickly emerged as powerful players in their own right, shaping regional and national politics. As governor of the Nizhniy Novgorod region, still only in his early thirties (he was only thirty-two when he became governor), Nemtsov was already a star — well before he entered national politics as deputy prime minister. Nemtsov led the democratic transformation of the Nizhniy Novgorod region, nurturing an atmosphere of political openness, attracting foreign investment, and supporting independent media and civil society. To scholars of Russian regional politics, Nemtsov's governorship of *Nizhegorodskaya* is associated with the most vibrant period in the history of Russian federalism. I hesitate to use the expression "golden age" of federalism because Yeltsin-era federal relations were associated with ad hocism and preferential politically-motivated deals with regional bosses that in some cases helped promote regional authoritarianism, nepotism, and corruption. Yet, regions like Nizhniy stood out as islands of sub-national openness, while governors like Nemtsov helped keep in check excessive concentration of power in the national executive and shaped national policy and public opinion. In 1996, for example, he organised a campaign

---

[1] A short version of this essay appeared as a LSE European Politics and Public Policy blogpost (Lankina 2015), http://blogs.lse.ac.uk/europpblog/2015/03/02/russian-citizens-owe-it-to-boris-nemtsov-to-keep-the-hope-of-democracy-in-russia-alive/ (as of 29 August 2017)

against the war in Chechnya, collecting one million signatures in the Nizhniy Novgorod region on a petition to President Yeltsin and calling on other regions to support his initiative.[2] President Vladimir Putin's recentralization drive of the early 2000s ensured that even the hitherto politically open regions would turn into dependencies of the Kremlin delivering blatantly fraudulent electoral support to the national incumbent.[3] Back in the 1990s however, the more politically competitive regions could, and did, shape national political landscapes. While the Rakhimovs, the Shaymievs, or the Ilyumdzhinovs—long-serving presidents of Bashkortostan, Tatarstan, and Kalmykia of that era will be associated in the public mind with patrimonialism and neo-Soviet sub-national authoritarianism,[4] Nemtsov will be remembered as a democratic, public-minded, governor.

This essay attempts to situate Nemtsov as an individual in the broader sweep of Russia's regional—and national—history. To what extent is the democratic development of particular regions down to the force, drive, and charisma of particular transformational leaders? And, to what extent is Nemtsov himself a product of the particular social milieu conducive to the genesis of the public-minded, self-sacrificing crusader for common good? If regional microcosms matter for understanding the genesis of the democratic leader, what are those elements of the longue durée of regional cultural, social, economic, and political fabrics that might help explain the phenomenon of Nemtsov? And how can Nemtsov's own life help illuminate what aspects of regional histories we should study to explain the paradox of democratic resilience in particular regions and the potential of these regions to help transform national poli-

---

2   Michael McFaul and Nikolay Petrov, *Politicheskiy al'manakh Rossii 1997* (Moscow: Moscow Carnegie Centre, 1998), 2.
3   Tomila Lankina and Rodion Skovoroda, "Sub-national Electoral Protests and the Spatial, Temporal, and Substantive Dynamics of Electoral Misconduct: A Theory and Empirical Test." (Unpublished Manuscript, 2015).
4   Tomila V. Lankina, *Governing the Locals: Local Self-Government and Ethnic Mobilization in Russia* (Lanham: Rowman and Littlefield Publishers, 2004); Jeffrey Kahn, *Federalism, Democratization, and the Rule of Law in Russia* (Oxford: Oxford University Press, 2002)

tics? This essay attempts to provide some answers to these questions. At the outset, I should say that I have never met Boris Yefimovich, nor am I familiar with all the known details of his biography. I am approaching this topic as a political scientist specializing in Russia's regional politics and as someone who had come to realize that to understand the post-1991 dynamics of regional political development we have to go beyond the preoccupation with the political leadership choices made in the post-communist period, and beyond even the structural variations imposed on the regions during the Soviet period. Rather, we should delve deeper into history, to explore how pre-communist developments may have already set regions on variable developmental and, ultimately, democratic trajectories; how these developments interacted with Soviet developmental goals and projects; and how these complex historical processes in turn continue to account for Russia's regional governance variations. Rather than emphasizing political and economic institutions as being central to the long-term reproduction of patterns of development, as would be consistent with a prominent strand of recent economic and political theorizing,[5] my approach is leaning more towards the human capital persistence and reproduction area of recent and established scholarship in economics, sociology, and political science.[6] Taking this approach endows our hero both with strong agency — the power to shape regional (and national) destinies — while also highlighting how the genesis of the particular values, mind-set, and actions that we associate with one particular individual is perhaps more likely in particular regional settings, and less so in others. In what follows, I begin by outlining the historical elements of regional development that ought to be considered as important drivers of the reproduction of the observed variations in regional governance over time. I then situate the phenomenon of

---

5   Daron Acemoglu, Simon Johnson and James A. Robinson, "The Colonial Origins of Comparative Development: An Empirical Investigation." *The American Economic Review* 91, no.5 (2001): 1369-1401.

6   Edward L. Glaeser, Rafael La Porta, Florencio Lopez-de-Silanes and Andrei Shleifer, "Do Institutions Cause Growth?" *Journal of Economic Growth* 9, no.3 (2004): 271-303; Pierre Bourdieu and Jean-Claude Passeron, *Reproduction in Education, Society and Culture* (London: Aage, 1990).

Boris Nemtsov in the particular constellations of regional variables propitious for nurturing non-conformist opinion—notably the development of Nizhniy's centers of scientific research in which he studied and worked—while also highlighting the democratic proclivities of the Yaroslavl' region, in which Nemtsov was elected as regional assembly deputy in 2013. A concluding section links the historical discussion about regional human capital to the wider debates about the role of the critical intelligentsia in keeping the hope of democracy in Russia alive.

The Longue Durée of Regional Histories

Following the collapse of the Soviet Union, it did not take long for scholars to observe that the substantial democratic variations that emerged early on among Soviet-bloc states are also characteristics of Russia's *sub*-national regions.[7] In fact, it was the persona of the media darling Boris Nemtsov—the young governor who shaped the democratic politics of the Nizhniy Novgorod region—that made these variations appear to be ever more glaring. The democratic politics of Nizhegorodskaya under Nemtsov's governorship—however messy and scandal-ridden[8]—nevertheless stood in stark contrast to the neo-Soviet, patrimonial, and corrupt regimes in the "ethnic" republics of Bashkortostan or Kalmykia; or to the conservative, nostalgic-Soviet, paternalistic politics in what quickly

---

[7] Lankina, *Governing the Locals: Local Self-Government and Ethnic Mobilization in Russia*; Vladimir Gelman, Sergei Ryzhenkov, Michael Brie, Boris Ovchinnikov and Igor Semenov, *Making and Breaking Democratic Transitions: The Comparative Politics of Russia's Regions* (Lanham: Rowman and Littlefield Publishers, Inc., 2003); Kelly M. McMann and Nikolai V. Petrov, "A Survey of Democracy in Russia's Regions." *Post-Soviet Geography and Economics* 41, no.3 (2003): 155–182; Tomila Lankina, "The Dynamics of Regional and National Contentious Politics in Russia: Evidence from a New Dataset." *Problems of Post-Communism* 62, no.1 (2015): 26–44; Tomila Lankina and Alisa Voznaya, "New Data on Protest Trends in Russia's Regions." *Europe – Asia Studies* 67, no. 2 (2015): 327–342; Tomila Lankina, Alexander Libman and Anastassia Obydenkova, "Authoritarian and Democratic Diffusion in Post-Communist Regions." *Comparative Political Studies*, 49, no.12 (2016), DOI: 10.1177/0010414016628270

[8] McFaul and Petrov, *Politicheskiy al'manakh Rossii 1997*.

became known as the "Red belt," "Russian" — that is, non-ethnically defined — *oblasti*. The ground-breaking indices of regional democracy composed by Nikolay Petrov and Alexey Titkov codified — in an innovative and highly systematic way — what was becoming known anecdotally about the democratic or authoritarian proclivities of particular regions.[9] Nizhny already emerged in these indices close to the top end of Russia's regional democratic achievers. The 1990s were the height of the dominance of transitology as the leading explanatory paradigm accounting for the emerging democratic variations among post-Soviet states. Scholarship on Russia's regions influenced by the transitology paradigm tended to explain the emerging variations in regional governance in terms of pacts and choices made among key individuals in regional leadership positions.[10] Others, however, were early on pointing to the significant Soviet-era structural legacies that may account for the particular regional elite constellations and the choices that these elites make in the context of democratic transition.[11] Again, Nizhniy Novgorod featured in some of these analyses as a region in which the Soviet-era industrial structure made consensual-style, democratic politics more likely than in those regions where such Soviet-imposed structural preconditions had been lacking. More recent scholarship on post-communist democracy and development has encouraged scholars to transcend their preoccupation with "temporally shallow"[12] causes and to more systematically explore how pre-com-

---

9   Nikolay Petrov and Alexei Titkov, *Reiting demokratichnosti regionov Moskovskogo tsentra Karnegi: 10 let v stroyu* (Moscow: Moscow Carnegie Center, 2013); Nikolai Petrov, "Regional Models of Democratic Development." In Michael McFaul, Nikolai Petrov and Andrei Ryabov, eds., *Between Dictatorship and Democracy: Russian Post-Communist Political Reform* (Washington, DC: Carnegie Endowment for International Peace, 2005).
10 Gelman, Ryzhenkov, Brie, Ovchinnikov and Semenov, *Making and Breaking Democratic Transitions: The Comparative Politics of Russia's Regions*.
11 Kathryn Stoner-Weiss, *Local Heroes: The Political Economy of Russian Regional Governance* (Princeton: Princeton University Press, 1997).
12 Herbert Kitschelt, "Accounting for Postcommunist Regime Diversity: What Counts as a Good Cause?" In Grzegorz Ekiert and Stephen Hanson, eds., *Capitalism and Democracy in Central and Eastern Europe: Assessing the Legacy of Communist Rule*, (Cambridge: Cambridge University Press, 2003), 125–152

munist histories might have a bearing on the long-term reproduction of variables that could be linked to spatial variations in democratic governance.[13] Much of this literature has tended to analyze national-level variations, though there were some exceptions.[14] Furthermore, recent research into the long-term influences of pre-communist legacies on post-communist democracy has mostly focused on Central European states. Russia has been curiously sidelined in this work, at best featuring as an observation in large-n national-level quantitative analyses.

Barring a handful of recent studies by economic historians into particular aspects of regional development, such as serfdom,[15] or the zemstvo movement,[16] there has been little systematic sub-national scholarship on how the pre-communist development of Russia's provinces could help us explain democratic — or autocratic — resilience in the regions. Research to date has tended to concentrate on a handful of regions; or to explore causal mechanisms contained within a particular historical era.[17] There is an even greater paucity of research into how regional pre-communist histories may have interacted with the communist project, and how the complex multi-

---

13   Tomila Lankina, "Unbroken Links? From Imperial Human Capital to Post-Communist Modernisation," *Europe-Asia Studies* 64, no.4 (2012): 623–43; Grigore Pop-Eleches and Joshua A. Tucker, "Communism's Shadow: The Effect of Communist Legacies on Post-communist Preferences, Evaluations, and Behavior" (Unpublished Manuscript, 2013); Stephen Kotkin and Mark R. Beissinger, "The Historical Legacies of Communism: An Empirical Agenda." In Stephen Kotkin and Mark R. Beissinger, eds., 1–27 (New York: Cambridge University Press, 2014); Keith Darden and Anna Grzymala-Busse, "The Great Divide: Literacy, Nationalism, and the Communist Collapse," *World Politics* 59 (2006): 83–115.

14   Lankina, "Unbroken Links? From Imperial Human Capital to Post-Communist Modernisation".

15   Evgeny Finkel, Scott Gehlbach and Tricia D. Olsen. "Does Reform Prevent Rebellion? Evidence From Russia's Emancipation of the Serfs." *Comparative Political Studies* 48, no.8 (2015): 984–1019.

16   Steven Nafziger, "Did Ivan's Vote Matter? The Political Economy of Local Democracy in Tsarist Russia," *European Review of Economic History* 15 (2011): 393–441.

17   Such as whether serfdom had the effect of deterring peasant rebellion in imperial Russia. See Evgeny Finkel, Scott Gehlbach, and Tricia D. Olsen. "Does Reform Prevent Rebellion? Evidence from Russia's Emancipation of the Serfs," *Comparative Political Studies* 48, no.8 (2015): 984–1019.

layered historical processes might, in turn, shed light on the developmental trajectories of particular regions.

The specific feature of Russia's regional development that I would like to highlight here is the inter-temporal resilience of human capital—and the institutions associated with the production and reproduction of human and cultural capital—transcending the distinct tsarist, communist, and post-communist periods and regime types. Already in the early 19th century, some regions of the Russian Empire that are now part of the Russian Federation possessed the beginnings of what would become some of the Empire's more advanced schooling systems. In the course of the 19th century, universities were also established in several of the *gubernii* corresponding to the territories of the present-day Russian Federation. These institutions were, of course, the manifestations of wider modernization processes in tsarist Russia, which affected the various territories in a highly uneven fashion. These modernization variations had been conditioned by a complex bundle of variables ranging from the differences in the practices associated with peasant bondage; to geographic location in proximity to key transport arteries; to the discovery of important natural resources and concomitant processes of industrialization in particular *gubernii*.[18] They were also conditioned by exogenous factors preceding industrialization, as would be the case with German settlers who had been invited by Catherine the Great to settle in the Volga area (*povolzhye*), and later settled also in Siberia, beginning in the 18th century.[19]

---

18   Jeffrey Brooks, *When Russia Learned to Read* (Princeton: Princeton University Press, 1985); Ben Eklof, *Russian Peasant Schools: Officialdom, Village Culture, and Popular Pedagogy, 1861–1914* (Berkeley University of California Press, 1986); Nafziger, "Did Ivan's Vote Matter? The Political Economy of Local Democracy in Tsarist Russia"; Carol Leonard, *Agrarian Reform in Russia: The Road from Serfdorm* (New York: Cambridge University Press, 2011); Donald W. Treadgold, *The Great Siberian Migration: Government and Peasant in Resettlment from Emancipation to the First World War* (Westport: Greenwood Press, 1976); David Moon, "Peasant Migration, the Abolition of Serfrom, and the Internal Passport System in the Russian Empire, c. 1800–1914." In David Eltis, ed., *Coerced and Free Migration: Global Perspectives, 324–57, 424–32* (Stanford, Calif.: Stanford University Press, 2002).

19   Fred C. Koch, *The Volga Germans in Russia and the Americas, from 1763 to the Present* (London: The Pennsylvania State University Press, 1977); Tomila V.

These German communities founded superb primary schools and gymnasia, while also providing the human capital pool for the nascent university system (as did other ethnic Germans, who had not been descendants of the settlers, but who had come to colonize Russia's higher educational and research establishments as scholars and who are given credit for the Germanization of the Empire's university system and research.[20] When reading the novelist Fyodor Dostoevsky's *The House of the Dead* or the explorer George Kennan's powerful *Siberia and the Exile System*, one is also reminded of the role of political exiles in creating small groups of cosmopolitan and highly educated communities—some transient, others leaving a profound mark on the local social-cultural milieu—in the most climatically harsh and undeveloped fringes of the Russian Empire.[21] Consequently, as is illustrated by the results of the first Imperial Census of 1897, at the turn of the 19th-20th centuries, on the eve of the Bolshevik revolution, Russia featured glaring spatial variations in literacy levels among its provinces. Furthermore, while some *gubernii* were only beginning to develop universal basic schooling, others already possessed world-class institutions of learning and research.

To illustrate these patterns, I provide some statistics on literacy in imperial Russia's *gubernii* and indicate where the more or less literate provinces ended up on regional democracy indices in the 1990s and early 2000s (Appendix, Table 1).[22] The literacy statistics

---

Lankina. "Religious Influences on Human Capital Variations in Imperial Russia." (Journal Article 2012): ; V. M. Kabuzan, *Nemetskoyazychnoe naselenie v Rossiyskoy imperii i SSSR v XVII-XX vekakh (1719-1989)* (Moscow: RAN: Institut rossiyskoy istorii, 2003); Michael Schippan and Sonja Striegnitz, *Wolgadeutsche: Gischichte und Gegenwart* (Berlin, 1992) ; Gerd Stricker, "Die Schulen der Wolgadeutschen in der zweiten Haelfte des 19. Jahrhunderts ." In Dittmar Dahlmann and Ralph Tuchtenhagen, ed., *Zwischen Reform und Revolution: Die Deutschen an der Wolga, 1860-1917* (Essen: Klartext, 1994).

20 Loren R. Graham, *The Soviet Academy of Sciences and the Communist Party, 1927-1932* (Princeton: Princeton University Press 1967).
21 George Kennan. *Siberia and the Exile System* (New York: The Century Co, 1891); Fyodor M. Dostoevsky. *Zapiski iz myortvogo doma* (Moscow: Pravda, 1982).
22 For a detailed discussion of these patterns and presentation of the relevant data, see Tomila Lankina, Alexander Libman and Anastassia Obydenkova, "Appropriation and Subversion: Pre-communist Literacy, Communist Party

are sourced from Russia's first imperial census of 1897,[23] while the regional democracy data are compiled by Petrov and Titkov. In developmental scholarship, female literacy in particular is considered to be an important indicator of human capital and modernization considering the significance of literacy and education for female participation in the labour force, reproductive decisions, and the likelihood of transmission of values conducive to educational aspirations to children.[24] Unsurprisingly, we observe that regions that had been most literate and ended up with comparatively high democracy scores are Moscow (56,3 overall literacy and 42,3 female literacy) and St. Petersburg (62,6 overall literacy and 51,5 female literacy).[25] What is less known is that, for instance, Samara and Yaroslavl', which had been considered among Russia's most politically open regions in the post-communist period, also had among the highest literacy levels, and particularly female literacy, in the imperial period (22,1 and 14 per cent; and 36 and 24 per cent, respectively). In territories that had been during the imperial period part of what constitutes the present-day Nizhegorodskaya *oblast*, the overall literacy rate was 22 per cent and female literacy was 11 per cent. These figures are modest if one compares Russia to Western European states with far higher literacy levels at the turn of the 19th- early 20th centuries, yet they are significantly above literacy rates in a large number of imperial Russia's other *gubernii*.

Now let us look at regions that had been among the least literate in the imperial period, in terms of both overall literacy and female literacy. The North Caucasus republics clearly stand out — with literacy of less than 15 per cent and with only 6 per cent females listed as literate in some regions (Kabardino-Balkaria, North

---

Saturation, and Post-Communist Democratic Outcomes," *World Politics* 68, no.2 (2016): 229–74.

23 N. A. Troynitskiy, *Obschii svod po imperii rezul'tatov razrabotki dannykh pervoy vseobschey perepisi naseleniya, proizvedyonnoy 28 Yanvarya 1897 goda*. I-II (St. Petersburg: Tipografiya N. L. Nyrkina 1905).

24 Tomila Lankina and Lullit Getachew, "Competitive Religious Entrepreneurs: Christian Missionaries and Female Education in Colonial and Post-colonial India." *British Journal of Political Science* 43, no.1(2013): 103–131.

25 Petrov and Titkov, *Reiting demokratichnosti regionov Moskovskogo tsentra Karnegi: 10 let v stroyu*.

Ossetia) — though, among the less literate regions, one also finds Siberian territories, like Omsk and Novosibirsk, that remained comparatively under-developed at the time of the 1897 census when it comes to overall levels of human capital (as distinct from the educational credentials of the small communities of exiles or tsarist administrators), but have been considered comparatively democratic in the post-communist period. What is also interesting is that Central Russian regions that in terms of their post-communist electoral geography had been characterized as belonging to the "red belt" of conservative regions with paternalistic political tendencies also had at the time of the 1897 census low levels of literacy, female literacy in particular. For instance, in Orel, the overall and female literacy rates were 17,6 and 7,3 per cent, respectively. In the "red belt" region of Briansk, overall literacy was 16,6 and female literacy was only 6,9 per cent.

Clearly, not all regions fit the pattern of high imperial literacy-high post-communist democracy, considering that a host of potential variables may impinge on regional democratic development. Nevertheless, systematic statistical analysis of the links between human capital and regional democratic variations suggests that the above-discussed patterns are non-random, in other words, that past literacy does have an effect on subsequent communist-era modernization, as well as on post-communist regional regime patterns.[26]

The spatial variations in human capital were to pose significant challenges to the rulers of the new Bolshevik state who were desperate to not only stamp out illiteracy and develop more advanced forms of education throughout the country, but to find sufficiently qualified cadre — the so-called red teachers (*krasnye uchitelya*) — to assist the Bolsheviks in the attainment of these noble objectives.[27] They also complicated the pursuit of the overall objective of the country's rapid modernization.

---

[26] Lankina, Libman and Obydenkova, "Appropriation and Subversion: Precommunist Literacy, Communist Party Saturation, and Post-Communist Democratic Outcomes".

[27] V. N. Varlamenkov, "Osobennosti kadrovoy politiki v obrazovatel'noy sfere v 20-kh godakh XX veka v Povolzhskom regione," *Vestnik samarskogo gosudarstvennogo universiteta* 1, no.60(2008): 350–361.

The underlying assumption in some of the scholarship on Soviet regional development has been that the Bolshevik Revolution of 1917 put a break on the reproduction of the above-discussed developmental—and, most importantly for this analysis, human capital—variations under the new order; and that the regional variations that we observe now are products of the spatially uneven application of the USSR's industrialization drive.[28] In fact, much of the earlier scholarship on communist-period regional development has tended to emphasize Soviet accomplishments in eliminating illiteracy, in building higher education, and in abolishing, or at least significantly reducing, the massive social inequalities that existed in the Tsarist period.

Thus, the claim of the creation of a New Soviet Man had been in some ways unreflectively internalized by scholars writing about Soviet modernization accomplishments. So has been apparently the notion that a *new* Soviet intelligentsia had been created, that is, an intelligentsia ostensibly untarnished by association with the *old* intelligentsia of educated or more or less privileged origin from the previous, tsarist order.[29] Yet, the undisputable record of social elevation of large numbers of hitherto underprivileged and uneducated members of the lower orders—and their metamorphosis into the *new* intelligentsia—has often tended to obscure the immense role of the literate, better-educated, and often (though not always) relatively privileged members of the *old* intelligentsia in this process, and of the corresponding eventual acquisition of respectable status of this *old* intelligentsia and their descendants under the Soviet regime.

The Soviets in fact built on the tsarist regime's modernization foundations, employing the educated strata of the past order to further their grand social engineering and economic modernization

---

28 Merle Fainsod, *How Russia is Ruled: Revised Edition* (Cambridge: Harvard University Press, 1970).
29 T. H. Rigby, *Political Elites in the USSR: Central Leaders and Local Cadres from Lenin to Gorbachev* (Aldershot: Edward Elgar, 1990); Fainsod, *How Russia is Ruled*; Nicholas De Witt. *Education and Professional Employment in the USSR* (Washington, DC: National Science Foundation, 1961).

projects.³⁰ The historical narratives about Bolshevik rule are littered with images of vandalism and destruction—of palaces, churches, and mansions. Yet, one story that features less prominently in these narratives is about the scores of institutions manufacturing human capital that the Bolsheviks unashamedly appropriated, preserved, patched up, and expanded to serve the regime's ambitious developmental objectives. It is little surprise then that territories corresponding to imperial *gubernii* with high concentrations of institutions of basic and advanced learning, or otherwise boasting high human capital development due to the long-term imperial-era modernization processes, also emerged as hubs of scientific endeavor and advanced industry in the communist period. So did those with perhaps more modest claim to being at the forefront of imperial education and scholarship—for instance, Ivanovo—but which due to the exogenous shock of war (the First World War during the Imperial period; and Secord World War during the Soviet period) ended up playing host, at first temporarily, and then permanently, to leading centers of learning or industry that had been evacuated from other regions for strategic reasons.³¹

Populating these institutions were real people, whose motivations for serving the communist regime were complex, but who played significant roles in the USSR's modernization endeavor. Until the Stalinist purges of the 1930s, available records allow us, with some degree of certainty, to establish the extent of reproduction of the generally literate strata and, indeed, the intellectual crème de la crème of the imperial academic establishments in the institutions of learning, scientific, and cultural endeavor under the Bolshevik regime. For instance, we know that a significant proportion of gymnasia teachers, as well as academicians, in such top imperial-era establishments like the Russian Academy of Sciences in St. Petersburg, had previously worked in those imperial academic institu-

---

30 Lankina, Libman and Obydenkova, "Appropriation and Subversion: Precommunist Literacy, Communist Party Saturation, and Post-Communist Democratic Outcomes".
31 Ibid.

tions and had been appropriated by the new regime to advance literacy, higher education, or science.³² The purges, of course, had an enormous toll on these educated strata of Soviet society.³³ Not only did they represent the physical extermination of hundreds of thousands of innocent citizens, but they also displaced and uprooted scores of others. Yet, statistics compiled by T. H. Rigby provide some indication as to the degree of what may be termed post-purge "restoration" of individuals with "undesirable" social origins in party and governance structures and in professional occupations.³⁴ For instance, the high proportion of "scientists" among post-purge, 1938–1939, party recruits suggests that many would have obtained their education under the old order—this would be in line with the policy of abandonment of rigid class-based criteria in admission to the party, and in advancement in the professions, by the late 1930s.³⁵ Analyzing the imperial backgrounds of Soviet academics, the Russian historian Sergey Volkov notes: "The scientific milieu ... corresponded the least to the Soviet understandings of 'correct' social origins;" this observation applied in particular to "physics, mathematics, and medicine."³⁶ Generally, some indication of the inter-generational reproduction of educational status, values, and preferences is provided by Sheila Fitzpatrick, Alex Inkeles and other leading scholars of Soviet politics, who documented the impetus of those who had been well-educated in the imperial era to transmit educational advantage to their offspring, even if, under

---

32   Graham, *The Soviet Academy of Sciences and the Communist Party, 1927–1932*; Varlamenkov, "Osobennosti kadrovoy politiki v obrazovatel'noy sfere v 20-kh godakh XX veka v Povolzhskom regione".
33   Michael Ellman, "Soviet Repression Statistics: Some Comments." *Europe – Asia Studies* 54, no.7 (2002): 1151–72; Steven Rosefielde, "Documented Homicides and Excess Deaths: New Insights into the Scale Killing in the USSR During the 1930s," *Communist and Post-Communist Studies* 30, no.3 (1997): 321–31; Robert Conquest, *The Great Terror: A Reassessment* (London: Pimlico, 2008).
34   T. H. Rigby, *Communist Party Membership in the U.S.S.R., 1917–1967* (Princeton: Princeton University Press, 1968).
35   Rigby, *Communist Party Membership in the U.S.S.R., 1917–1967*: 222.
36   He writes: "Nauchnaya sreda iz vsekh professional'nykh grupp intellektual'nogo sloya, po-vidimomu, v naimen'shey stepeni otvechala sovetskim predstavleniyam o 'pravil'nom' sotsial'nom sostave."

the new order, in new form, name, and substance.[37] The result had been a considerable degree of reproduction of social and professional identifications—with a corresponding set of value orientations—between two apparently vastly contrasting imperial and communist regimes.[38]

In a recent paper, Tomila Lankina, Alexander Libman, and Anastassia Obydenkova, conceptualize the above-discussed social repositioning of the imperial regime's educated strata under the new communist regime as a form of *appropriation*.[39] Whether these individuals and their descendants became genuine converts to Marxist-Leninist faith, or simply professed enthusiasm for the new regime to get on with their lives and careers, many ended up joining the Communist Party of the Soviet Union (CPSU). In fact, as a large body of sovietological scholarship testifies, the educated, upwardly mobile strata tended to be over-represented in the CPSU in proportion to the share of these groups in the USSR's population.[40] Some public opinion surveys conducted in the post-soviet period (and in various other post-communist states) suggest that, contrary to expectations of modernization theorizing, the highly educated former communist party members ended up espousing values less democratic than those who had never been party members during the communist period.[41] These data might indicate that there was

---

37 Sheila Fitzpatrick, *Education and Social Mobility in the Soviet Union, 1921–1934* (Cambridge: Cambridge University Press, 1979); David Lane, "The Impact of Revolution: The Case of Selection of Students for Higher Education in Soviet Russia, 1917–1928." *Sociology* 7, no.241(1973): 241–52; Alex Inkeles, "Social Stratification and Mobility in the Soviet Union: 1940–1950." *American Sociological Review* 15. No.4 (1950): 465–79.
38 Sergey Volkov, *Intellektual'nyy sloy v sovetskom obshchestve* (St. Petersburg: Russian Academy of Sciences, 1999)
39 Lankina, Libman and Obydenkova, "Appropriation and Subversion: Precommunist Literacy, Communist Party Saturation, and Post-Communist Democratic Outcomes".
40 Milovan Djilas, *The New Class: An Analysis of the Communist System* (San Diego: Harcourt Brace Jovanovich 1983); Rigby, *Communist Party Membership in the U.S.S.R., 1917–1967*.
41 Ada W. Finifter and Ellen Mickiewicz, "Redefining the Political System of the USSR: Mass Support for Political Change," *The American Political Science Review* 86, no.4 (1992): 857–74; Russell J. Dalton, "Communists and Democrats: Democratic Attitudes in the Two Germanies," *British Journal of*

something about socialization within the party that had an undemocratic effect on value orientations; it may also point to the undemocratic effects of *service* to the communist regime more generally insofar as party membership may proxy for involvement with the political-managerial and governance side of Soviet professions.[42] Paradoxically, those very same areas of present-day Russia that had been rich in human capital—and democratic potential—before the Bolshevik revolution of 1917, ended up becoming the more robust suppliers of educated party cadre; this in turn, as Lankina, Libman, and Obydenkova conjecture, would have a *subversive* effect on the democratic trajectories of particular regions in the post-communist period.

So, if the *appropriation and subversion* thesis is correct, how, then, do we begin to explain why not all educated strata engaged in regime-reinforcing ideological dogma and professions? And what kind of a regional milieu would have been least conducive to the processes of democratic subversion-through-service discussed above? To address this question, I turn again to T.H. Rigby, whose work has been rather unjustly neglected in recent scholarship on the historical legacies of communism, but who provides the, in my view, still unsurpassed analysis of the professional, demographic, and social characteristics of the members of CPSU over time.[43] As noted above, the highly educated professionals had been drawn to the party. Academia and research were not immune to this trend

---

Political Science 24, no.4 (1994): 469–493; Robert Rohrschneider, "Report from the Laboratory: The Influence of Institutions on Political Elites' Democratic Values in Germany," *The American Political Science Review* 88, no.4 (1994): 927–941; Arthur H. Miller, Vicki L. Hesli and William M. Reisinger, "Conceptions of Democracy Among Mass and Elite in Post-Soviet Societies," *British Journal of Political Science* 27, no.2(1997): 157–190.

42 Alexander Libman and Anastassia V. Obydenkova, "CPSU Legacies and Regional Democracy in Contemporary Russia," *Political Studies* 63, no S1: 173–190, April 2015; Alexander Libman and Anastassia Obydenkova, "CPSU Legacies and Regional Democracy in Contemporary Russia"; Alexander Libman and Anastassia Obydenkova, "Communism or Communists? Soviet Legacies and Corruption in Transition Economies," *Economics Letters* 119 (2013): 101–103.

43 Rigby, *Communist Party Membership in the U.S.S.R., 1917–1967*; Rigby, *Political Elites in the USSR: Central Leaders and Local Cadres from Lenin to Gorbachev.*

insofar as many academics and scientists represented the party's "lay" membership—uninvolved with the party apparat, but possessing membership cards, usually for the purposes of career advancement. Specific branches of scholarship, however, stood out in their comparatively low statistics for membership in the USSR's "leading and guiding force." It is well-known that the hard sciences, in particular, had served as breeding grounds for the USSR's dissident movement. Rigby's statistics confirm that certain branches of scholarly endeavor had been indeed comparatively low party-saturated. The party records data that he cites are for the late 1940s, but they provide some illustration of what continued to represent a trend in party membership rates among scientists over time. For instance, while in 1947, a mere 17 per cent of engineering professors were CPSU members, 58 per cent of professors in the social sciences and philosophy possessed CPSU membership cards.[44]

Here, as the sociologist Georgi Derluguian notes, an element of self-selection is likely to have been at work, as those most critically-inclined towards the regime had been perhaps more likely to join the least-ideologically indoctrinated professions.[45] Rigby also speculates that "first-rate" scientists valued by the regime for their contribution to the USSR's stellar achievements had been perhaps also comparatively immune from the pressures of membership—and the administrative burdens that come with ritualized regime-reinforcing "public" activities associated with being a Komsomol or party member. Finally, the Russian historian Sergei Volkov highlights the element of the inter-generational reproduction of a particular mind-set amongst descendants of pre-Soviet academic intelligentsia that continued to discreetly hold on to their values while laboring in scientific environments far removed from the "ideological vanguard of communist construction." He writes:

> Despite the artificial nature of the soviet intellectual strata in general, in its midst had been preserved, or even newly formed, isolated strata and groups

---

44   Rigby, *Communist Party Membership in the U.S.S.R., 1917–1967*, 445.
45   Georgi M. Derluguian. *Bourdieu's Secret Admirer in the Caucasus: A World-System Biography* (Chicago: University of Chicago Press, 2005).

qualitatively different—and better—than the rest... I mean first and foremost the academic milieu and the sphere of military-technical research and development. In a number of the branches of these spheres, as is well-known, can be found the intellectual potential of world quality, at least in a professional sense. Having found themselves for a variety of reasons... outside of the sphere of rigid ideological control, these strata had partially succeeded in conserving the features characteristic of the normal intellectual elite. It is also characterized by a comparatively high level of self-reproduction. This is also the strata that had partially succeeded in preserving certain traditions of the pre-soviet intellectual layer of society.[46]

I conjecture that the social milieu propitious for democracy in post-communist Russia would be one situated around the kinds of islands of non-conformism discussed above, which would be, in turn, conditioned by the long-term historical legacies of development in particular regions; these islands would be also most immune to the pressures of communist-era *appropriation* that may have been more strongly felt by other comparatively well-developed areas. These would be also the kinds of spatial islands of critical thought and opinion that would generate support structures for Russia's post-communist democratic movement. In the next section, I illustrate the various insights that I have sketched out above, about the temporal, spatial, and social dimension of the reproduction of imperial and communist legacies, based on the example of the Nizhniy Novgorod region, while also briefly highlighting the conditions similarly propitious for democratic resilience in the Yaroslavl' region, where Nemtsov performed his final formal political role as deputy to the regional legislature.

The Nizhniy Novgorod Region and Boris Nemtsov

Territories of what is now the Nizhniy Novgorod region had been in the XIV century part of the independent Nizhegorodsko-Suzdal'skoe Principality. Located at the intersection of the Volga and Oka river basins and key transport arteries linking central Russia

---

46   Volkov, *Intellektual'nyy sloy v sovetskom obshchestve*.

with the Urals and Siberia, Nizhniy Novgorod City, by the 19th century, emerged as a leading center of trade and commerce. From 1817, it played host to Russia's largest market, the Makaryevskaya Trade Fair. In the Soviet period, Nizhniy Novgorod became a "hyper-industrial" region, surpassed only by the city of Moscow and the Moscow and Sverdlovsk *oblasti* in industrial production levels. While the region is well-known for its machine-building industries, a third of its industrial production during the Soviet period had been in the defense sector. The Nizhniy Novgorod region had been off-limits to foreigners during the Soviet period because it housed the highly secretive "numbered" towns like Arzamas-16 (Sarov), which abandoned its closed status only in 1995. As had been the case with the USSR's other hubs that serviced the military-industrial complex, the Nizhniy Novgorod region became a leading center of scientific research. By the time of the USSR's collapse, scientific research, education and services related to knowledge-production (along with culture and the arts) constituted the second largest area of employment in the *oblast*.

The Lobachevsky State University, in which Nemtsov studied, started its life as the Warsaw Polytechnic Institute named after Nicholas II. It had been founded in 1898 and was among Imperial Russia's leading scientific establishments. Like the Ivanovo Polytechnic in the Ivanovo region (which ended up hosting the Riga Polytechnic Institute), the university had been evacuated to the region during the First World War. In 1916, it became Nizhniy Novgorod's "People's University." Although the Institute had been an acquisition from Imperial Russia's more advanced territories, the choice of Nizhniy as its new home had been influenced by a sustained campaign of the *guberniya* residents to raise funds for the relocation of the Institute's staff and facilities to their region. Here, the tradition of *metsenatstvo* (philanthropy) in this historically trading region played a role as Nizhniy's leading industrialists pooled funds to ensure that the project would be viable. The presence of relatively developed educational infrastructure and human capital pool, which would be leveraged during the early days of the polytechnic's relocation, also played a role in the selection of Nizhniy as the Institute's new home. When the Bolsheviks came to power, the

Institute became the Nizhegorodsky Polytechnic Institute. In 1956, it was named after the feted Soviet mathematician Nikolay Lobachevsky.[47]

The academic institution which Nemtsov joined as a student; and the Radio-physics Research Institute in which he subsequently worked as a scientist, would have been microcosms of the liberal hard sciences milieu that, as noted above, had been propitious to the nurturing of unconventional values and thought. These institutions would have been beneficiaries of the Bolshevik regime's privileged treatment of the sciences that had been introduced from the outset of Soviet rule. As early as 1921, a Central Commission for the Improvement of the Livelihoods of Scientists was created, which provided, inter alia, for special *akademicheskie payki* (academic supplements); financial incentives in the form of premiums for academic publications and inventions had been also introduced. The greatest generosity had been shown towards those working in the "hard" sciences. A special 1921 decree essentially put scientists on a par with "workers" in status, which implied that they would not face discrimination due to their "undesirable," bourgeois origins; this also implied that these individuals and their offspring would not face discrimination in university admissions (or even that they would get the same preferential treatment as those ascribed a "worker" category).[48] In-depth studies of the bureaucratic politics of the USSR's leading scientific institutions—an example of which would be Loren Graham's study of the Russian Academy of Sciences in St. Petersburg—highlight how they remained oases for the reproduction of scientific—and cultural—capital inherited from the imperial era, despite the pressures they faced in the form of the introduction of monitoring and supervision by mediocre party *appratchiki*. Derluguian provides an illustration of how communities of the liberal-minded would have been nurtured in institutions like

---

47   University of Nizhny Novgorod, http://www.unn.ru/general/brief.html; http://www.nntu.ru/content/istoriya (as of 5 July 2015).
48   Mervin Matthews, "Stanovlenie sistemy privilegiy v Sovetskom gosudarstve," *Skepsis* http://scepsis.net/library/id_439.html; original publication in *Voprosy istorii*, № 2–3 (1992): 45–61 http://scepsis.net/library/id_439.html (as of June 2015).

the Lobachevsky University and the Radio-physics Research Institute even in the later decades of the Soviet period.[49] The "hard" sciences represented, he writes, "the main breeding ground for liberal dissidents, ... especially the advanced fields of nuclear research and space exploration. During the 1950s and 1970s, these scholarly communities [along with other professions like linguists] enjoyed privileged funding, exceptionally high public acclaim, and relatively unrestricted intellectual exchanges with their Western colleagues." The pursuit of such "obscure interests... beyond the focus of official Marxist-Leninist ideology... helped to foster cohesive communities with a sense of professional dignity and kinship with the intellectual community outside the USSR. It is no small matter that such disciplines normally required a familiarity with esoteric concepts and at least a basic knowledge of foreign languages, which tended to deter administrative careerists."

The presence of a large community of intelligentsia, continuously nurtured in Nizhniy's centers of learning and research, provided important foundations for Nizhniy's *perestroika*-era democratic politics. As elsewhere in the Soviet Union, the origins of the region's politically-transformative societal activism could be traced to the environmental movement, which often featured the scientific intelligentsia as activists, and it is not coincidental that Nemtsov's political career began in Nizhniy's environmental campaigns of the 1980s. It is also not coincidental that in this region, a democratic politician like Nemtsov stood a chance of resisting and checking the power of the former communist *nomenklatura*. A study that ranked Russia's regions according to the degree of their involvement in EU-funded projects in the 1990s found Nizhniy Novgorod — a region formerly featuring cities that had been closed to foreigners — to be one of the most active regional participants in initiatives that involved EU-Russia civil society development and other democracy-promotion projects.[50] Nemtsov's sheer drive, determination,

---

49   Georgi Derluguian, *Bourdieu's Secret Admirer in the Caucasus: A World-System Biography* (Chicago: University of Chicago Press, 2005).
50   Tomila V. Lankina and Lullit Getachew, "The Virtuous Circles of Western Exposure in Russian Regions: A Case for Micro-Polity Analysis of Democratic Change," *The Journal of Communist Studies and Transition Politics* 24, no.3

and charisma during his governorship had been undoubtedly instrumental in creating the policy windows for investment and public and private projects with external partners in the region. Yet, he also operated in a regional environment with the cultural, intellectual, and human capital that would make such politics and policies possible.

Nemtsov's subsequent career outside of Nizhniy Novgorod further supports the argument developed above, namely that particular regions are propitious for both nurturing politicians like Nemtsov, while also serving as hubs of democratic resilience attracting "refugees" with high moral and political principle from more democratically "hostile" national or regional environments. I have noted already that in the imperial period, territories forming part of what is now Yaroslavl' region were at the very top of imperial Russia's literacy achievers, next only to Moscow and St. Petersburg and surrounding districts now in the Moscow and Leningrad *oblasti*; the scholars Nikolay Petrov and A. Mukhin note that already in the 18th century, Yaroslavl was imperial Russia's major industrial center. In the early 1990s, they note, "Yaroslavl' became a second after N. Novgorod Mecca for foreigners, the showcase of reforms of provincial Russia;" and a "bastion of democracy."[51] As Putin consolidated power and sought to undermine regional political pluralism by subordinating regional assemblies to loyalists affiliated with the pro-Kremlin United Russia party, Yaroslavl surprised even seasoned observers of regional politics by electing an opposition-supported candidate Yevgeniy Urlashov. Urlashov boasted a law degree from Yaroslavl University, one of the country's oldest higher educational establishments and a successor to the Demidov School of Higher Sciences (*Demidovskoye uchilishche*

(2008): 338–64; Tomila V. Lankina and Lullit Getachew, "A Geographic Incremental Theory of Democratization: Territory, Aid, and Democracy in Post-Communist Regions," *World Politics* 58, no.4(2006): 536–82; Tomila Lankina, "Explaining European Union Aid to Russia," *Post-Soviet Affairs* 21, no.4 (2005): 309–34.

51 Nikolay Petrov and A. Mukhin, "Yaroslavskaya oblast." In Michael McFaul and Nikolay Petrov, eds., *Politicheskiy al'manakh Rossii 1997* (Moscow: Moscow Carnegie Centre, 1998).

vysshikh nauk) founded in 1803 during the reign of Alexander I. Nemtsov would subsequently courageously publicly defend Urlashov when he became subject to politically-motivated prosecution. Alexander Kynev, a leading expert on regional electoral politics referred to Ulrashov's victory as among "the most stunning successes of the opposition in regional and local elections in Russia in recent years."[52] Other commentators likewise singled out Yaroslavl' as an unusual example of how "the opposition, by uniting forces and capabilities, may not just calmly, but convincingly win in the elections—here, in Putin's Russia, now, in the first year of Putin's third term."[53] It is in Yaroslavl' in 2013, that Nemtsov likewise impressed observers of regional politics by winning one seat in the regional assembly as lead candidate from the Party of People's Freedom, formerly the Republican Party of Russia (RPR-PARNAS) declaring that "the freeing of the country from swindlers and thieves will start here in Yaroslavl;" and that "the dismembering of the Putin regime will start at the regional level."[54]

Discussion

The account presented above alerts us to the phenomenon of intertemporal reproduction of particular regional societal microcosms that have endured decades of communist rule and continue to survive under the current authoritarian system. Where, then, does the agency of a transformational leader like Boris Nemtsov fit into this account? The concept of *appropriation* introduced earlier in the essay

---

52 Alexander Kynev, "Voyna i mir: Prichiny i posledstviya ataki na Yevgeniya Urlashova," *Forbes* (Russia) 4 July 2013, http://www.forbes.ru/mneniya-column/vertikal/241665-voina-i-mer-prichiny-i-posledstviya-ataki-na-evgeniya-urlashova (as of 23 December 2015).

53 Stanislav Belkovskiy, "Net vybora, krome vyborov," MKRU, 5 April 2012, http://www.mk.ru/politics/2012/04/05/689843-net-vyibora-krome-vyiborov.html (as of 23 December 2015).

54 "Boris Nemtsov ofitsial'no stal deputatom Yaroslavskoy obldumy," *FederalPress*, 25 September 2013, http://fedpress.ru/news/polit_vlast/news_polit/1380081577-boris-nemtsov-ofitsialno-stal-deputatom-yaroslavskoi-obldumy (as of 23 December 2015).

is useful here because it highlights how rationalist and adaptive impulses can dictate accommodation to a new regime by members of the past order that one would not expect to embrace the new regime. There remains, however, a minority, that will resist such impulses. As noted in this discussion, many educated members of the tsarist regime ended up joining the communist party, some even becoming true believers in the process. Likewise, we observe how many a prominent *perestroika*-era democrat or democratic commentator has now morphed into a tacit or even active and vocal apologist for the Putin regime. Fear, survival instincts, or perhaps a genuine change of political orientation would perhaps account for the remarkable metamorphosis of an apparently democratic leader into an endorser of Putin's political propaganda; or a former liberal TV commentator into a host of a kitsch show on TV Rossiya.

I have noted how some social/professional strata—even under a far more ideologically-indoctrinated and repressive—soviet—environment than the one found in present-day Russia—had been more likely to resist such forms of appropriation, and that perhaps an element of self-selection may have been at work in that those most principled and independent-minded would have navigated their way into a safe haven of sanity and moral integrity. Together, these individuals constitute the moral core of an apparently demoralized society, and represent the hope for change. Here it is appropriate to remind ourselves of the long-forgotten polemic between Seymour Martin Lipset and Richard Dobson, on the one hand, and Martin Mailia, on the other. Writing in the early 1970s, at the height of Communism in Russia, Lipset and Dobson sought to identify the common features shared by the non-conformist academic milieus in contexts as diverse as the United States and the Soviet Union. From amongst the educated strata, they distinguish specifically the "critical intelligentsia." They write:

> The critical intelligentsia is composed of those who not only have the ability to manipulate symbols with expertise, but who have also gained a reputation for commitment to general values and who have a broad evaluative outlook derived from such commitment. The characteristic orientation of these "generalizing intellectuals" is a critically evaluative one, a tendency to appraise in terms of general conceptions of the desirable, ideal conceptions

which are thought to be universally applicable. Such generalizing intellectuals have been described by Lewis Coser as follows: Intellectuals exhibit in their activities a pronounced concern with the core values of society. They are the men who seek to provide moral standards and to maintain meaningful general symbols . . . Intellectuals are men who never seem satisfied with things as they are, with appeals to custom and usage. They question the truth of the moment in terms of higher and wider truth; they counter appeals to factuality by invoking the "impractical ought." They consider themselves special custodians of abstract ideas like reason and justice and truth, jealous guardians of moral standards that are too often ignored in the market place and the houses of power.[55]

Lipset and Dobson identify America's and the USSR's leading centers of academic research as the repositories and the producers of the critical intellectual. In the USSR, some examples of such hubs that they find notable, in particular, are the Moscow area towns of Dubna and Obninsk, and the science town, *Akademgorodok*, in Novosibirsk, with its over twenty specialized scientific institutions. Even within America's top institutions, they argue, one finds those with an instinct to conserve the status quo. So it is also with Soviet centers of scientific innovation where the mediocre not unfrequently labor alongside the brilliant and the critical-minded. Nevertheless, it is within such leading spatial clusters of the production of knowledge that Lipset and Dobson saw strong potential for the germination of values ultimately corrosive of the Soviet regime. "While such settlements may serve to isolate scientists and scholars from the rest of the population, they also seem to afford a fertile setting for the gestation of critical thought, and they clearly pose new obstacles to the party's persistent efforts to maintain ideological controls," they write.[56] In a response to Lipset and Dobson's essay, Malia begged to disagree. The natural sciences, he argued, could be indeed singled out for relative non-conformism against the overall background of the "flat quality of Soviet intellectual

---

55   Seymour Martin Lipset and Richard B. Dobson, "The Intellectual as Critic and Rebel: With Special Reference to the United States and the Soviet Union," *Daedalus* 101, no.3 (1972): 137–98.
56   Lipset and Dobson, "The Intellectual as Critic and Rebel: With Special Reference to the United States and the Soviet Union," 161.

life."[57] Yet, the critical intellectual who, like Andrei Sakharov, would dare to challenge the political system appears in Malia's essay as more of an exception, not the rule in Soviet research establishments, while the picture of the general structure of USSR academia is presented as one that arguably discourages the germination of the kinds of critical faculties that may be characteristic of centers of research and innovation in some other settings.

History, of course, proved Lipset and Dobson's observations to be more prophetic than those of Malia's. Not only did many academic intellectuals contribute to the democratization—and ultimate collapse—of the Soviet system,[58] but, as any scholar of post-Soviet Russian regional politics would testify, it is the regions that had been hubs of knowledge production like Novosibirsk, Nizhniy, or St. Petersburg that have consistently ranked high in democratic ratings over the last twenty five years, and therefore could be considered as possessing latent potential for confronting the national political regime much like the science towns did during the Soviet period.

What is particularly important about the observations of Lipset and Dobson, and indeed those of Malia when he discusses the origins of the Russian intelligentsia, is the emphasis on the "pronounced concern with the core values of society," rather than on the production of new knowledge per se. By many accounts, Nemtsov had been a first rate scientist.[59] As vividly described by his press-secretary, he was no book-worm though, and not someone who could anchor his polemics in high-brow philosophical, literary, or ethics debates.[60] His political biography, however, is testimony to consistency in adherence to high principle and code of conduct in that he continued to be a democrat long after it ceased to be

---

57 Martin Malia, "The Intellectuals: Adversaries or Clerisy?" *Daedalus* 101, no.3 (1972): 2016-16.
58 Archie Brown, *The Gorbachev Factor* (Oxford: Oxford University Press, 1996).
59 "Nuzhen pamyatnik Borisu Nemtsovu," *Radio Svoboda*, 7 April 2015, http://www.svoboda.org/content/transcript/26942688.html (as of 3 July 2015).
60 Liliya Dubovaya *Nemtsov, Khakamada, Gaidar, Chubais: Zapiski Press-sekretarya* (Moscow: AST, 2015).

fashionable, expedient, lucrative, and safe. Nemtsov's life and political engagement is, of course, that of the *un*-appropriated—of the Soviet scientific intelligentsia that inherited the high moral credentials of its imperial antecedents—relatively immune to the pressures of daily reaffirmations of ideological dogma; and, later, during the times of Putinism, that of an almost quixotic figure, a romantic adhering to principles so at odds with the prevailing environment.

I have chosen to take a broad-brush historical approach to explain how historically, because of their advanced levels of human capital development, some regions of Russia have tended to become both producers of the intelligentsia in the highest sense of the term, but also to attract—as refuge-seekers from other regions—the non-conformist, the sceptic, and the critical-minded. Putin's federal recentralization drive, his neglect of Russia's research and academic establishments, and the cultivation of an atmosphere of intolerance for political dissent are gradually chipping away at what remains of the "custodians" of high moral principle. Will such islands of democratic obstinacy survive in Russia? If the record of the decades of resilience of regional hubs of human capital that strides the imperial and communist periods is any guide, I would answer that question in the affirmative. Yet, we also know that it would take the agency of a new Boris Nemtsov to inspire and mobilize these latent forces.

Governing Nizhny Novgorod: Boris Nemtsov as a Regional Leader

Vladimir Gel'man and Sharon W. Rivera

Introduction[1]

In the early 1990s, the prospect of major changes in Russia's political elite was on the horizon. A number of newcomers had entered the political arena due to the unintended effects of the "stunning" elections, to use Samuel Huntington's phrase,[2] which put an end to the previous ruling monopoly of the Communist Party in the late Soviet period and opened up the possibility of a new pool of talent coming to power. In reality, however, the scope of change in the elite turned out to be smaller than expected, especially in Russia's provinces, where by the mid-1990s, in sharp contrast to post-Communist Poland and Hungary,[3] most of the key positions were still held by representatives of the Soviet-era nomenklatura.[4] Many of those who entered Russia's national and regional politics during the democratic breakthroughs of 1989–91[5] subsequently lost their newly acquired positions in the wake of turbulent political and economic changes. The deep and protracted economic recession of the 1990s, on the one hand, and the lack of skills and connections necessary for political survival, on the other, swept a number of new

---

[1] We would like to thank David Rivera and Artem Kochnev for their comments on previous drafts of this article. This chapter draws in part on Sharon Werning Rivera, "Nemtsov and Democracy in Nizhny Novgorod," *Demokratizatsiya: The Journal of Post-Soviet Democratization* 24, no.1 (2016): 36–38.

[2] Samuel P. Huntington, *The Third Wave: Democratization in the Late Twentieth Century*. (Norman, OK: University of Oklahoma Press, 1991), 174–80.

[3] Eric Hanley, Natasha Ershova, and Richard Anderson, "Russia–Old Wine in a New Bottle: Circulation and Reproduction of Russian Elites," *Theory and Society* 24, no. 5(1995): 639–68.

[4] Olga Kryshtanovskaya and Stephen White, "From Soviet *Nomenklatura* to Russian Elite," *Europe-Asia Studies* 48, no.5 (1996): 711–33.

[5] M. Steven Fish, *Democracy from Scratch: Opposition and Regime in a New Russian Revolution* (Princeton: Princeton University Press, 1996)

"democrats" to the periphery of Russian politics, and they were replaced by a second-tier of Communist-era elites, both at the national and sub-national levels.[6] In many ways, this limited nature of elite change in Russia contributed to sub-optimal outcomes, including numerous stalled reforms and inefficient policy changes.

Paradoxically, understanding the causes of this failed revolution in the political elite might require an in-depth analysis of one of the few "success stories," where newcomers to Russian regional politics in the 1990s were able to achieve significant advancements in politics and governance and also managed to effect a measure of change in the attitudes and behavior of regional elites. From this perspective, the case of Nizhny Novgorod Oblast'[7] in 1991–97 can be regarded as an outlier in the political landscape of Russia's regions.[8] Boris Nemtsov, one of the youngest new governors and an outsider to the deeply entrenched regional politics of Nizhny Novgorod, was initially appointed by President Boris Yeltsin in 1991 to head this large and important industrial region. He became a successful leader who made efficient deals with key stakeholders both within and outside the region; co-opted old and new actors into his informal ruling coalition; pursued a number of policy initiatives; won gubernatorial elections in 1995 amidst major economic distress; and in 1997 was promoted to the post of first deputy prime minister in the federal government. While his proposed role as a potential successor to Yeltsin[9] remained nothing but a wild and unrealistic dream after the 1998 economic crisis, the impact of

---

[6] Sharon Werning Rivera, "Elites in Post-communist Russia: A Changing of the Guard?" *Europe-Asia Studies* 52, no.3 (2000): 413–32; Joel C. Moses, "Who Has Led Russia? Russian Regional Political Elites, 1954–2006," *Europe-Asia Studies* 60, no.1(2008): 1–24.

[7] Between 1932–1991, it was named Gor'ky Oblast.

[8] Kathryn Stoner-Weiss, *Local Heroes: The Political Economy of Russian Regional Governance* (Princeton: Princeton University Press, 1997); Michael McFaul and Nikolay Petrov, eds. *Politicheskii al'manakh Rossii 1997*, 2 vols. (Moscow: Carnegie Moscow Center, 1997); Vladimir Gel'man, Sergey Ryzhenkov and Michael Brie, *Making and Breaking Democratic Transitions: The Comparative Politics of Russia's Regions* (Lanham, MD: Rowman and Littlefield, 2003).

[9] In August 1994, Yeltsin told *Vesti*'s correspondent in Nizhny Novgorod that Nemtsov had become so mature during his time in office that he "could aspire

Nemtsov as a regional leader warrants further consideration. How did Nemtsov achieve a measure of success in governing Nizhny Novgorod Oblast? To what extent was he able to transform the political culture of elites working with him in the region? This chapter intends to shed new light on these questions, using both previous case study research[10] and evidence from a survey of Russian elites (including regional elites in Nizhny Novgorod) conducted in 1996.[11]

The structure of the chapter is as follows. After making a brief case for an elite-driven approach to analyzing post-Communist political transformations and for understanding the role of "elite settlements" in regime change, we describe the politics of Nizhny Novgorod Oblast before, during, and after Nemtsov's governorship against the background of the turbulent dynamics of Russian politics in the 1990s. We argue that Nemtsov's leadership contributed greatly to the advancement of democratization and economic reforms in the region, although these successes were short-lived, fading soon after his departure from the region in 1997. Some implications for the study of post-Communist politics will be discussed at the end of the chapter.

Elites, Leadership and Transformation: Building New Coalitions

Needless to say, elites and especially political leaders are essential to the success of major transformations, including post-Communist ones. At critical junctures, leaders set the agenda for political, economic, and societal change. Although their visions, ideas, and preferences are important for enacting these changes, leaders rarely act alone; rather, the larger circle of elites within which they operate is crucial to the success of any program or reform. That is why leaders

---

to become president [of Russia]." "Yeltsin Lauds Nemtsov as Possible Successor," *RFE/RL Daily Report*, 16 August 1994.

10   Gel'man, Ryzhenkov, and Brie, *Making and Breaking Democratic Transitions*, Chapter 4.

11   Rivera, "Elites in Post-communist Russia."

must establish and maintain their "winning coalitions" of supporters[12] among elites, that is, stakeholders who are able to use their formidable resources to affect major political and policy decisions in a systematic way.[13] The problem becomes that elite changes occurring during the transition process can also cause major conflicts, and the polarization of elites and societies at large can make the building of post-Communist states, markets, and institutions much more difficult for political leaders.[14] At the same time, if changes in elite political culture are shallow and remnants of the Soviet-era elite remain, these too can limit the prospects of a successful transition and even result in stagnation.

Some post-Communist political leaders attempted to overcome the collective action problem among elites through a series of major compromises, or "elite settlements," which aimed to avoid zero-sum conflicts and left room for the pursuit of often competing interests within the framework of formal institutional settings.[15] Yet these attempts rarely brought successes even slightly comparable to the famous 1977 Moncloa Pact in Spain or the 1989 Roundtable Agreement in Poland, both of which paved the way for sustainable democratization through peaceful and orderly elite turnover and the design of new democratic institutions through a cooperative process. More typically, political leaders have to rely on ad hoc compromises with various segments of a fragmented elite and find ways to prevent major conflicts from erupting. This is especially true in post-Communist transitions, when elite changes are often accompanied by, and also contribute to, a higher level of elite fragmentation. In their turn, elites often consider these ad hoc compromises to be tacit agreements, and their cooperative efforts may be short-lived—even provoking a new round of conflicts at times. Still, even these partial and incomplete "elite settlements" result in more

---

12 Bruce Bueno de Mesquita, Alastair Smith, Randolph M. Siverson, and James D. Morrow, *The Logic of Political Survival* (Cambridge, MA: MIT Press, 2003).
13 John Higley and Michael Burton, *Elite Foundations of Liberal Democracy* (Lanham, MD: Rowman and Littlefield, 2006)
14 Timothy Frye, *Building States and Markets after Communism: The Perils of Polarized Democracy* (Cambridge: Cambridge University Press, 2010)
15 Higley and Burton, *Elite Foundations of Liberal Democracy.*

positive outcomes than the two extremes—either polarized, conflict-ridden elite pluralism or the political monopoly of a single leader who tends to concentrate control over a monolithic elite structure through a "single power pyramid."[16] In a sense, therefore, such tacit deals between elites and leaders may be regarded as a second-best (yet imperfect) solution to the dilemma of the post-Communist transition.

Post-Soviet Eurasia is replete with examples of elite and leadership turnover that resulted in decidedly unsuccessful outcomes in terms of democratization and state-building.[17] For instance, Russia in the 1990s was epitomized by a raft of zero-sum conflicts among elites and leaders who battled with each other for dominance amidst a major economic downturn: in 1991 (between Gorbachev and Yeltsin), in 1993 (between Yeltsin and the Russian parliament), and then again in 1996 (between Yeltsin and his Communist rivals).[18] Similar intra-elite conflicts in Ukraine contributed greatly to mass mobilization and leadership changes in 2004 and 2014.[19] On the opposite side of the ledger, post-Communist Central Asian states such as Uzbekistan or Kazakhstan demonstrated a high degree of elite continuity and the emergence of a political monopoly of entrenched leaders throughout the entire post-Soviet period. In the 2000s, Russia too experienced a major decline in elite pluralism and the consolidation of Vladimir Putin's dominance against the background of an "imposed consensus" among elites.[20] In various ways, these examples illustrate how certain post-Communist elite arrangements are incompatible with democratization, the construction of an efficient and modern state, and policy reforms. Indeed, elites and leaders themselves bear much of the

---

16 Henry E. Hale, *Patronal Politics: Eurasian Regime Dynamics in Comparative Perspective* (New York: Cambridge University Press, 2014)
17 Hale, *Patronal Politics*; Lucan A. Way, *Pluralism by Default: Weak Autocrats and the Rise of Competitive Politics* (Baltimore: Johns Hopkins University Press, 2015)
18 Vladimir Gel'man. *Authoritarian Russia: Analyzing Post-Soviet Regime Changes* (Pittsburgh: University of Pittsburgh Press, 2015)
19 Way, *Pluralism by Default*.
20 Gel'man, *Authoritarian Russia*.

blame for the consolidation of authoritarianism, crony capitalism, and bad governance in the region.

Is it correct to view post-Soviet elites and leaders as destined to produce sub-optimal outcomes after the collapse of Communism? For instance, one might attribute the irresponsible behavior of post-Soviet elites and leaders to the *nomenklatura* background and continuity of the former, Soviet-era elite;[21] the complexities of building market economies from scratch;[22] the path-dependency of patron-client ties among elites;[23] identity-based divisions among elites and state weakness;[24] and the overall characterization of post-Soviet leaders as ruthless power maximizers.[25] Yet these explanations, however persuasive, do not rule out the possibility of more mutually beneficial relationships emerging among elites and leaders in post-Soviet Eurasia. To illustrate this point, we can see that major elite changes resulted in workable compromises in some countries of Central and Eastern Europe (such as Poland, Hungary and Estonia), which made great strides after the collapse of Communism in terms of democratization and good governance.[26] So, if such outcomes were possible in Central and Eastern Europe, why did not they not emerge in post-Soviet Eurasia? And even if these opportunities were largely missed during the troubled post-Communist transition process, does it necessarily mean that post-Soviet elites and leaders were completely unable to build more efficient, mutually beneficial "winning coalitions" instead of creating political monopolies and/or viewing politics as a zero-sum game?

The key is that elites and leaders must arrive at compromise solutions and prefer cooperation to confrontation. In essence, this

---

21 Kryshtanovskaya and White, "From Soviet *Nomenklatura* to Russian Elite."
22 David Lane and Cameron Ross, *The Transition from Communism to Capitalism: Ruling Elites from Gorbachev to Yeltsin* (New York: St.Martin's Press, 1999)
23 Hale, *Patronal Politics.*
24 Way, *Pluralism by Default.*
25 Gel'man, *Authoritarian Russia.*
26 John Higley, Jan Pakulski and Włodzimierz Wesołowski, eds. *Postcommunist Elites and Democracy in Eastern Europe* (New York: St. Martin's Press, 1998); Neil Abrams and M. Steven Fish, "Policies First, Institutions Second: Lessons from Estonia's Economic Reforms," *Post-Soviet Affairs* 31, no. 6 (2015): 491–513.

will happen if and when they realize that their chances for victory in zero-sum conflicts are low and that cooperation can bring certain benefits—or at least prevent major losses. During the transition process, fragmented and unstable elite factions are often incapable of maintaining cohesion, and even attempts to strike tacit deals cannot be sustained over time and/or easily devolve into fruitless bargaining. Under these circumstances, the role of political leadership is pivotal: leaders become the major (if not the only) actor capable of initiating and promoting elite settlements under their direction. Although leaders may derive benefits from such deals themselves, they also need a vision that extends beyond themselves as well as the power of persuasion to make such elite compromises workable and sustainable over time. Leaders of this kind are in short supply everywhere, but their acute shortage in post-Soviet Eurasia negatively affected the transition process almost everywhere in the region. Even some pro-democratic elite coalitions that emerged in Russia in 1991 and in Ukraine in 2004 disappeared soon after their victories due to major conflicts erupting among elites and the lack of leadership that could have kept those coalitions alive. Yet a closer look at the post-Soviet political landscape reveals a few attempts by emerging leaders to build intra-elite coalitions that proved to be successful in terms of politics and governance. With some caveats, we argue that the governance of Nizhny Novgorod under the leadership of Boris Nemtsov (1991–1997) is one of those rare "success stories."

Nizhny Novgorod Oblast under Governor Nemtsov: Conflicts and Compromises

During the Soviet era, Gor'ky Oblast was a typical industrial region. The share of its urban population in 1989 was 77 per cent, more than 50 per cent of the population in the region lived in the capital city, and it was home to major military enterprises that were governed by federal branch ministries.[27] The car manufacturing giant *GAZ* (with over 100,000 employees), the shipyard *Krasnoe Sormovo* (with almost 20,000 employees), the *"Nitel"* radio-electronics enterprise (with 13,000 employees), and other enterprises as well as institutions devoted to research and development provided major jobs in Gor'ky, while the city itself was closed to foreigners, a point that was instrumental in its selection as the location for dissident Andrei Sakharov's exile between 1980 and 1986.

The liberalization of Soviet politics during the perestroika period naturally affected political developments in the region. While Gorbachev's purges of regional elites led to the replacement of the Communist leadership in Gor'ky, the rise of bottom-up political activism, especially in the wake of the 1989 and 1990 electoral campaigns in Russia, contributed to the emergence of an alternative actor—the democratic movement in Gor'ky. In just a few years, that group moved away from focusing on local ecological initiatives to becoming a mass protest movement. During the 1990 elections for the Russian Congress of People's Deputies (RCPD) and local councils (soviets), the region followed the bipolar model of the "Communists vs. the anti-Communist opposition" that was typical of a number of highly urbanized regions.[28] Given the rising public discontent accompanying the sharp decline of the late Soviet economy and the weakening of central control by the Communist Party of the Soviet Union (CPSU), it is no wonder that mass mobilization resulted in the triumphal election of the young leader of the local democrats—the 30-year-old physicist Boris Nemtsov—as a representative of the city of Gor'ky to the RCPD in 1990. Moreover, about half of the members of the city soviet were democrats, and this group also won 52 of the 280 seats in the oblast (regional) soviet. During this period, the influence of Gor'ky's regional Communist leadership was attenuated; it had declined, in part, due to internal

---

27   Peter Rutland, *The Politics of Economic Stagnation in the Soviet Union: The Role of Local Party Organs in Economic Management* (Cambridge: Cambridge University Press 1993), 91–108; Stoner-Weiss, *Local Heroes*, 20; Gel'man, Ryzhenkov, and Brie, *Making and Breaking Democratic Transitions*, 108.

28   Fish, *Democracy from Scratch*; Robert W. Orttung, *From Leningrad to St.Petersburg: Democratization in a Russian City* (New York: St.Martin's Press 1995).

conflicts. The Communists, the democrats, and the industrial directors all struggled for control over scarce resources in the region, and they more or less counterbalanced each another. As such, the elite structure in Nizhny Novgorod Oblast at that time was, in essence, fragmented.

The collapse of Communist rule in Moscow after the August 1991 coup led to a major reshuffling of elites in Nizhny Novgorod. Since the regional Communist leadership and the oblast soviet under its control had expressed loyalty to the coup plotters, Communist leaders were dismissed and replaced in the oblast soviet, and a representative of the democrats, Evgeny Krest'yaninov, became the soviet's chairman. Nemtsov, who had taken an active part in the resistance to the coup in Moscow and was one of the Yeltsin's closest allies in the RCPD, was soon appointed presidential representative in the region. However, major changes in the composition of the regional elite soon resulted from Yeltsin's decision (approved by the Russian parliament in November 1991) to appoint the heads of the regional administrations (with approval by the regional soviets) in most of Russia's regions. Although the democrats in Nizhny had been able to install one of their own as chairman of the oblast soviet, they were still in the minority in the regional legislature. As a result, they were unable to secure the nomination of one of their candidates to head the regional administration (since formal nomination by the oblast soviet was considered to be a precondition for an appointment to that post by Moscow).

Instead, the post-Communist faction in the oblast soviet, which was strong enough to serve as a veto group, put forward the candidacy of Ivan Sklyarov. Sklyarov was a member of the Russian parliament and the former Communist Party secretary of the city of Arzamas. Nemtsov made use of this situation. Supported by Krest'yaninov, he managed to reach an informal agreement with Sklyarov on the division of powerful positions between the two factions. Sklyarov consented to Nemtsov's nomination as the head of the regional administration (hereafter–governor) on the condition that he would be nominated as Nemtsov's first deputy. At the oblast soviet session, Sklyarov withdrew his candidacy for head of the regional administration and openly called on his supporters to vote for Nemtsov. As a result, the overwhelming majority of deputies recommended Nemtsov's candidacy. Nemtsov was soon appointed governor by Yeltsin and also retained his post as presidential representative in the region as well.[29]

The Nemtsov-Sklyarov informal "pact" was not an ordinary compromise of the sort that results from a temporary alignment of personal interests among elites. On the contrary, after ratification by both old and new elites in the regional legislature, it became the foundation of an "elite settlement" in the region. The principal factions of the regional elite, which had previously been in serious conflict with each other, now agreed on both the new configuration of actors and the new rules of the game. This ran counter to the tendency for elites to be in conflict with each other—a pattern that had dominated Nizhny Novgorod's political landscape since 1990. This settlement resulted in a new, relatively stable "winning coalition" that stabilized the regional political regime. It also stood in sharp contrast to the protracted political conflicts that were ongoing between old and new elites in many of Russia's regions at that time, such as in St. Petersburg or Saratov Oblast.[30]

As a political outsider, Nemtsov did not have his own cadre of administrators and thus faced the necessity of choosing a strategy of appointments that would enable him to navigate the political waters in the region. It goes without saying that Nemtsov's most important political resource was his influence in Moscow, primarily his close links with Yeltsin. Few of the other regional leaders in Russia enjoyed such an advantage. Yet Nemtsov's effective use of this resource would be possible only if there was stability in the regional government. Hypothetically, Nemtsov could have chosen to distribute major posts in the administration to his political supporters. However, he chose another strategy—appointing some of his supporters while both retaining and appointing former regional officials to his government. In fact, newcomers were appointed as

---

29 Stoner-Weiss, *Local Heroes*, 96; Gel'man, Ryzhenkov, and Brie, *Making and Breaking Democratic Transitions*, 110.
30 Orttung, *From Leningrad to St.Petersburg*; Stoner-Weiss. *Local Heroes*; McFaul and Petrov, *Politicheskii al'manakh Rossii 1997*; Gel'man, Ryzhenkov, and Brie, *Making and Breaking Democratic Transitions*.

heads of local district (raion) administrations in only six of the 48 districts in Nizhny Novgorod Oblast. In the regional government, members of the former nomenklatura comprised almost 40 per cent of the top administrators and 75 per cent of the mid-level civil servants.[31] The most significant new appointment Nemtsov made was the promotion of his aide and legal expert Dmitry Bednyakov as the mayor of the city of Nizhny Novgorod in December 1991.

Simultaneously, Nemtsov managed to neutralize the most influential actor in the region—the directors of large industrial enterprises—even if he was unable to win them over to his side. He did this by concluding several formal and informal cooperation agreements with them, such as with the boards of directors (sovety direktorov) of industrial enterprises.[32] The directors generally preferred to avoid participation in local politics, but given that the country was in a deep economic recession, the social stability of the region depended to a large degree on this group. Using his ties in Moscow, Nemtsov managed to arrange for part of the tax payments from large enterprises to be paid into an extra-budgetary fund for defense conversion; in addition, he preserved the system of distributing food at discount prices through enterprises (*produktovye zakazy*). In return, some of the directors provided political support and assistance to Nemtsov; others, at least, did not oppose him. As a result, some of those enterprises gained informal access to the regional decision-making process, and the assistant to the director of GAZ was appointed deputy governor. Overall, the cooperation between the governor and old and new economic actors greatly contributed to the establishment of efficient regional governance. In fact, based on numerous indicators, Nizhny Novgorod was rated higher than several other of Russia's provinces in terms of its quality of governance in the mid-1990s.[33]

The oblast soviet supported Nemtsov not only with respect to his appointment as governor but in his subsequent activities as

---

31 Gel'man, Ryzhenkov, and Brie, *Making and Breaking Democratic Transitions*, 111.
32 Stoner-Weiss, *Local Heroes*, 175–76.
33 Ibid., 90–130.

well. Mostly thanks to the influence of Krest'yaninov, who controlled the majority of the deputies, Nemtsov was granted additional powers. In various ways, the assembly's loyalty to Nemtsov was rewarded. After the Yeltsin administration's conflict with and dissolution of the Russian Congress of People's Deputies in September-October 1993, many of the regional soviets across Russia were dismissed as well.[34] In Nizhny Novgorod, however, the oblast soviet continued to exercise its powers until the next election in March 1994. Despite a degree of continuity between deputies in the former oblast soviet and Nizhny Novgorod's new Legislative Assembly (*Zakonodatel'noe Sobranie*), Nemtsov's authority after the 1994 elections grew even greater, not least because the status of the assembly within the new balance of power in Nizhny Novgorod proved to be considerably lower than that of the former oblast soviet. About half of the new deputies were executive officials from the regional administration, and the assembly did not exert any significant independent influence on political outcomes in the region.[35]

Nemtsov further consolidated his dominant position in Nizhny Novgorod's regional politics through success in federal elections. In December 1993, Nemtsov and Krest'yaninov ran in elections to the Federation Council in a two-mandate district and received 66 per cent and 57 per cent of the vote, respectively. (No other candidates attempted to compete against them in this election. In order to ensure a formally competitive vote, a puppet candidate was put up, a representative of the students' labor union.) During the elections to the State Duma that took place at the same time, a pro-reform electoral coalition named Fond Vybor was set up under Nemtsov's patronage; although it acted independently, it was associated with the nationwide pro-reform bloc, Vybor Rossii (Russia's Choice). The two groups coordinated their campaigns and

---

34 Orttung, *From Leningrad to St.Petersburg*; McFaul and Petrov, *Politicheskii al'manakh Rossii 1997*.
35 Gel'man, Ryzhenkov, and Brie, *Making and Breaking Democratic Transitions*, 112.

ran candidates in five out of six single-member districts in the region. In the end, four out of five Vybor candidates emerged victorious in their districts, and yet another candidate loyal to Nemtsov received a seat in the Duma.[36]

If the creation of such an "elite settlement" in Nizhny Novgorod was mainly due to an effective exchange of resources and political support between the dominant actor and other (subordinate) actors, then its maintenance was the result of an active strategy on Nemtsov's part. He not only spent much of his time in Moscow lobbying for regional interests, but also spearheaded a number of regional policy innovations. In June 1992, a group of Moscow-based economists led by Grigory Yavlinsky launched a regional economic program called Nizhegorodskii prolog (Nizhny Novgorod Prologue), which proposed a detailed plan of economic reforms in Nizhny Novgorod Oblast. The plan included several policy measures aimed at encouraging inter-regional trade, the development of small and medium business, and the like.[37] One respected Western journalist writing at that time highlighted the "energy [that] emanates from Governor Nemtsov" and noted "[t]he proposed role for Nizhny Novgorod as a crucible of economic revolution."[38] Not two years later, echoing the consensus view of the 34-year old Nemtsov prevailing at the time, another journalist characterized him as a "charismatic reform-minded Governor."[39] Indeed, Nizhny's economic policy attracted so much attention by the federal media that Nizhny Novgorod became a showcase of economic reforms. Nemtsov, however, did not always follow the guidelines emanating from the Kremlin and often even opposed some of its policies. In 1995, Nemtsov openly disagreed with the war in Chech-

---

36 Nigel Gould Davis, "Nizhnii Novgorod: The Dual Structure of Political Space." In *Growing Pains. Russian Democracy and the Election of 1993*, ed. Timothy J. Colton and Jerry F. Hough (Washington, D.C.: Brookings Institution Press 1998), 431–61.
37 Stoner-Weiss, *Local Heroes*, 106–107.
38 Serge Schmemann, "New Leaders of Ancient City Try to Lead Russia to Reform," *New York Times*, 9 August 1992.
39 Alessandra Stanley, "Nizhny Novgorod Journal; Camelot on the Volga, With 2 Bold Antagonists," *New York Times*, 29 April 1994.

nya (which was extremely unpopular among Russians) and initiated a large-scale petition campaign in the region calling for halting the military operation there. After this campaign, Nemtsov's relationships with Yeltsin's administration remained chilly for a time.[40] This was probably the only such example of defiance related to the first Chechen War among Russia's regional leaders.

Although Nemtsov managed to dominate the political scene in Nizhny Novgorod, his leadership was far from unchallenged by regional elites within and beyond the limits of the "elite settlement." This resulted in a series of conflicts between Nemtsov and other actors in 1994–95. The first of those conflicts arose between Nemtsov and incumbent mayor and former ally Bednyakov during the mayoral elections held in 1994.[41] In addition to the dispute between regional and city authorities over the use of regional resources (primarily property and finances), the conflict was fueled by the fact that a popularly elected city mayor had the potential to become an even more powerful actor—one not controlled by the governor. Backed by Nemtsov, Krest'yaninov announced that he too would run for the post of mayor. Before the election, when polls revealed that both candidates' chances were equal, Krest'yaninov withdrew from the race. Since no other candidates except for Bednyakov had registered, the election was canceled. On Nemtsov's initiative, Bednyakov was fired; a decree issued by Yeltsin replaced him with Sklyarov. It is thus no wonder that Nemtsov was rightly criticized for his manipulation of the outcome of the mayoral election.[42]

In addition to these conflicts with political elites, Nemtsov also encountered resistance from powerful economic elites in the region. Nemtsov broke openly with the managers of GAZ over the issue of privatizing the enterprise. Supported by the workers' collective, the directors of GAZ tried to take control of a 50 per cent stake in the company, while Nemtsov, supported by the Russian government, was in favor of selling the shares on the open market and forcibly

---

40   Boris Nemtsov, *Provintsial* (Moscow: Vagrius 1997).
41   Gel'man, Ryzhenkov, and Brie, *Making and Breaking Democratic Transitions*, 113.
42   Kelly M. McMann and Nikolai V. Petrov, "A Survey of Democracy in Russia's Regions," *Post-Soviet Geography and Economics* 41, no. 3 (2000): 163.

dividing the enterprise into smaller units. However, GAZ's resources were too vast for Nemtsov to gain control and Nemtsov and the directors agreed to a compromise: the controlling stake was formally left in the hands of the workers' collective, while the former director of GAZ retained his position. He soon resigned, and shortly thereafter, the position was filled by Nikolai Pugin, who was a former director of GAZ (and earlier, a Soviet minister) and had become a strategic ally of Nemtsov.[43] This conflict demonstrated the limits of both Nemtsov's and the directors' influence: both sides were forced to compromise. While these conflicts had the potential to erode the "elite settlement," in reality they fostered a consolidation of the regional political regime. In other words, the ability to forge consensus and promote interaction among elite factions was not only not weakened but was, in fact, strengthened.

It might be said that Nemtsov's most successful public victory was the December 1995 gubernatorial election. Nemtsov won 58.4% of the vote, which was almost twice the share won by his closest competitor, the entrepreneur Vyacheslav Rasteryaev, who was supported by the Communists and their allies.[44] Nemtsov, in fact, was one of the few new regional leaders lacking a Soviet-era nomenklatura background who was able to win in a competitive gubernatorial election amidst Russia's deep and protracted economic recession.[45] According to local experts, the deciding factor for the electorate in that election was not the difference in ideology between the liberal reformer Nemtsov and his main rival, but rather, the degree of loyalty they felt to Nemtsov personally.[46] The result of holding simultaneous mayoral elections in city of Nizhny Novgorod was also very important for Nemtsov, as his choice for mayor, Ivan Sklyarov, won instead of Dmitry Bednyakov.

In sum, Nizhny Novgorod's "elite settlement" of 1991 led to a consolidation of regional elites, which was maintained throughout

---

43 Gel'man, Ryzhenkov, and Brie, *Making and Breaking Democratic Transitions*, 113–114.
44 Ibid., 114–115.
45 McFaul and Petrov, *Politicheskii al'manakh Rossii 1997*.
46 Gel'man, Ryzhenkov, and Brie, *Making and Breaking Democratic Transitions*, 115.

the entire period of Nemtsov's governorship—that is, until March 1997 when Nemtsov was appointed first deputy prime minister of the Russian government and moved to Moscow. It proved to be mutually advantageous for the regional leader and for various sectors of the elite, who were able to manage elite conflict and maintain stability in the region.[47] Once this "elite settlement" had been achieved, the Nizhny Novgorod regional government led by Nemtsov showed itself to be quite efficient in implementing economic reforms; it enacted legislation on privatization, land reform, budget restructuring, and housing reforms. At that time, in contrast, many of the regional governments in Russia were demonstrating neither the capacity nor the willingness to put forth proactive economic policies aimed at promoting market reforms.[48]

Empirical Support for the Impact of Leadership

We have seen that Nemtsov's leadership, and with it, the region's "elite settlement," were instrumental in managing conflict, maintaining stability, and producing the conditions necessary for successful economic reforms in Nizhny Novgorod Oblast. But did Nemtsov's reformist vision filter down to the political elites whose support was needed to implement his program? A plausible case for the impact of Nemtsov's leadership on elite political culture in the region can be made by examining an original survey of elites that Rivera conducted between February and July of 1996 in coop-

---

[47] Other observers praised the mutual cooperation among various political forces and commitment to compromise that was fostered in Nemtsov's administration, as well as the region's relative political stability. See A. Magomedov, "Politicheskie elity rossiiskoi provintsii" [Russia's Regional Political Elite]. *Mirovaya ekonomika i mezhdunarodnye otnosheniya* 4 (1994): 72–79; Kathryn Brown, "Nizhnii Novgorod: A Regional Solution to National Problems?" *RFE/RL Research Report* 2, no.5 (1993): 17–23. For a dissenting view, see Gulnaz Sharafutdinova, *Political Consequences of Crony Capitalism inside Russia*. Notre Dame (IN: University of Notre Dame Press 2010), Chapter 2.

[48] Stoner-Weiss, *Local Heroes*, 90–130; Gel'man, Ryzhenkov, and Brie, *Making and Breaking Democratic Transitions*, 115–116.

eration with the Russian Academy of Sciences' Institute of Sociology. Elites in both the legislative and executive branches were surveyed in three locations—in Moscow, Nizhny Novgorod, and Tatarstan.[49]

The interviews reveal that Nizhny's regional administrators and legislators were indeed more favorable to pluralist institutions and market economics—as well as more amenable to being interviewed—than their counterparts in both Tatarstan and the federal government. The results displayed in Table 1 demonstrate these attitudinal differences. Nizhny's elites were virtually unanimous that all citizens should have an equal opportunity to affect government policy, compared to slightly more than three-fourths of the Moscow sample and less than two-thirds of Tatarstan's elites. In the realm of economic policy, Nizhny officials were again the most reform-oriented: whereas three-fourths of Tatarstan's officials agreed that all heavy industry should be state-owned, only slightly more than half of those in Nizhny supported this proposition.[50]

Moreover, as Rivera and her local collaborators fanned out to interview department heads in Nizhny's regional administration and deputies in the regional legislature, they found that access to both government buildings and their respondents was remarkably easy to obtain. They noted that such an environment provided a welcome respite from the long days they had spent in Moscow trying to secure interviews with highly placed federal bureaucrats and State Duma deputies.[51] It stood in even starker contrast to Tatarstan

---

49 For complete survey results, see Rivera, "Elites in Post-communist Russia."
50 On elite politics in Tatarstan, see Kimitaka Matsuzato, "From Ethno-Bonapartism to the Centralized Casiquismo: Characteristics and Origins of the Tatarstan Political Regime, 1990–2000," *Journal of Communist Studies and Transition Politics* 17, no. 4 (2001): 43–77; Gulnaz Sharafutdinova. "Elite Management in Electoral Authoritarian Regimes: A View from Bashkortostan and Tatarstan," *Central Asian Affairs*, 2, no. 1 (2015): 117–39; Katherine E. Graney. *Of Khans and Kremlins: Tatarstan and the Future of Ethno-Federalism in Russia* (Lanham. MD: Lexington Books 2009).
51 On the challenges of interviewing Russian elites, see Sharon Werning Rivera, Polina M. Kozyreva and Eduard G. Sarovskii, "Interviewing Political Elites: Lessons from Russia," *PS: Political Science and Politics* 35, no.4 (2002): 683–88.

under Mintimer Shaimiev, where they were denied access to republic-level officials altogether. Instead, a representative of the republic's presidential administration conducted the interviews for them and forbade the sessions to be tape-recorded, as had been their practice in Moscow and Nizhny.

Table 1. Attitudes of Political Elites in Nizhny Novgorod, Moscow, and Tatarstan in 1996

(% Agree)	Nizhny Novgorod n=25	Moscow n=73	Tatarstan n=25
All citizens should have an equal chance to influence government policy	92.0	76.7	64.0
All heavy industry should belong to the state and not be in private hands	56.0	58.9	76.0

Source: Rivera's 1996 survey of Russian elites.
Note: Figures represent all those who responded "completely agree" or "somewhat agree," as a percentage of all responses, including "don't know" and "no answer."

The interview data also support our contention that one of the hallmarks of Nemtsov's leadership was his ability to facilitate elite compromises and forge a workable "elite settlement." We have argued that Nemtsov led by example in this regard, by reaching across parties and political eras to include old and new elites the regional government. As discussed above, Nemtsov had retained many "old cadres" in the regional administration, at least early in his tenure.[52] As the survey data show, this pattern held toward the end of his term: those with prior experience in leadership positions in the Communist Party had not been excluded from office but were, in fact, holding important positions in Nemtsov's government. Of the fourteen high-ranking officials from the regional administration who were interviewed, ten had been members of the CPSU, two had held an elected post on a party committee at the

---

52 See also Michael McFaul and Nikolay Petrov, eds. 1995. *Politicheskii al'manakh Rossii 1995* (Moscow: Carnegie Moscow Center, 1995), 456; and Natalia Zhelnorova, "Kak zhivete, gospodin gubernator?", *Argumenty i fakty*, 28 July 1994.

district (raion) level or higher, four had held a full-time (*osvobozhdennyi*) party job at the district level or higher, and two had worked full-time for the Komsomol, the Communist Youth League. Moreover, eight years earlier (in 1988), five of these bureaucrats had belonged to the Soviet-era nomenklatura—"a hierarchical network of important posts dotted over the country, where CPSU party committees held the exclusive right to appoint individuals to (and dismiss individuals from) those positions."[53] Those five individuals were working in positions that were likely to have been in the nomenklatura of a party committee at the oblast level or higher.[54]

In addition to the inclusion of a variety of elites in the regional government, an "elite settlement" can be more easily maintained if there are clear and broad avenues of communication between regional officials and other important local and regional actors. Increased interaction, in other words, can facilitate greater cooperation. The survey data suggest that a culture of reaching across traditional lines and interacting with key groups in the region was a feature of Nizhny's political life in the mid-1990s. All respondents (both regional administrators and legislators) were asked how often they came into contact with representatives of various economic, civic, and political entities in the course of their jobs. Figure 1 displays the percentage of respondents who answered "regularly" (in comparison with "occasionally" or "rarely or never"). With only one exception (contacts with civic organizations), more—or at least an equal percentage of—political elites in Nizhny reported meeting regularly with significant local and regional groups than did their counterparts in Tatarstan.

---

53 Rivera, "Elites in Post-communist Russia," 419.
54 Data are from Rivera's 1996 database. For more information, see Figure 2 and Table 2 in Rivera, "Elites in Post-Communist Russia." Note that both Figure 2 and Table 2 in that article include all regional elites in Nizhny (both regional deputies and administrators), whereas the demographic data presented in the text here refer to regional bureaucrats only.

Figure 1. Percentage of Elites Reporting Regular Contacts with Various Regional Groups, 1996

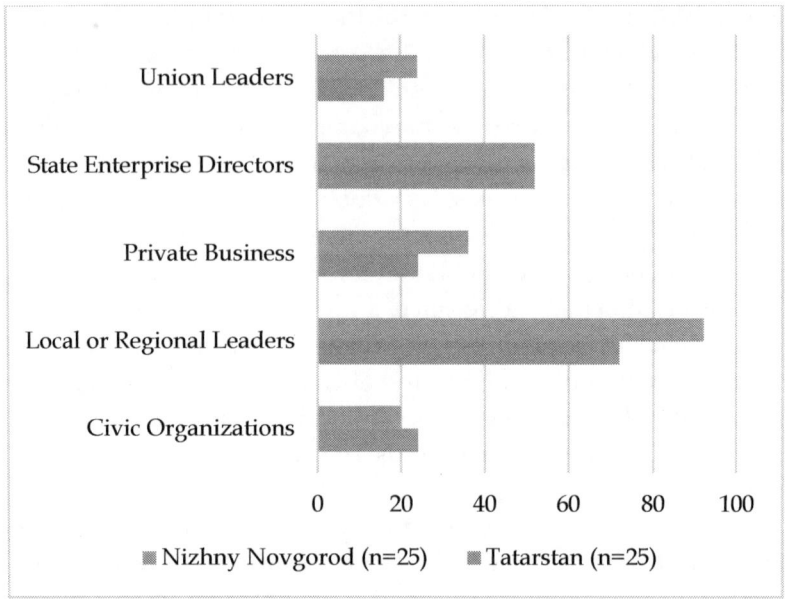

Source: Rivera's 1996 survey of Russian elites.
Note: The question reads as follows: "In your job how often do you come into contact with...?" The bars represent all those who responded "regularly," as opposed to "occasionally" or "rarely or never," as a percentage of all responses, including "don't know" and "no answer."

In comparison with Tatarstan as well as the federal "centre," then, Nizhny Novgorod during Boris Nemtsov's governorship stood out for the higher level of democratic and market-oriented values espoused by its regional leadership, as well as its openness to survey research. Moreover, in comparison with their counterparts in Tatarstan, Nizhny elites were generally in more regular contact with business groups, local and regional leaders, and unions across the region.

Nizhny Novgorod after Nemtsov

The "elite settlement" in Nizhny Novgorod under Nemtsov's leadership was short-lived. His departure from the region in March

1997 to assume the position of first deputy prime minister in the federal government put an end to the consensus among regional elites that had held during his tenure. Sklyarov, who became acting governor after Nemtsov left, faced serious resistance to his election to this post in June 1997. Ultimately, he won only 52 per cent of the vote, while his major rival, former Communist leader of the region Gennady Khodyrev, received 42 per cent.[55] Since Sklyarov had left his post as mayor of the city of Nizhny Novgorod, the vacancy was filled by a popular vote. The election was marked by vigorous competition among various segments of the regional elite, and surprisingly, resulted in the victory of an outsider, entrepreneur Andrei Kliment'yev. Kliment'yev had had numerous conflicts with Nemtsov while he was governor and was under criminal investigation during the campaign. Due to the victory of the candidate that was considered by the regional and federal elite to be undesirable, the election was annulled.[56] In a new round of balloting, Yury Lebedev, a former deputy governor in the Nemtsov administration, won the race despite his open confrontation with Sklyarov. The ensuing period was marked by numerous elite conflicts, and governance in the region was only faintly reminiscent of the Nemtsov period.[57] Sklyarov did not pursue proactive reform policies, his lobbying efforts in Moscow were minimal, his public appearances were rare and unimpressive, and his leadership was widely criticized. As a result, Nizhny Novgorod lost its role as the vanguard of regional change in Russia—a role that it had held during the Nemtsov years. As one observer gloomily summed up the situation in 2001: "...[I]n the four years following Nemtsov's departure,

---

55 "'Party of Power' Wins Nizhnii Novgorod Election," *RFE/RL Newsline*, 14 July 1997.
56 Technically the electoral commission in Nizhny Novgorod ruled that the election was invalid because of campaign violations on all sides. "Annulment of Nizhnii Election Draws Criticism," *RFE/RL Newsline*, 2 April 1998. See also the coverage in Michael R. Gordon,"Heavy Hand Squelches Yeltsin Foe," *New York Times*, 14 April 1998.
57 Gel'man, Ryzhenkov, and Brie, *Making and Breaking Democratic Transitions*, 119–122.

Nizhnii Novgorod, which was once considered to be at the forefront of economic reform, reverted to being a provincial backwater."[58]

Cross-regional empirical data confirm that the departure of Nemtsov, and with him, the disintegration of the "elite settlement," led to a degradation of democracy in the region. When asked to assess the levels of democracy in 57 regions of Russia in mid-1997—just after Nemtsov's tenure as governor had ended—40 experts selected for their knowledge of Russia's provincial politics listed Nizhny Novgorod Oblast as the third most democratic region in the Russian Federation.[59] As the authors of the study write, "The experts...mentioned 'the autonomy of different groups' and the leeway afforded the political opposition" in Nizhny Novgorod."[60] When experts were again asked to identify the "most democratic regions" in an abbreviated version of the same survey conducted just two years later, "Nizhegorod fell from their ranks." As McMann and Petrov write, "With the departure of Governor Boris Nemtsov, Nizhegorod lost its role as the showcase of reform, emphasizing the importance of leadership in the country."[61]

Undoubtedly, Nemtsov played an outstanding role in building elite cohesion in Nizhny Novgorod in the 1990s. Yet his advancements did not contribute to the institutionalization of political competition, which is a vital component of democracy. Governor Sklyarov's initial failure to hold a successful mayoral election in Nizhny Novgorod amid intra-elite conflicts stands in sharp contrast to Nemtsov's leadership. In fact, Nemtsov's political achievements were short-lived in terms of democracy and governance, which is why Nizhny Novgorod's politics in the 1990s received a certain amount of criticism in cross-regional comparisons with some other regions of Russia.[62] Still, the Nemtsov period remains a unique and

---

58 Oleg Rodin, "Election Rematch Set for Nizhnii Novgorod," *RFE/RL Newsline*, 19 July 2001.
59 McMann and Petrov, "A Survey of Democracy in Russia's Regions," 160.
60 Ibid., 162.
61 Ibid., 175.
62 Gel'man, Ryzhenkov, and Brie, *Making and Breaking Democratic Transitions*, Chapter 9.

positive experience of political development in Russia's regions during the turbulent 1990s.

Conclusion and Implications: Lessons from Nizhny Novgorod

Overall, the case study and survey data support the contention that Nizhny Novgorod under Boris Nemtsov was an outlier in the political landscape of Russia's regions. Although he was one of the youngest new governors as well as an outsider to the deeply entrenched regional politics of Nizhny Novgorod in the initial post-Communist period, Nemtsov was able to pursue important policy initiatives and, to some degree, shape the elite political culture in the region in a manner that would provide fertile soil for the enactment of economic reforms.

All of this highlights the crucial role of leadership in achieving success in the post-Communist transitions, even on the sub-national level. Indeed, numerous authors highlight the role played by leaders in their countries' transitions from communism and generally advance the proposition, sometimes only implicitly, that the beliefs, values, skills, and character traits of these chief executives have been important determinants of the evolution of their polities.[63] Although these and other full-length works of political history emphasize the role of political leaders, much less theorizing exists about the specific actions taken by leaders in the early post-Communist era that can lead to positive results. Our article offers some insight in this regard: it shows that an "elite settlement" characterized by efficient deal-making with key stakeholders and the co-optation of old and new actors into a ruling coalition can prove to be highly effective. Although a case can be made that "pacted"

---

63 See, for instance, Timothy Colton and Robert Tucker, eds. *Patterns in Post-Soviet Leadership* (Boulder, CO: Westview Press, 1995); Archie Brown and Lilia Shevtsova, *Gorbachev, Yeltsin, and Putin: Political Leadership in Russia's Transition* (Washington, D.C., 2001): Carnegie Endowment for International Peace; Michael McFaul. "Explaining Party Formation and Nonformation in Russia: Actors, Institutions, and Chance," *Comparative Political Studies* 34, no.10 (2001): 1159–87.

transitions have their drawbacks, we find that this mode of governance—at least during the turbulent 1990s—was the most effective of the options available in Nizhny Novgorod at the time.

Finally, as we have noted, Nemtsov had not personally appointed all of the political elites in the oblast; regional deputies had been popularly elected in 1994, and Nemtsov had retained many "old cadres" in the regional administration. But as governor, he surely set the tone regarding the values and priorities of his administration. Nizhny Novgorod under Boris Nemtsov illustrates how the spirit of free market competition and pluralism can be fostered when a courageous reformer is in charge. Nizhny—and Russia as a whole—would seem to need more governors like him.

Boris Nemtsov 1959-2015: The Rise and Fall of a Provincial Democrat

Andre Mommen

Boris Nemtsov's political career stretched from the early 1990s until his death in 2015. Among Russian liberals, Nemtsov was the most outspoken protagonist of market reforms. In his region Nizhny Novgorod he immediately launched a comprehensive program of privatizations for which he obtained foreign technical and financial aid to combat industrial decline and poverty. When visiting Nizhny Novgorod, President Boris Yeltsin and several Western politicians were enticed by Nemtsov's dynamism and successful economic reforms. His informal behavior and boyish good looks contrasted sharply with the behaviour of the former Soviet bureaucrats. In addition, he also liked windsurfing and playing tennis, not hunting or fishing, which were the preferred hobbies of the former nomenklatura. However, the Western journalists would soon discover another side of his personality. Nemtsov was also "loud, brash, boastful, vain and a tireless womanizer."[1]

His reputation as a handsome politician and intelligent administrator was nonetheless growing. Yeltsin, who now needed a crown prince to help him shore up his presidential power and to speed up stagnating economic reforms, appointed Nemtsov and Anatoly Chubais as first deputy prime ministers in March 1997. In the West, these appointments were hailed as a victory for the anticorruption "young reformers" promising Russia a Western form of capitalism and democracy.

Nemtsov immediately launched several reforms in order to combat Russia's "cowboy capitalism" in which corrupt bureaucrats and criminal gangs seemed to rule unchecked. From this time on,

---

[1] Keith Gessen, "Remembering Boris Nemtsov", *London Review of Books* 37, no. 6 (2015): 5-6.

government tenders had to be open and transparent. Russia's natural monopolies had to be broken up and fair, free-market competition had to be introduced. Taxes were to be collected in time. Hence, Nemtsov's auction of the telecommunication firm Svyazinvest, which went to George Soros and Oneximbank, was presented as the cleanest state sale ever held. But it nonetheless became a subject of debate when it was discovered that Oneximbank had distributed bribes to several "young reformers," including Chubais. Though Yeltsin kept Nemtsov and Chubais in government, Nemtsov's reputation had suffered a severe blow: he had lost his political innocence.

In August 1998 the devastating financial crisis swept the "young reformers" away. Divided and out of power, these liberals passively witnessed the nascence of Vladimir Putin's state-controlled capitalism and authoritarian rule. In the beginning, Nemtsov's opposition to Putin's rise to power was rather flimsy. Because of the latter's support for a free-market economy, the liberals in the State Duma thought they would be back soon. But in 2003 the liberals lost their seats in the State Duma. Then Nemtsov tried to reorganise the divided opposition around himself, but without any tangible result. From then on Nemtsov's driving goal was his relentless opposition to Putin's adventurous foreign policy and authoritarian rule.

Democracy in One Region

In Nizhny Novgorod, where democratic grass-roots movements were mushrooming in 1986 after Mikhail Gorbachev called for reforms, young activists started contesting authoritarian rule. Among these activists was a young physicist named Boris Nemtsov. Like many of his fellow activists, Nemtsov was born into a family of intellectuals. Together with his mother, a pediatrician, he had successfully campaigned against the building of a nuclear power plant in Nizhny Novgorod. This initial success inspired him to join the local democratic movement. Like most of the young democrats, Nemtsov was a member of the local Komsomol. As a defender of free speech and property rights, he tried to compete in the 1989 elections for the Soviet Congress of People's Deputies, but the selection commission did not endorse his candidacy. Then, in 1990, he easily won a seat in the RSFSR Supreme Soviet, where he joined Yeltsin's faction. Democratic Russia (DemRossiya) captured some 40 percent of the seats. In its wake, a multitude of political parties had already appeared.[2] The democratic movement was ideologically diverse and loosely organized. The liberals were "realists" and oriented to electoral participation, while the radicals were "romantics" and sometimes in favor of the use of revolutionary means. Socialists and "reform communists" organized their own parties as well.

In the local and regional elections of 4 March 1990, democratic groups obtained significant victories. In Moscow they took 52 out of 64 seats, and 28 out of 44 seats in Leningrad.[3] But in Nizhny Novgorod they only took 52 of the 280 mandates in the Oblast Soviet (the regional legislature). After the failed coup of August 1991, the Democrats immediately replaced the Communists in the executive committee (ispolkom) of the Oblast Soviet and President Yeltsin nominated Nemtsov as his "representative" (later called "governor") in Nizhny Novgorod Oblast. The conservatives, who still dominated the Oblast Soviet, refused to approve Nemtsov's appointment. Nemtsov ultimately reached an informal deal with Oblast Soviet Chairman Yevgeny Krestyaninov on sharing power with the former Communist Ivan Sklyarov as his first deputy. Making informal deals with local Communists was in line with Yeltsin's tactical behaviour vis-à-vis Communists. For example, Yeltsin's vice-president was war hero Alexander Rutskoi of the Democratic Party of Communists of Russia (DPKR).[4]

Sharing power with the former Communist bosses did not tarnish Nemtsov's democratic image since he acted in a deliberate

---

2   Vladimir Lysenko, "The Russian Democratic Movement: Past, Present, and Future." *Demokratizatsiya: The Journal of Post-Soviet Democratization* 5, no. 4 (1997): 477–481.

3   Stephen White, Graeme Gill and Darrell Slider. *The Politics of Transition: Shaping a Post-Soviet Future* (Cambridge: Cambridge University Press, 1993): 161.

4   Timothy J. Colton. *Yeltsin: A Life* (New York: Basic Books, 2008): 190.

manner to appoint his own men to strategic positions. In 1990 Nemtsov appointed as his personal advisor Alexey Likhachev, who, like Nemtsov, was a graduate from the Radio Physics department at the local university and had just been elected to the Nizhny Novgorod city council even as he led the local industrial insurance company Aval.[5] Nemtsov also tried to control local city politics by appointing Dmitri Bednyakov—a teacher at the local police academy—to the post of mayor of Nizhny Novgorod. By cooptation he enrolled former members of the *nomenklatura* and businessmen in his team.[6] Foreign experts from international organizations and NGOs drafting guidelines for administrative reforms were recruited.[7]

Like most populist leaders, Nemtsov frequently organized informal face-to-face meetings with entrepreneurs and ordinary citizens. He neutralized the powerful directors of the large enterprises by arranging tax deals and giving them access to the administration's decision-making process. His old friend Andrey Klimentyev managed the Council of Entrepreneurs. As local residents knew, Klimentyev had been convicted of petty crimes (card sharping and selling pornography, including the movie *Emmanuelle*). In June 1992 Nemtsov proposed the founding of an Oblast Coordinating Council in which the chairman of the Oblast Soviet, the chairmen of the different city Soviets and the heads of the Oblast and city administrations would be represented. Although this new administrative body would not take into consideration the opinions of the democratically elected assemblies, Nemtsov's initiative met no serious political opposition.

The 1994 election results for the new Oblast Legislative Assembly nonetheless confirmed Nemtsov's growing popularity.

---

5   Ministry of Economic Development of the Russian Federation. "Alexey Likhachev", http://economy.gov.ru/wps/wcm/connect/economylib4/en/home/about/management/lihachev (as of 7 May 2015).
6   Andrei Shleifer and Daniel Treisman, *Without a Map: Political Tactics and Economic Reform in Russia* (Cambridge, MA: The MIT Press, 2000): 9.
7   Andrey S. Makarychev. *Ten Years of Integration to the Global World: The Case of Nizhny Novgorod's International Adjustment*. Policy Paper (Budapest: OSI, 2001), http://www.policy.hu/makarychev/eng9.htm (as of 7 May 2015).

About a half of the Oblast legislators were now employed as his executive officials. His political star was rising within the national firmament as well. In December 1993 he formed a tandem with Kresyaninov when running in the region's two-mandate district for the Federation Council elections. In order to stress his political importance, he recruited liberal icons like Yegor Gaidar and Gregory Yavlinsky to support him in the media. Ultimately, Nemtsov won 66 percent and Klimentyev 57 percent of the popular vote. However, these excellent results were also due to puppet candidates Nemtsov had organized for the race. Elections to the State Duma took place the same day. In order to have "liberal" candidates elected, Nemtsov's private foundation *Vybor* (Choice) ran candidates in five out of six single-mandate districts. The Nemtsov liberals won four seats.

However, personal animosities, bureaucratic neuroses and growing mutual distrust undermined the early harmony in Nemtsov's little kingdom. In 1994-95, several political incidents tarnished Nemtsov's reputation as a democrat who opposed any form of political manipulation. These incidents revealed that Nemtsov's democratic reforms were suffering from the interference of interest groups, ambitious bureaucrats, and business people. During the mayoral elections of 1994, incumbent mayor Bednyakov, who had been appointed to the post by Nemtsove, aspired to win the popular vote. Nemtsov, fearing the rise of a legitimate and autonomous mayor in his city, pressed Krestyaninov to run for mayor as well. On election eve, however, Krestyaninov suddenly withdrew. Since there was no other candidate registered to run against Bednyakov, the election had to be cancelled. Two days later, on Nemtsov's initiative, Mayor Bednyakov was dismissed by Yeltsin and replaced by Sklyarov. Krestyaninov received Nemtsov's former post as Yeltsin's representative in the Oblast.[8]

The Nemtsov-Klimentyev alliance would not last for long. In the beginning of 1995, a conflict arose between the two men about

---

8   Vladimir Gel'man, "Russia's Elites in Search of Consensus: What kind of Consolidation?." *Demokratizatsiya: The Journal of Post-Soviet Democratization* 10, no. 3 (2002): 349.

an alleged misuse of credits earmarked for a local ship-building factory. The conflict acquired a political dimension when Klimentyev announced that he would run for the post of governor in the coming elections that year. To prevent that eventuality, a criminal case was opened against him. Klimentyev was arrested, preventing him from running for governor.[9] Subsequently, Nemtsov won the gubernatorial election of December 1995 with 58.4 percent of the popular vote against the leftist candidate Vyacheslav Rasteryaev who scored only 26.2 percent. During the simultaneously held mayoral elections, Bednyakov lost to Sklyarov, who won 64 percent of the vote.

Presidential Candidate

As Nemtsov's concern about political developments in Russia grew, he became directly involved with the war in Chechnya. In early 1996 he had a serious clash with Yeltsin when he presented him with a million signatures on a petition protesting the on-going war in the republic. This conflict had no serious consequences for Nemtsov's relations with Yeltsin. During his 1996 re-election campaign, Yeltsin asked Nemtsov for help. In Chechnya Yeltsin signed a peace accord with the rebels. Nemtsov, who had accompanied Yeltsin, was suddenly confronted with the latter's outspoken populist leanings: Yeltsin ordered him to deliver some GAZelle trucks and Volga cars, which were manufactured in Nemtsov's region, to the poor Chechen farmers living in misery.[10]

Nemtsov's closeness to Yeltsin must have awaken the ambition of playing a role in national politics. It was no longer a secret that Yeltsin's health was bad and that the question of his succession was dividing the ruling elites. Possible candidates to succeed Yelt-

---

9   Information and Analytical Center of Nizhny Novgorod Society for Human Rights. 1998. "Section 3: Observance of Fundamental Political Freedoms." In *1998 Report on Human Rights Status in the Nizhny Novgorod Region*, http://www.uic.unn.ru/hrnnov/eng/nnshr/analyst/report98/report4.htm (as of 7 May 2015).

10 Colton, *Yeltsin: A Life*, 170, 364, 379.

sin had good reason to present themselves to the public by influencing the media, which where largely controlled by a small number of tycoons. Hence, having the support of these tycoons and their influential friends in and around the Kremlin would be of crucial importance for any candidate.

In January 1997, Nemtsov sought a national audience by publishing a booklet in which he revealed some aspects of his rebellious youth and his views on several political leaders.[11] This booklet, published in Moscow, explicitly sought to inform the Russian media and the political and economic elites about the ambitions of a provincial politician. The public discovered that Nemtsov had moved with his divorced mother from Sochi to Nizhny Novgorod. Having once upon a time run away from home, he had survived for a while by doing odd jobs and sleeping in a basement. He nonetheless obtained a degree in radio-physics with first class honors. As a student, Nemtsov greatly admired famous dissidents like Andrey Sakharov and Mstislav Rostropovich. But this "golden boy" also liked playing tennis and practising windsurfing. He appreciated Yeltsin as a man "who could be reckless, careless and often brave, but also sleep like a bear." Nemtsov claimed that "In contrast to the Russian tsars, Yeltsin is a 'good' Russian tsar. [...] Of course, his physique plays a role: such an enormous guy from the Urals. [...] He is the tsar, he feels deeply his responsibility for what is happening." Prime minister Chernomyrdin appeared to him as a "good man [...] who thinks quickly enough," but "not someone who is prepared to act as a prime minister during a crisis." "Why? Not because he is lacking experience," Nemtsov explained.[12] Of course, comparing Yeltsin to a tsar born in an Ural village was not done, but Yeltsin liked it.[13]

Nemtsov's book "created a small sensation with his open criticism of the Kremlin leaders."[14] Subsequently, the media described

---

11 Boris Nemtsov, *Provintsial* [A Provincialist] (Moscow: Vagrius, 1997).
12 Nemtsov, *Provintsial*, 81, 88.
13 Colton, *Yeltsin: A Life*, 325–6.
14 Sergei Shargorodsky, "Nemtsov tells his story in 'The Provincial Man'." *The Moscow Times*, 10 April 2008, http://www.themoscowtimes.com/news/a

Nemtsov as a possible presidential candidate. These presidential ambitions would soon meet opposition from other candidates backed by political parties and interest groups. But Nemtsov opposed any effort to found a "political party" by referring to the evils of totalitarianism and the advantages of democracy. This libertarian stance was common to most former members of the democratic movement or informal groups, leaving them with neither a unified set of political perspectives, nor a single organisational apparatus.[15]

Capitalism in One Region

Nemtsov's project consisted of building capitalism in one region by privatising state and city properties and inviting foreign investors to work together with local entrepreneurs. These ideas had been developed within the democratic movement and were common to all neoliberal economic reformers. According to the prevailing theory, market reforms would strengthen civil freedoms by creating a large middle class. Some economic reformers were also tempted by the Chilean or South Korean model of developing market capitalism under strong authoritarian guidance.[16] Opting for economic shock therapy, Yeltsin appointed Yegor Gaidar as his acting prime minister and he set in train a series of market reforms. In March 1992, the Russian government announced its privatization program. The first stage in this transformation process consisted of a fast privatization of small and medium-sized businesses. In April 1992, a presidential decree announced that all citizens would receive vouchers they could use to bid for shares in privatizing enterprises. By the end of January 1993, about 144 million Russians obtained the 10,000 ruble vouchers that they also could sell or use for participating in an investment fund.

---

rticle/from-the-archive-nemtsov-tells-his-story-in-the-provincial-man/516717.html (as of 7 May 2015).
15 Boris Kagarlitsky, *Russia under Yeltsin and Putin* (London: Pluto Press, 2002): 71.
16 Russell Bova, "Political Dynamics of the Post-Communist Transition. A Comparative Perspective." In Nancy Bermeo, ed. *Liberalization and Democratization. Change in the Soviet Union and Eastern Europe* (Baltimore: The Johns Hopkins University Press, 1991): 134.

Though the democratic movement had been much stronger in Moscow and Leningrad, Nizhny Novgorod was the pioneering region with regard to privatisations largely due to Nemtsov's initiatives and his team. The first auctions of state property were launched on 4 April 1992 under supervision of Robert Gale of the International Finance Corporation (IFC), an a member of the World Bank Group. Local officials were assisted by experts from Czechoslovakia and Poland and lawyers from Sweden. The IFC compiled a "manual" showing what was necessary in order to privatize all small enterprises, but also to explore "the possibility of using Nizhny Novgorod as a model for privatising small-scale enterprises in other Russian cities."[17] Deputy Prime Minister Yegor Gaidar, Anatoly Chubais (chief of the Russian Privatisation Program), Deputy Minister Dimitri Vasilyev, IFC Vice President Wilfried Kaffenberger and national and international journalists attending the inauguration ceremony. It was a success. An IFC report published in September 1992 noted that about 75 percent of retail trade workers had been rehired by the new shop owners.[18] Later that year, state trucks were auctioned. The drivers and other private citizens were able to use their 10,000-ruble vouchers to buy the trucks. *The Moscow Times* reported nonetheless that this time the procedure would be different: "The crux of the privatization plan for Nizhny Novgorod's trucking industry […] will not occur on the auction block but behind the scenes. The first stage of the sell-off to directors, employees and the public is important to disentangle enterprises from the Transport Ministry and involves no real change […]. Only later will truckers be forced to sink or swim in the market."[19]

---

17 *Small Scale Privatization in Russia. The Nizhny Novgorod Model: A City Official's Guide*. 1992. A Publication of the Government of the Russian Federation. Prepared by IFC International Finance Corporation. Jointly financed by the United States Government and the International Finance Corporation (Washington, D.C.: International Finance Corporation).

18 Kathryn Kaje Brown, "Nizhny Novgorod: A City Privatizes." *The Moscow Times*. 22 October 1992, http://www-cf.themoscowtimes.com/news/article/tmt/220581.html (as of 7 May 2015).

19 Ibid.

Despite these problems, privatization of small shops, restaurants and services was a big success. But privatizing large firms and industrial or agrarian conglomerates proved to be extremely complicated, creating opportunities for abuses.[20] About 600 large firms producing heavy equipments, steel tubes, submarines, television sets, cars and MiG jets dominated the Nizhny Novgorod industrial landscape. In order to compete in the new conditions, many firms had to modernize their production lines, develop new products, and find (new) markets for them. These big firms had to be corporatized before selling at least 29 percent of their shares at voucher auctions. Only much later could they sell their remaining shares to large-scale investors. Weapons manufacturers, in particular, were in crisis.

The Sokol aircraft factories producing MiG fighters (Sokol Nizhny Novgorod) worked with heavy losses. In order to reduce its dependency on arms sales, Sokol even began producing cutlery. In order to save its core business, producing medium-sized airplanes for commercial use was the only solution. In 1996 the medium-sized Yakovlev Yak was developed, but production began only in 2009. Nemtsov also had to lobby in Moscow to gain support for the deeply unprofitable GAZ company,[21] which then employed about 120,000 workers and produced, apart from the Volga car, heavy trucks, busses, engines and weaponry. During the privatization process, Nemtsov clashed with the directors who had tried to take control of a 50 percent stake in GAZ. After a court decision ruled in favour of the managers, Nemtsov made a deal with them.[22] A light pick-up (Burlak) and a van (GAZelle) were developed for the Russian market. Western firms signed modernization agreements with the company, but, because of the abundance of better

---

20   Ruslan Dzarasov, *The Conundrum of Russian Capitalism. The Post-Soviet Economy in the World-System* (London: Pluto Press, 2004).
21   Martha de Melo and Gur Ofer, *The Russian City in Transition: The First Six Years in Ten Volga Capitals*. Working Paper 2165 (Washington, DC: World Bank, 1999): 22.
22   Vladimir Gel'man, "Russia's Elites in Search of Consensus: What kind of Consolidation?" *Demokratizatsiya: The Journal of Post-Soviet Democratization* 10, no. 3 (2002): 349.

foreign cars, the Volga was priced at the bottom of the market. Following a desperate search for investors, the oligarch Oleg Deripaska acquired GAZ and transformed the motorcar division into a subcontractor assembling cars for Western clients.

On 15 May 1992 Nemtsov founded the Nizhegorodsky Bankirsky Dom (NBD Bank) in order to support conversion programs, privatizations, local private businesses and social and economic development projects. The bank also opened an account for the Foundation for Arms Conversion Assistance, which the weapon makers had to fund by paying contributions.[23] Though Nemtsov stimulated several new initiatives in services, R&D, electronics and IT by opening Nizhny Novgorod to foreign investors, his region remained a crisis-ridden industrial province dependent on subsidies from Moscow. Five years after the implosion of the USSR, social and economic indicators were still negative. About 40 percent of the population were pensioners. According to a report published by the Troika Dialog Bank in 1996, the local average living standard of US$1,211 per capita lagged behind the country's average of US$1,797. The region's population was constantly shrinking (from 3,714,322 people in 1989 to 3,524,028 in 2002 – and even to 3,310,597 in 2010). Though the Nizhny Novgorod Oblast could balance its budget, the region owed large sums to Gazprom – together with Moscow, St. Petersburg and Tatarstan.[24] Accumulating arrears was, however, a tactic all Russian authorities and industrial firms were practising. In the meantime Gazprom had amassed a huge debt to the budget in unpaid taxes.

Nizhny Novgorod belonged among the top ten regions (together with Moscow, St. Petersburg, Tyumen, Sverdlovsk, Samara, Tatarstan, Chelyabinsk, Irkutsk and Krasnoyarsk) because of its good investment climate.[25] Not everybody was, however, convinced of Nemtsov's extraordinary talents. Agricultural production had declined during his early tenure. Many start-up innovation

---

23 *Businessweek Russia*, 23 September 2007.
24 Andrei Shleifer and Daniel Treisman, *Without a Map: Political Tactics and Economic Reform in Russia* (Cambridge, MA: The MIT Press, 2000): 73.
25 *The Territories of the Russian Federation* (London: Europa Publishers, 2002): 15

projects were not fully realized. The effort to convert arms producers to civilian production was not successful. Cases of embezzlement and fraud soon came to light. For example, Nemtsov's local business friend Boris Brevnov had taken over the Dzherzhinsky Balakhna Pulp and Paper Mill OAO—Russia's largest paper mill—at the knockdown price of US$7 million, but after having stripped the firm of its assets, he sold his shares to the Moscow branch of CS First Boston Bank, led by tycoon Boris Jordan.[26]

In the mean time, Nemtsov started selling his "model city" to the media by attracting celebrities to his region. In March 1993, former president of the USSR Mikhail Gorbachev visited the city at the invitation of Nemtsov's *Vybor* Foundation,[27] as would Margaret Thatcher with her husband Dennis during the summer of that year.[28] "I had heard back in London that the Governor of the [Nizhny Novgorod] province, Boris Nemtsov, was [...] committed to a radical program of what some call Thatcherism, but what I had always regarded as common sense," Thatcher recounted in her book *Statecraft*.[29] British prime minister John Major, his French counterpart Alain Juppé and even Republican politician Newt Gingrich came and admired Nemtsov's miracle. A scientific conference entitled "Nizhny Novgorod: History of Russian Success?" met at Columbia University in February 1994 where the region's economic reforms were acclaimed by economists.

A Passage to Moscow

Recovering from a multiple bypass surgery in December 1996, Yeltsin was confronted with increasing financial problems due to poor tax collections and Russia's general economic decline. With a need

---

26   *Businessweek Russia*, 23 September 2007.
27   Mikhail Gorbachev, *Memoirs* (London: Doubleday, 1996): 694.
28   "Margaret Thatcher's Visit to Russia and Armenia." Film. Net Film Document 22598. http://www.net-film.ru/en/film-22598/ (as of 7 May 2015).
29   Margaret Thatcher, *Statecraft: Strategies for a Changing World* (New York: HarperCollins, 2002). Quoted in: http://jtf.org/forum/index.php?topic=68 394.50 (as of 7 May 2015).

to take dramatic action, in March 1997 he suddenly decided to reshuffle his government. In order to better control Prime Minister Chernomyrdin, Yeltsin appointed Chubais first deputy prime minister. The oligarchs, who had much contributed to Yeltsin's 1996 reelection campaign, had pushed him back into the new government.[30] Two days later, on 17 March 1997, Nemtsov, was added to the government, also with the rank of first deputy prime minister. These two "young reformers" promised to carry out a set of economic and institutional reforms that the former government under Chernomyrdin had failed to implement.

Nemtsov's sudden departure as a governor caused increased political tensions in Nizhny Novgorod. Two serious candidates ran to succeed Nemtsov: Nizhny Novgorod Mayor Sklyarov and businessman Gennady Khodyrev. The latter was a former Communist boss, having received the backing of the Communist Party of the Russian Federation and nationalist Vladimir Zhirinovsky. Sklyarov, who was described "at best as a reluctant reformer"[31] was supported by Nemtsov, Yeltsin, Chernomyrdin and Yavlinsky. In the run-off election, Sklyarov narrowly won with 52 percent of the popular vote,[32] which indicated that Nemtsov's neoliberal reformism had lost much of its initial popularity. Keeping Nizhny Novgorod under the influence of neoliberal reformism would soon become a hazardous enterprise.

The elections for the oblast's Legislative Assembly in March 1998 were simultaneously organized with snap Nizhny Novgorod mayoral elections following Sklyarov's election as governor. The dominant interest groups this time were unable to present a common mayoral candidate, which created a chaotic situation. Klimentyev, who was still awaiting trial on charges of having misused a US$2 million loan from the Ministry of Finance, suddenly

---

30 Juliet Johnson, *A Fistful of Rubles. The Rise and Fall of the Russian Banking System* (Ithaca, NY: Cornell University Press, 2000): 182.
31 *Monitor*, 14 July 1997.
32 Yevgenia Borisova, "Nizhny Novgorod." *The Moscow Times* 9 September, 2000. http://www.themoscowtimes.com/sitemap/free/2000/9/article/nizhny-novgorod/258957.html (as of 7 May 2015).

emerged as a dangerous outsider candidate[33] backed by nationalist Zhirinovsky. This time Klimentyev, whose campaign loudly defended the interests of pensioners and the unemployed, won the elections on 31 March 1998. Nemtsov called Klimentyev's election a "serious mistake, first and foremost on the part of the Oblast authorities" and noted that the mistake "must be corrected by legal means."[34] Subsequently, the City Electoral Commission invalidated the results, citing irregularities that had occurred during the campaign. Klimentyev was arrested. Yuri Lebedev, who was then Yeltsin's representative in Nizhny Novgorod Oblast, was forced to resign from his post after accusing the local authorities of attempting to falsify the election results. Dmitry Bednyakov, who was one of the losing candidates, said in an interview that the annulment of the election had "created a major political problem, and the jailing created a human rights problem."[35] In September-October 1998 new mayoral elections were held, this time without the still imprisoned Klimentyev. Lebedev, backed by local entrepreneurs, easily won the voting and immediately started a campaign to unseat Governor Sklyarov.[36]

The Klimentyev affair, which blemished Nemtsov's "highly touted bastion of reform" also had a negative impact on his democratic credentials. It was now clear that he had left behind a city where the "military factories lie idle, wages are chronically in arrears and pensioners are strapped."[37] Moreover, Nemtsov's political system was also showing authoritarian traits similar to those prevailing in other Russian regions. These tendencies certainly

---

33 *Kommersant*, 5 August 1997.
34 Christian Lowe, "New Nizhny Mayor 'Concerns' Yeltsin." *The Moscow Times*, 1 April, 1998. http://www.themoscowtimes.com/news/article/new-nizhny-mayor-concerns-yeltsin/293096.html (as of 7 May 2015).
35 Michael R, Gordon, "Heavy Hand Squelches Yeltsin Foe." *The New York Times*, 14 April 1998.
36 Vladimir Gel'man, "Russia's Elites in Search of Consensus: What kind of Consolidation?." *Demokratizatsiya: The Journal of Post-Soviet Democratization* 10, no.3 (2002): 343–361.
37 Gordon, "Heavy Hand."

were connected with Yeltsin's new constitutional system, which established a strong executive at the top[38] and set a precedent for the development of local politics.[39]

As a young, "telegenic" and liberal person not linked to the oligarchs, Nemtsov could entice a Russian public that was largely disappointed by the results of the successive economic reforms. Nemtsov's passage to the Russian government was therefore seen as a victory of the "young reformers" over the old party bosses and Mafioso. Nemtsov, however, was less optimistic about his chances: he saw himself as "a kamikaze appointee, sent in to do an impossible job."[40] Nemtsov's presence in the government was an asset[41] for Yeltsin at a moment when his popularity was fading. In addition, several names of plausible candidates for his succession were already circulating in the media. Among them was not only ex-general Alexander Lebed or Yuri Luzhkov, the popular mayor of Moscow having been re-elected in 1996 with some 90 percent of the popular vote, but now also Nemtsov, who was Yeltsin's preference, a perspective that was disliked by other contenders, like Luzhkov,[42] and some oligarchs courting Yeltsin. They saw in Nemtsov an impostor dictating Yeltsin's decrees. For instance, on 1 April 1997 Yeltsin signed a decree forbidding officials to drive foreign cars. The only alternative was the Volga, produced by GAZ in Nizhny Novgorod. Moreover, in Nemtsov's presence, all foreign cars owned by his staff were publicly auctioned. This kind of action fueled Nemtsov's rising popularity.

---

38 David Kotz and Fred Weir, *Revolution from Above. The Demise of the Soviet System* (London: Routledge, 1997): 210–248.
39 Jeffrey W Hahn, "Democratization and Political Participation in Russia's Region." In Karen Dawisha and Brice Parrott, eds. *Democratic Changes and Authoritarian Reactions in Russia, Ukraine, Belarus, and Moldova* (Cambridge: Cambridge University Press, 1997): 141–51.
40 *The Economist*. 22 March 1997.
41 Elena Kremencova, "Nemtsov's Role in the Plunder of Russia in the 1990's: Links to Berezovsky, Khodorkovsky and Soros." *Fort Russ*, 9 March 2015. http://fortruss.blogspot.be/2015/03/nemtsovs-role-in-plunder-of-russia-in.html (as of 7 May 2015).
42 Boris Kagarlitsky, *Russia under Yeltsin and Putin* (London: Pluto Press, 2002): 131.

From now on, Yeltsin, who "loved public adulation,"[43] kept Nemtsov at his side. He sent him in advance to Tokyo for a meeting with Japanese businessmen when preparing for a diplomatic visit to Japan in April 1998.[44] Because of Nemtsov's popularity, Yeltsin could use him for carrying out urgent, but unpopular, reforms, such as imposing fiscal rigor, taming the energy monopolies, implementing pension reforms, and ending subsidies to households. Keeping powerful pressure groups devouring subsidies out of the decision-making process was the new government's priority. Pressed by the IMF, it drafted a new tax code slowing down capital flight, encouraging private investment and collecting higher tax revenues. Then, the State Duma accepted cuts in public spending as a condition for resuming disbursements of the US$10 billion IMF loan suspended since the beginning of 1997. A downsizing of the army from 1.7 million to 1.2 million men in uniform sought to bring defense spending below 3.5 percent of GDP. Some army generals warned that the cuts would lead to a further under-provisioning of the army in a period of painful restructurings. Meanwhile working-class unrest was growing.[45] For the "young reformers" in the government, it was now a matter of preventing a state default.

Nemtsov's policy consisted of implementing thoroughgoing reforms in various economic and social sectors. Breaking up the energy monopolies and cutting social-security spending (pensions, housing subsidies, sickness and maternity benefits, child and unemployment allowances) received priority, but met fierce resistance from entrenched interests in the energy sector and several segments of the population. Higher utility bills and housing costs

---

43 Serhii Plokhy, *The Last Empire: The Final Days of the Soviet Union* (New York: Basic Books, 2014): 28.
44 Peggy Falkenheim Meyer, "Russo-Japanese Relations: Opportunity for a Rapprochement." *Demokratizatsiya, The Journal of Post-Soviet Democratization* 6, no. 2 (1998): 363–379; Roy Medvedev, *Post-Soviet Russia: A Journey through the Yeltsin Era* (New York: Columbia University Press, 2000): 312.
45 Peter Reddaway and Dmitri Glinsky, *The Tragedy of Russia's Reforms: Market Bolshevism against Democracy* (Washington, DC: United States Institute of Peace, 2001): 570; Timothy L. Thomas and Lester W. Grau. "A Military Biography: Russian Minister of Defense General Igor Rodionov: "In with the Old, in with the New." *Journal of Slavic Studies* 9, no.2 (1996): 443–452.

would threaten the population's standard of living. On 27 April 1997 Yeltsin signed a decree urging that a Russian welfare state reform plan be submitted to the State Duma. Nemtsov's proposal was that by 2003 households would pay 100 percent of their true maintenance and utility costs. In 1996, households paid only 27 percent of the actual cost. Hence, Russia was spending 6 percent of GDP on subsidies to households, while the average household was spending a mere 2 to 3 percent of its income on housing. Though about 40 percent of Russia's housing stock was already privately owned, local governments continued to supply cheap services to owner-occupiers and tenants regardless of their income. Under the reformed system, in order to keep the poorest layers of the population afloat, cash payments would go exclusively to citizens whose housing costs amounted to more than 16 percent of their income.

Nemtsov's neoliberal reforms proved difficult to implement. Introducing individual metering and billing systems required expensive outlays, while disconnecting poor families was socially unacceptable. Local authorities would be tempted to go on supplying cheap energy. Nemtsov, who had just assumed the function of energy minister, urged Gazprom to pay about US$2.5 billion in back taxes to the federal government. But Gazprom refused. The company promised to hand over roughly half of that sum while forcing Nemtsov to leave undisturbed an earlier deal which handed most of the state's 40 percent share in the firm to its managers. Other serious reasons for cleaning up the tax code and the oil and gas legislation were that Yeltsin was looking for foreign direct investment, membership in the World Trade Organization and an invitation to join the G7 elite of democratic market economies. With "young reformers" Chubais and Nemtsov at his side, Yeltsin could demonstrate that he was preparing thoroughgoing market reforms.

Meanwhile, the Russian oligarchs tried to acquire the state's remaining valuable assets. Vladimir Potanin of Uneximbank allied with international investor George Soros to acquire a 25 percent stake in a new telephone investment company, Svyazinvest, which held controlling stakes in several regional phone companies. A consortium led by Soros paid US$1.8 billion at auction for the shares. Observers claimed that the deal went through because Potanin had won the sympathy of Chubais. But Nemtsov revealed that other Russian oligarchs had tried to obtain the Svyazinvest stake at a lower price. According to Nemtsov, this auction was a victory of market forces over "bandit capitalism." Soros explained that his interest in Russia was based on his confidence in the "young reformers" surrounding Yeltsin.[46] But a few months later, the media reported that one of Chubais' assistant had received a bribe of US$90,000 from a Swiss firm connected to Potanin for a book that was not yet written on the history of Russian privatizations.

The Svyazinvest scandal damaged the image of Chubais and Nemtsov. Though they remained in government, both lost a considerable part of their influence on 20 November 1997. Nemtsov's face-to-face meetings with Yeltsin dropped from two audiences a week to one every several weeks[47] and his important position as minister of fuel and energy went to his friend Sergey Kiriyenko. Soros, who had also bought Potanin's shares in Svyazinvest, lost a good part of his fortune in this adventure.

Nemtsov's reputation was then tarnished by the Brevnov affair, which revealed how deeply he had been involved in the old-boy networks of Nizhny Novgorod. On 1 April 1997 Nemtsov had appointed his friend Boris Brevnov, the 29-year-old NBD Bank president in Nizhny Novgorod, head of the United Energy Systems (UES) board of directors. At a shareholders' meeting on 5 May 1997, Brevnov took over the position of president and chairman of the governing board.[48] But less than a year later, on 25 March 1998, he had to submit his resignation on charges of corruption and abuse of office and left Russia for the U.S.[49]

In May 1997 Yeltsin appointed Kiriyenko first deputy minister of fuel and energy under Nemtsov. One may assume that this appointment happened at Nemtsov's request. Kiriyenko and

---

46   Timothy O'Brien, "George Soros has seen the Enemy. It Looks like Him.'" *The New York Times*. 6 December, 1998.
47   Timothy J. Colton, *Yeltsin: A Life* (New York: Basic Books, 2008): 406.
48   *Kommersant*, 13 November 2001.
49   Enovation Partners. "Boris Brevnov," http://enovationpartners.com/team/boris-brevnov/; Zoominfo. (n.d.). "Boris Brevnov," http://www.zoominfo.com/p/Boris-Brevnov/50797254 (as of 7 May, 2015).

Nemtsov had always been close friends. Both spent their early youth in Sochi and then later in Nizhny Novgorod's Komsomol youth organization and the democratic movement. In 1990 Kiriyenko was elected to the Oblast Soviet. Kiriyenko had been a manager of a Komsomol-owned trading firm and then he organized scratch-card lotteries. In 1993 he became director of Garantiya, a commercial bank in Nizhny Novgorod. By 1996 he chaired the board of Norsi-Oil, a big oil refinery in Kstovo[50] with access to the Moscow market.[51] Kiriyenko's appointment as first deputy minister of fuel and energy under Nemtsov surprised many, but Yeltsin already knew him well after having met him during a visit to Nizhny Novgorod.[52] On 20 November 1997 Kiriyenko was appointed minister of fuel and energy, a portfolio he took over from Nemtsov.

The "young reformers" did not succeed in imposing all the reforms they hoped for within a year. Speeding up economic reforms was an idea Prime Minister Chernomyrdin did not share. Yeltsin was now forced to intervene and in March 1998 he fired his prime minister. Yeltsin tried to impose Kiriyenko as his next prime minister, but the State Duma twice opposed Kiriyenko's appointment (143 votes in favor to 186 against; 115 votes in favor to 271 votes against). In order to avoid new parliamentary elections to be held after a third rejection of Kiriyenko's candidacy, Yeltsin was forced to compromise with the opposition in the State Duma. The public announcement that the deeply unpopular Chubais would take up the post of chairman of the UES board of directors, thus leaving the government, meant that Kiriyenko's candidacy no longer aroused the opposition and the State Duma voted in his favor by a tally of

---

50   Gary Peach, "The Analyst: Norsi Oil: The Headache LUKoil Can't Live Without," *The Moscow Times*, 16 December, 1997 http://www.themoscowtimes.com/news/article/the-analyst-norsi-oil-the-headache-lukoil-cant-live-without/296430.html (as of 7 May 2015).

51   Heiko Pleines, "FSU Refineries: Norsi-Oil." *Alexander's Gas and Oil Connection*. An Institute for Global Energy Research. 17 January 2000. http://www.gasandoil.com/news/russia/66e179e5bf1c31f23c8066269808b341 (as of 7 May 2015).

52   Colton, *Yeltsin: A Life*, 580.

251–25. At Yeltsin's demand, Nemtsov stayed in his post as a deputy prime minister, helping Kiriyenko deal with some difficult situations. In July 1998 he represented the government at the controversial interment ceremony of the imperial Romanov family in St. Petersburg. Kiriyenko asked him to meet with striking coal miners who had occupied two branches of the Trans-Siberian Railroad.[53] To the outside world it was clear that Nemtsov no longer played an important political role. The financial crisis of August-September 1998 transformed the entire political scene, ending Nemtsov's ministerial career.

Leader of the Opposition

After giving up his post as deputy prime minister on 28 August 1998, Nemtsov's political career came to a standstill. He resigned this position voluntarily even though Yeltsin had asked him to stay on. No party organization or social movement was backing him. The evaporated democratic movement had already given birth to a multitude of political organizations and initiatives led by social celebrities or politicians. Having moved to Moscow, Nemtsov had also lost his popular base in Nizhny Novgorod. Hence, he decided to reinvent himself. Therefore, he refused Yeltsin's offer to become the head of a newly formed Municipal Council, a club of Russia's mayors. Instead, he announced at a press conference in St. Petersburg that he would run for a seat in the State Duma in 1999. He refrained from answering questions about his political future: running as an independent candidate or joining an existing political party. He explained his indecision by referring to his political philosophy: "I have never been a member of a political party. I don't even like the word party. At the same time, I understand that it is necessary to enter an election with the support of some kind of social or political organization. Maybe we can think up a new name for such a thing." He also said that Russia's main problem was the weakness of it political system: "The problem in Russia is the weak political authority and a system of oligarch capitalism. They say the

---

53   Colton, *Yeltsin: A Life*, 413; *The Chicago Tribune*, 21 May 1998.

oligarchs run the country, but this isn't because they are so strong, but because the authorities are so weak. By strong political authority, I don't mean a dictatorship. We already have had that and it gave us nothing. What I mean is a state that is not corrupt, can collect taxes, is independent of financial interests, and is under the control of citizens and society. When we have such a state, our financial problems will take care of themselves."[54]

The perspectives for starting a political career were at that time unfavorable for a "young reformer" who had been involved in privatization policies and defending neoliberal ideas. With former intelligence chief Yevgeny Primakov now heading the government, the nationalist and communist currents were gaining momentum. The danger of a communist-backed nationalist or authoritarian take-over was possible. A unification of all democratic forces in one democratic bloc had thus become urgent. Forming that united democratic bloc would be, according to Vladimir Lysenko (a former leader of the democratic movement and a member of the Republican Party), difficult because "all democrats are so well known and loved by the people that each believes that he is the one most adored by the voters."[55] Lysenko distinguished three possible evolutions. In the first scenario, a democratic bloc would unite the whole democratic movement. But neither Yavlinsky nor Gaidar had been capable of doing this in the recent past. The democratic bloc therefore could be better formed around the unifying person of Nemtsov, because the latter had the highest ratings among the democrats in the regions. "If this bloc receives 15 to 20 percent in the Duma elections, then Nemtsov has a real chance to perform very successfully in the presidential elections."[56] In the second scenario, the communists and national-patriots could form a bloc under Alexander Lebed's leadership and come to power by winning the parliamentary elections of 1999 and the presidential elections of

---

54 Brian Whitmore, "Nemtsov Will Run for State Duma in 1999 Elections." *The Moscow Times*, 25 September 1998.
55 Vladimir Lysenko, "Republican Party Calls for Reunification of Democratic Forces." *Demokratizatsiya: The Journal of Post-Soviet Democratization* 5, no. 4 (1999): 147.
56 Ibid., 148.

2000. A third possible variant could be the installation of an authoritarian regime with a *coup d'état* followed by rigged elections. But how that democratic electoral bloc could be forged out of a collection of governmental "retirees" with their own personal ambitions was not made clear.[57]

Reviving the democratic opposition was one of Nemtsov's aims when he registered "Young Russia" (*Rossiya Molodaya*) as his political movement in January 1999. However, this political vehicle did not succeed in attracting other "young reformers." Kiriyenko founded his own rival civic movement "New Force" (Novaya Sila) when campaigning for a "weaker presidency."[58] In August 1999 the former "young reformers" founded the "Union of Right Forces" (Soyuz Pravykh Sil, SPS) with Kiriyenko as elected party leader and with Gaidar, Nemtsov and Chubais as his deputies. According to journalist Oleg Davydov, these people resembled one another so closely and were so devoid of any independent political identity that they could be regarded as a single individual.[59] The SPS remained a media phenomenon lacking a real party structure and it membership consisted mainly of technocrats who were sitting in the waiting room of the Kremlin.[60] Yavlinsky's social-liberal Yabloko party refused to join the right-wing liberal SPS, which focused on defending private property rights and representing business interests. Ultimately, the two liberal parties decided to compete separately in the Duma elections held on 19 December 1999.

The two liberal parties had little chance to win the Duma elections. After a decade of revolution, many Russians were desperate for leadership and the parliamentary process inhibited that, as did

---

57   Vladimir Lysenko, "The Russian Democratic Movement: Past, Present, and Future." *Demokratizatsiya: The Journal of Post-Soviet Democratization* 5, no.4 (1997): 479.

58   Andrei Zolotov Jr., "Kiriyenko Floats Idea of Weaker Presidency." *The Moscow Times*, 13 August, 1999 http://www.themoscowtimes.com/news/article/kiriyenko-floats-idea-of-weaker-presidency/273718.html (as of 7 May 2015).

59   Boris Kagarlitsky, *Russia under Yeltsin and Putin* (London: Pluto Press, 2002): 254.

60   Lilia Shevtsova, *Russia – Lost in Transition. The Yeltsin and Putin Legacies* (Washington, DC: Carnegie Endowment for International Peace, 2007): 113–17.

a constitution that was next to impossible to amend. They were thus willing to see the parliamentary system temporarily suspended by a "strong leader." Luzhkov, Primakov and their electoral coalition Fatherland-All Russia led the opinion polls at that point, but Yeltsin had already appointed his security man Vladimir Putin to the post of prime minister with the task of stabilizing the regime and winning the Duma elections. Putin assembled a new party, the Interregional Movement "Unity" (*Yedinstvo*) that quickly rose in the opinion polls during the campaign. After the voters had spoken, Unity obtained 73 seats to 113 seats for the KPRF and 68 seats for Fatherland-All Russia. The two liberal parties, SPS and Yabloko, won 29 and 20 seats respectively. Immediately after the elections Fatherland-All Russia split into two factions. Primakov was left with the Fatherland banner. Because the "independents" had scored 114 seats among the single member district constituencies from the overall total of 450 Duma seats, "Unity" was able to form a presidential bloc with the independents and some smaller parties. On 31 December 1999 Yeltsin, who seemed completely broken, suddenly resigned. His prime minister automatically became "acting president." Snap presidential elections followed on 26 March 2000.

Against this quickly changing political landscape, the SPS leaders decided to back Putin, rather than Yavlinsky for the presidency — specifically Chubais, Gaidar and Kiriyenko voted for Putin, while Nemtsov and Khakamada did not. Their main concern was that economic policy be liberal.[61] After Putin's election, the divided SPS leadership nonetheless preferred remaining in opposition, although Chubais had already openly pleaded for following a more "realist" course. Foreign observers could agree on the fact that Putin's election marked the end of revolution. For the first several years of the last decade, Russian politics were polarized by the struggle between communists and anti-communists. [...] Putin's coming to power signaled for many an end to this volatile period — the Thermidor of Russia's current revolution. Coined during the French revolution, the Thermidor of any revolution marks the cooling off of the revolutionary fever and the beginning of a period

---

61   Kagarlitsky, *Russia under Yeltsin and Putin*, 263.

when old institutions are revived and melded into the new practices of the post-revolutionary order. Thermidor is also the moment in a revolutionary transition when the state becomes stronger and nationalism replaces the more idealistic slogans of the earlier revolutionary period. The parallels between contemporary Russia and the periods of Thermidor in other great revolutions are striking.[62]

In the beginning, Putin kept a low profile. Seeking to coopt the liberals, he appointed Kiriyenko as his representative in the newly created Volga Federal District. Having become a "Putinist," Kiriyenko left the SPS leadership and the Duma. Later on Putin would appoint him at head of the state firm Rosatom. Putin reinforced his personal power by centralizing the decision-making process, firing opponents, and subjecting the oligarchs to his authority. Several oligarchs left the country after having been stripped of their Russian assets (Boris Berezovsky, Vladimir Gusinsky in 2001) or went to prison (Mikhail Khodorkovsky in 2003). Facing the parliamentary elections of December 2003, the two liberal parties, Yabloko and SPS, were once more talking about merging their Duma factions and party organizations.[63] Again, however, no accord could be reached and neither SPS nor Yabloko crossed the 5 percent threshold. The SPS kept only three single-mandate seats. These three parliamentarians now preferred sitting with Putin's Unity faction. SPS leaders Nemtsov, Chubais, Gaidar and Khakamada resigned. The fatal divide between the two liberal parties can be explained by their different electorates.[64] Yabloko mainly appealed to academics and teachers interested in human rights, whereas SPS was "a party

---

62 Michael McFaul, "Russia's 2000 Presidential Elections: Implications for Russian Democracy and U.S.-Russian Relations 2000." *Carnegie Moscow Center*, 1 April 2000 http://carnegieendowment.org/2000/04/01/russia-s-2000-presidential-elections-implications-for-russian-democracy-and-u.s.-russian-relations-pub-421 (as of 7 May 2015).
63 Letter to Boris Nemtsov and Irina Khakamada from Grigory Yavlinsky and Sergei Ivanenko on SPS. *Proposals*, 28 January 2003. http://eng.yabloko.ru/Activities/letter_290103.html (as of 7 May 2015).
64 David White, "Going Their Own Way: The Yabloko Party's Opposition to Unification." *Journal of Communist Studies and Transition Politics* 21, no. 4 (2005): 462–486.

[...] closely connected with the oligarchic system, often on a personal level."⁶⁵

Constantly Fighting Putinism

After this crushing electoral defeat, Nemtsov dreamt of a complete reshuffling of Russia's political landscape by winning the next presidential elections. In January 2004 he founded a Committee for Free Elections in the Year 2008, seeking to bring together all opposition politicians and also some prominent Russian "dissidents", like Garry Kasparov and Vladimir Bukovsky, in a campaign for fair presidential elections. The SPS abstained from presenting a presidential candidate in the March 2004 presidential elections, but Khakamada nonetheless decided to run as an "independent" candidate, winning only Nemtsov's backing. Her campaign, she said, was financed by Leonid Nevzlin, a large shareholder of Yukos.⁶⁶ After winning just 3.9 percent of the popular vote, Khakamada founded her own, all-but-still-born political party Our Choice (*"Nash Vybor"*), which she eventually merged with Mikhail Kasyanov's People's Democratic Union (PDU).

When the Orange Revolution broke out in Kyiv at the end of 2004, Nemtsov was the only Russian public figure who identified himself completely with the insurgency. In a television debate on NTV on 9 December 2004, he argued that the Putin regime had supported pro-Russian presidential candidate Viktor Yanukovych, who twice had been convicted of criminal charges, against Westernizer Viktor Yushchenko.⁶⁷ After the revolution, Yuschchenko appointed Nemtsov his private (but unpaid) business adviser, which created some confusion in Russian public opinion. Nemtsov

---

65 Anastasia Matveyeva, "YABLOKO Does Not Sell Itself." *Gazeta*, 29 January 2003. http://www.eng.yabloko.ru/Publ/2003/PAPERS/gazeta_300103.html (as of 7 May 2015).
66 *Vremya Novostei*, 15 January 2004.
67 Robert Horvath, *Putin's 'Preventive Counter-Revolution': Post-Soviet Authoritarianism and the Spectre of Velvet Revolution* (London: Routledge, 2013): 34.

explained his new position by pointing out that "I must attract Russian investments, and thus help improve Ukraine's investment climate. I am not a Ukrainian government official and I am not a Russian government official, so there won't be any thick-headed lobbying."[68] Yavlinsky, who supported the insurrection as well, had always refrained from becoming personally involved in Ukrainian affairs. However, some of his party activists, like Ilya Yashin and Andrey Piontkovsky, did nonetheless participate in the Orange Revolution before joining Nemtsov's team.

The events in Kyiv made clear that electoral competition in a repressive environment would remain unproductive without mass movements on the streets. Only a well-organized upheaval of the urban masses could destroy an authoritarian regime's legitimacy. But the conditions for applying such a scenario were at that moment absent in Russia, where the living standard was continuously rising and welfare provisions could be financed out of oil and gas revenues. Hence, a liberal revolution would not have any chance to succeed. At a meeting of the All-Russian Civic Congress For Democracy, Against Dictatorship at the Kosmos Hotel in Moscow on 12 December 2004, Nemtsov told the audience that he was tormented by the fact that the Russian liberals had surrendered. There would be no democratic revolution in Moscow as long as "the ambition of our politicians—and I don't exclude myself from this category—is outrageously high and, unfortunately, is placed ahead of the national interests of Russia."[69] The only workable solution was uniting all democratic liberal political forces in order to rescue the institution of free elections.[70]

In the meantime Nemtsov's popularity had evaporated. On 13 December 2008 he joined "eternal dissident" Gary Kasparov in

---

[68] Valeria Korchagina, "Nemtsov to advise Ukraine's President." *The Moscow Times*, 15 February 2005 http://www.themoscowtimes.com/business/articl e/nemtsov-to-advise-ukraines-president/225149.html, (as of 7 May 2015).

[69] Robert Horvath, *Putin's 'Preventive Counter-Revolution': Post-Soviet Authoritarianism and the Spectre of Velvet Revolution* (London: Routledge, 2013): 40.

[70] "Press Conference with Serge Ivanenko, Garry Kasparov, Boris Nemtsov and other Committee officials". *Interfax* 18 May 2004. http://www.eng.yablok o.ru/Publ/2004/AGENCIES/040518_interfax.html, (as of 7 May 2015).

founding a new opposition movement entitled "Solidarnost," which had difficulty attracting media attention. In 2009 he decided to run for mayor in his native town Sochi, where the 2014 Winter Olympics were planned. Though Nemtsov had campaigned energetically in the streets of Sochi, he only obtained an insignificant 14 percent of the popular vote, while Putin's favored candidate won 77 percent. In this period Nemtsov had become persona non grata in leading political circles. His "reformist" colleagues (Kiriyenko, Gaidar, Khakamada, Chubais) had left politics. By 2008 Chubais had reformed UES out of existence. Putin offered him the job of general manager of Rosnanotech, a state-backed corporation. Gaidar headed a Moscow-based economic research institute. Following his unexpected death in December 2009, the Russian Presidency organizes an international Gaidar Forum for the business elite each year in mid-January. Khakamada went back to the university. In November 2012, Putin appointed her a member of the Presidential Council for Civil Society Institutions and Human Rights. Nemtsov did not bury his political ambitions. In September 2010 he founded the party For Russia without Lawlessness and Corruption, later renamed as the People's Freedom Party (PARNAS), fighting Putin's corrupt regime. Because the Ministry of Justice refused its registration, PARNAS merged with Vladimir Ryzhkov's already registered Republican Party of Russia (RPR). Ryzhkov, Kasyanov and Nemtsov co-chaired the RPR-PARNAS combination. In 2013 Nemtsov was elected as a RPR-PARNAS candidate to the Yaroslavl Oblast parliament.[71] Despite his return to public office, one could hardly speak of a political comeback for the former "golden boy."

Meanwhile, Nemtsov's image had been tarnished by some of his business affairs. In February 2004, he had been appointed director of Neftyanoi Bank, which was Russia's 76th largest bank (in 2006) and chairman of the oil firm Neftyanoi located in Nizhny

---

[71] Vladimir Kara-Murza, "Boris Nemtsov: Elected by Voters, Prosecuted by Kremlin." *World Affairs Journal*, 20 September 2013. http://www.worldaffairsjournal.org/blog/vladimir-kara-murza/boris-nemtsov-elected-voters-prosecuted-kremlin (as of 7 May 2015).

Novgorod. Bank owner Igor Linshits subsequently became the subject of an investigation following allegations of fraud and money laundering. That he was "supporting liberal political parties and harbored political ambitions of his own"[72] was not a secret. In 2003 he had run unsuccessfully for a State Duma seat on the Communist ticket. But he had also supported Nemtsov's SPS. In December 2005 Nemtsov resigned from his positions and Linschits disappeared to Israel. Nemtsov's advisory work for Ukrainian President Yushchenko's disastrous administration was subjected to heavy criticism. In Ukraine, Nemtsov's position had become untenable and in October 2006 he was relieved of all his duties. Though Nemtsov had contacts in the financial sector — at that time his daughter Zhanna Nemtsova was vice president of Mercury Capital Trust in Moscow — little came of Nemtsov's promise to bolster Russian investment in Ukraine.[73]

When in September 2011 Putin unilaterally announced that he would run for a third presidential term, a protest movement soon materialized. This unforeseen outburst of discontent brought together a growing number of young urban professionals, teachers and workers aspiring for a more open society. During several well attended street demonstrations, various speakers and politicians addressed the crowd in Moscow. The emblematic blogger Aleksey Navalny emerged as the movement's informal leader and icon. Though Nemtsov's protests were intellectually better articulated, his speeches did not always resonate with the crowd. Nemtsov had

---

72 Maria Antonova, "Criminal Charges Dropped for Former Neftyanol Bank Owner." *The Moscow Times*, 18 May 2010. http://www.themoscowtimes.com/business/article/criminal-charges-dropped-for-former-neftyanoi-bank-owner/406166.html (as of 7 May 2015).
73 *The Moscow Times*. 15 May 2004.

already frequently castigated Putin's crony capitalism,[74] the bankrupt oligarchs,[75] Gazprom's monopoly,[76] blatant economic mismanagement,[77] and widespread corruption.[78] Most of the time, he only repeated what Western authors had already published.[79] He also tried to develop a discourse giving priority to the rule of law.[80] Nemtsov's problem was that he was easily identified as an old friend of the oligarchs, including the jailed Khodorkovsky. As a free-market fundamentalist, he liked combatting "nationalization, price-fixing" and "anti-globalization,"[81] but he refused, along with almost all the rest of his cohort, to reflect on what had gone wrong in the 1990s, "a bad omen. [...] Instead he blamed everything that went wrong in the next 15 years on Putin."[82]

As in 2004, Nemtsov appeared in Kyiv in February 2014 where a popular upheaval had ousted Yanukovich. He sided with liberal European politicians supporting Petro Poroshenko's bid for power.

---

74 Nikolaus von Twickel, "Nemtsov assails Putin's rule in new report." *The Moscow Times*, 16 June 2010. http://www.themoscowtimes.com/news/article/nemtsov-assails-putins-rule-in-new-report/408320.html (as of 7 May 2015).
75 Boris Nemtsov. "Bankrotim oligarkhov – Spasaem Rossiyu [By bankrupting the oligarchs, we will save Russia]." *Yezhednevii zhurnal*, 18 February 2010. http://www.ej.ru/?a=note&id=8825 (as of 7 May 2015).
76 Boris Nemtsov and Vladimir Milov, *Putin and Gazprom: An Independent Expert Report*, 2 August 2008, http://en.novayagazeta.ru/politics/8107.html (as of 7 May 2015).
77 Boris Nemtsov and Vladimir Milov, "Putin i krizis" [Putin and Crisis]. *Grani.ru* 29 February 2009. http://goo.gl/i5cQP (as of 7 May 2015).
78 V. Milov, B. Nemtsov, V. Ryzhkov and O. Shorina, "Putin. Corruption. An Independent White Paper." Moscow: Putin-Itogi, 2011. http://www.putin-itogi.ru/putin-corruption-an-independent-white-paper/ (as of 7 May 2015); Putin-Itogi. *Razgovor s Borisom Nemtsovym na "Radio Svoboda", 2012* [Interview with Boris Nemtsov on "Radio Svoboda"]. Moscow http://www.putin-itogi.ry/category/novosti/ (as of 7 May 2015).
79 Robert W. Ortung, "Russia" *Nations in Transit 2014*, Freedom House 2014. https://freedomhouse.org/report/nations-transit/2014/russia#.VUPYNFIcSpo (as of 7 May 2015).
80 *The Economist*, 6 January 2011.
81 Olivia Ward, "Russia's Boris Nemtsov: From 'Boy Governor' to Opposition 'Grandfather.'" Thestar.com 2012 http://www.thestar.com/news/world/2012/02/12/russias_boris_nemtsov_from_boy_governor_to_opposition_grandfather.html (as of 7 May, 2015).
82 Gessen. 2015.

Poroshenko and his appointee as Odessa governor, former Georgian president Mikheil Saakashvili, became his close friends. In Moscow, Nemtsov also mobilized against Putin's annexation of the Crimea and the subsequent outbreak of fighting in eastern Ukraine. But his regular visits to the United States, where he met Republican senator John McCain and independent Senator Joe Lieberman or banker Soros, made it easy for the Kremlin to label him an "American agent" who could be associated with foreign funds provided by the National Endowment for Democracy (NED)[83] and Soros's Open Society Foundations (OSF).

While he was walking home on the night of 27 February 2015, Nemtsov, then aged 55, was shot dead on Bolshoy Moskvoretsky Bridge near the Kremlin two days before he would take part in a rally against Russia's involvement in the fighting in Ukraine. Several theories about the murder appeared in the media. One group claimed that Nemtsov shared his Ukrainian girlfriend Anna Duritskaya with Kyiv mafia boss Pyotr Listerman, giving him reason to commit the crime.[84] Others argued that he was killed by Muslim fundamentalists. Some thought that enemies in Nemtsov's own party could have ordered the crime, while sources close to Nemtsov held Putin personally responsible for the murder. The Kremlin rejected any involvement, claiming that in political terms Nemtsov was no threat to Putin. Rumors also spread that Chechen leader Ramzan Kadyrov had ordered Nemtsov's execution[85] because Nemtsov was preparing a report on Putin's and Kadyrov's involvement in Ukraine. As Nemtsov interviewed people and collected documents for this publication, his research certainly attracted the attention of the Russian or Chechen secret services. Despite Nemtsov's killing, the report was nonetheless completed by

---

83   William F. Engdahl, "Regime Change in the Russian Federation? Why Washington Wants 'Finito' with Vladimir Putin." *Gobal Research* 10 January 2012, http://www.globalresearch.ca/regime-change-in-the-russian-federation-why-washington-wants-finito-with-vladimir-putin/28571?print=1 (as of 7 May 2015).
84   *Le Figaro*. 3 March 2015.
85   *The Economist*. 15 March 2015.

his research team and presented on 12 May 2015;[86] it was received in the West as an important document describing Putin's involvement in the war in eastern Ukraine.

Conclusions

Nemtsov was perhaps Russia's most outspoken political leader, articulating the democratic and social demands of the new middle classes in the big cities. More than the other "young reformers" serving under President Yeltsin, he was a political propagandist defending western opinions about politics and society. Nevertheless, he started his political career as a local activist and member of the democratic movement in Nizhny Novgorod. He left his "model region" in 1997 for Moscow. At one point, he was considered a serious candidate for the presidency. The Svyazinvest affair and the financial crisis of 1998 marked an abrupt end for his ministerial career.

Nemtsov's rise and fall was driven by several social and political factors. Thanks to the democratic movement, he had obtained a leading role in Nizhny Nogorod's politics. Following the collapse of this movement, he used administrative and political power to consolidate his authority. He easily captured the attention of the media when promoting his "model region" in Russia and abroad. For Yeltsin and the technocrats in the Kremlin, he became an ally in the struggle against the vested economic interests affiliated with the oligarchs. The 1998 crisis that finished Nemtsov's ministerial career ultimately paved the road to Putin's authoritarian regime.

In order to combat Putin's regime, Nemtsov tried to form an electoral bloc of all liberal forces. This project had little chance of success. In 2003 Nemtsov's SPS lost the State Duma elections. Nemtsov was now forced to combat Putin in the (new) media, set up platform organizations, and reorganize the opposition. But the Putin reforms and the rising standard of living for the population had meanwhile led to more political and social stability. When in

---

86 "Putin. The War: about the Involvement of Russia in the Eastern Ukraine and the Crimea". *European Union Foreign Affairs Journal*, Special Edition. May 2015.

2011–12 the urban masses were demonstrating in the streets for more political transparency and against Putin's renewed presidential ambitions, Nemtsov's voice was hardly heard. By then, he was identified as a political dissident linked to the bygone Yeltsin era.

The Nemtsov Vote: Public Opinion and Pro-Western Liberalism's Decline in Russia[1]

Henry E. Hale

With Boris Nemtsov's untimely and violent death in 2015, scholars were reminded of just how powerfully pro-Western liberal opposition has been marginalized in Russia during the era of Vladimir Putin.[2] Often seen in the mid-1990s as a leading young voice for democracy, market reforms, and a Europe-leaning foreign policy who might one day challenge for the presidency, Nemtsov by the 2010s was widely regarded as a spent political force, out of step with Russian reality. Indeed, back in 1997 he held the post of first deputy prime minister and could boast 22 per cent support for president, bested only by Communist leader Gennady Zyuganov's 24 per cent.[3] But fifteen years later, his ratings in the race for Russia's top job were near zero and another poll found that 46 per cent of the population considered him a man "whose time has passed," with only 11 per cent still thinking his "time is yet to come." Over a fifth of the population did not even recognize his name in 2012.[4]

---

1   This paper was made possible in part by a grant from Carnegie Corporation of New York. Funds from the National Council for Eurasian and East European Research (NCEEER) (under authority of a Title VIII grant from the U.S. Department of State), the National Science Foundation (NSF), and from the U.S. Department of State also supported work leading to this paper. The statements made and views expressed within this text are solely the responsibility of the author, who is grateful to all whose support made this project possible.
2   Vladimir Gel'man, *Authoritarian Russia: Analyzing Post-Soviet Regime Changes*, 1 edition (Pittsburgh, Pa: University of Pittsburgh Press, 2015).
3   *Argumenty i Fakty*, no. 23, May 1998, as reported in RIA Novosti and circulated in Johnson's Russia List no.2207.
4   Data come from the 2012 Russian Election Studies (RES) nationwide survey of the Russian Federation population organized by the present author and Timothy J. Colton. Details on the survey can be found in Timothy J. Colton and Henry E. Hale, "Putin's Uneasy Return and Hybrid Regime Stability: The

To whom did Nemtsov's brand of pro-Western liberalism appeal during the Putin era? The answer is not merely of academic interest as we remember Nemtsov in this special journal issue marking the first anniversary of his passing. It also has implications for how we understand the Putin era in Russia more generally. Indeed, while some scholars have argued that Western-oriented liberalism lacked a base in Russian public opinion,[5] surveys have consistently documented strong support for many important liberal ideas — including core principles of democracy and a market economy that would appear quite in line with what Nemtsov advocated — during the same period liberal parties have struggled.[6] Key to pro-Western liberals' political marginalization, then, is the question of why they were unable to mobilize votes among people who, surveys suggest, generally supported many of their ideas. While an obvious answer is Putin's repressive apparatus,[7] liberals' marginalization occurred well before this apparatus had come full flower; repression is thus a better explanation for why liberalism has not come back than for why it became marginal in the first place. To explain the political demise of pro-Western liberal forces in Russia,

---

2012 Russian Election Studies Survey," *Problems of Post-Communism* 61, no. 2 (April 2014): 3–22.

[5] Some portray it as essentially anathema to Russian culture while others blame the unpopular 1990s reforms in the name of pro-Western liberalism. For different views, see: Alexander N. Domrin, "Ten Years Later: Society, 'Civil Society,' and the Russian State," *The Russian Review* 62, no. 2 (2003): 193–211; M. Steven Fish, "The Travails of Liberalism," *Journal of Democracy* 7, no. 2 (1996): 105–17, doi:10.1353/jod.1996.0024; Andrei P. Tsygankov, *The Strong State in Russia: Development and Crisis* (Oxford ; New York: Oxford University Press, 2014); William Zimmerman and Judith S. Kullberg, "Liberal Elites, Socialist Masses, and Problems of Russian Democracy," *World Politics* 51, no. 3 (1999): 323–58.

[6] Timothy J. Colton and Michael McFaul, "Are Russians Undemocratic?," *Post-Soviet Affairs* 18, no. 2 (April 1, 2002): 91–121, doi:10.1080/1060586X.2002.10 641515; Henry E. Hale, "The Myth of Mass Russian Support for Autocracy: The Public Opinion Foundations of a Hybrid Regime," *Europe-Asia Studies* 63, no. 8 (September 1, 2011): 1357–75, doi:10.1080/09668136.2011.601106.

[7] E.g., Karen Dawisha, *Putin's Kleptocracy: Who Owns Russia?* (New York: Simon & Schuster, 2014); M. Steven Fish, "Democracy Derailed in Russia: The Failure of Open Politics (New York: Cambridge University Press" 2005; Christopher Walker and Robert W. Orttung, "Breaking the News: The Role of State-Run Media," *Journal of Democracy* 25, no. 1 (January 2014): 71–85.

therefore, it becomes important not only to identify which views they shared with the electorate, but to identify which of the appeals they made were able to win them votes in the face of competition (including pressure from the Kremlin) and which were not.

Accordingly, the following pages examine patterns in Nemtsov's electorate during the only episode in which he actually appeared on the ballot for a nationwide office as the top leader of a political force, in 2003, prior to the maturing of Putin's political machine. It finds that among the constituencies to which Nemtsov appealed, he was able to win votes disproportionately from youth, residents of Russia's very largest cities, ethnic minorities, and proponents of Western democracy. But despite his calls for market reform and a Western foreign policy orientation, people who supported these values were generally no more likely to vote for him than were others. Nor did he, as some believed, appeal mainly to people who identified with big business, small business, or the middle class. These findings are argued to be consistent with the argument that the decline of Nemtsov's variety of pro-Western liberalism in Russia owes in large part to Putin's ability early on to co-opt some of liberalism's most popular ideas while leaving people like Nemtsov with less promising sources of appeal, a co-optation that could be enforced and deepened as the Kremlin's ability to repress and manipulate politics developed.[8]

Nemtsov's 2003 Duma Campaign as Electoral Career Pinnacle

Despite being regularly in the discussion about possible future presidents, Nemtsov never pursued such a run to the end. Through the mid-late 1990s, he was a loyal man of then-incumbent Boris Yeltsin. His ratings in the presidential race began to soar with his rise to the central government in early 1997, but his time in power did not serve him well as economic problems continued and he became embroiled in certain scandals, as described elsewhere in this

---

8   Henry E. Hale, *Why Not Parties in Russia: Democracy, Federalism, and the State* (New York, NY: Cambridge University Press, 2006).

special issue. He staged a remarkable political comeback in 1999 atop the newly formed Union of Right Forces (*Soiuz pravykh sil*, or SPS), which surged into parliament with a surprisingly strong 9 per cent of the party-list vote, good enough for fourth place. But he was only the second figure on this party list, with top honors going to former Prime Minister Sergei Kirienko, and in any case SPS benefited by hitching itself to the fast-rising star of then-Prime Minister Putin, whom Yeltsin had already anointed his preferred successor.[9]

Nemtsov shifted into what he called "strict opposition" to federal authorities shortly after Putin's election as president in 2000, criticizing among other things Putin's efforts to take control over television,[10] though he at other times cautioned that his opposition was "constructive" and would not be oriented to harsh criticism of Putin.[11] Thus when the topic of the approaching 2004 presidential election came up, Nemtsov told a group of students that "A realistic prognosis with a high degree of probability is that the president in 2004 will be Vladimir Vladimirovich Putin." Consequently, Nemtsov went on to say, he did not want to "set up for myself a masochistic experiment, 'how many votes will I get?'"[12] Instead, he would concentrate on winning the 2003 parliamentary elections for a liberal force on the political right.

This 2003 election can in some sense be seen as the pinnacle of Nemtsov's participation in elections. It was only then that he ever led a political force in a nationwide campaign that made it onto the ballot. He personally topped the SPS party list, which accentuated relatively young, pro-market politicians and also included businesswoman-politician Irina Khakamada and Yeltsin's "privatization tsar" Anatoly Chubais in its "troika" of lead candidates. Nemtsov brashly declared this the "party of winners" as opposed to the party of "losers" from the reforms of the 1990s, such as the Communist Party and the intelligentsia represented by a rival pro-

---

9 Ibid.
10 Third Monitor, *Polit.Ru*, 17 November 2000.
11 Boris Nemtsov. "Interview, *Kommersant-Vlast'*," Moscow, in Russian, 7 July 2003, translation circulated in Johnson's Russia List, no.7249.
12 *Gazeta*, 20 May 2003, 17:36.

market force, the Yabloko Party. "The task that we set before ourselves is the following: We have conducted reforms from which 20 million Russians came to live better. Now it is necessary to conduct reforms from which the majority will benefit," Nemtsov declared in June 2003.[13]

Ultimately, the party fell just short of the 5 per cent needed in the party-list voting to form a delegation in the Duma, and in an interview shortly afterwards Nemtsov gave two reasons for this defeat. Most importantly, he said, the party failed to take a clear stance on whether to oppose or support Putin, with Nemtsov personally inclined to oppose him but Chubais leading a large group in the party who thought it best to back the incumbent president given Putin's continued advocacy of pro-market reforms. Nemtsov also blamed the dramatic arrest of Mikhail Khodorkovsky less than two months before the voting; he said SPS did the right thing by criticizing this move but at the cost of "another million votes" because the "oligarch" was quite unpopular and widely believed guilty.[14]

Nemtsov was never again the primary leader of a run for nationwide office in an election. For the 2008 presidential contest, he was initially nominated by SPS but withdrew in December 2007 in favor of former Prime Minister Mikhail Kasianov, who had joined the "democratic" camp after having served under Putin a few years earlier.[15] Presumably Nemtsov's thinking was influenced by polls such as one by the respected Levada Center that had been reported just a few days earlier: Only one per cent supported Nemtsov in the presidential race.[16] SPS — badly split between those who favored cooperation with the Kremlin for the sake of economic reforms and those who advocated strong opposition largely over the Kremlin's expanding authoritarianism — then dissolved itself in late 2008 to meld into a new party called Right Cause (Pravoe Delo) that was widely considered a Kremlin project. Nemtsov strongly resisted this move.[17] After this point, Nemtsov became a central figure in a

---

13   Boris Nemtsov. Interview. *Gazeta*, 19 June 2003, p.1, online version.
14   *Polit.Ru*, 25 December 2003, 17:08.
15   *RFE/RL Newsline*, 27 December 2007.
16   *RFE/RL Newsline*, 19 December 2007.
17   *Kommersant.ru*, 17 November 2008; *Polit.ru*, 15 November 2008, 17:11.

small but vigorous anti-Putin movement, taking on various leadership roles in organizations of various names ranging from Committee 2008-Free Choice to Solidarity to the Party of National Freedom, though these never made it onto a national ballot.

Perhaps ironically, while Nemtsov was among the first to be arrested for protesting against fraud in the 2011 Duma election,[18] just a few days later absolutely massive protests erupted that ultimately catapulted new figures to the forefront of the democracy movement, notably Aleksei Navalny. Thus while the majority of those who recognized Nemtsov's name in the first half of 2012 saw him as a figure of the past rather than the future, the majority of those who knew enough about Navalny to venture an answer categorized him as a man whose time was yet to come (though two-thirds still did not know him). Nemtsov was even more clearly eclipsed on this particular metric by oligarch-turned-politician Mikhail Prokhorov, who claimed to support liberal, especially pro-market values and was seen in 2012 as someone whose time was yet to come by over 60 per cent of respondents.[19] And of course, by early 2015, any political future Nemtsov had was taken violently from him.

Research Design

To examine sources of Nemtsov's appeal, it makes sense to consider patterns of support for him when he was at his electoral pinnacle and when he personally was the leader of an electoral force for which people could vote, as he was as the leader of SPS's list of candidates in the 2003 Duma race. While it might be interesting as well to consider what underlay his standing when he was at the peak of his national popularity in 1997, I do not have at my disposal opinion data that would capture this and that would also include a full range of variables necessary for pinpointing where exactly he stood out from other candidates in potential voters' minds. One might also consider examining support for his potential candidacy

---

18   RFE/RL, 6 December 2011.
19   2012 RES Survey.

for president in 2004, but the surveys around this time find that hardly anyone wanted him in Russia's top job at that time; in the dataset used here, only four people in the entire survey sample said they would vote for him, a figure representing not even half of one per cent of the population.[20] Obviously, this makes a meaningful statistical analysis impossible. The 2003 Duma election, though, does supply a useful opportunity for data analysis since SPS under Nemtsov's leadership received a small but substantial share of the vote, 4 per cent, according to official results.[21] The primary complication, of course, is that a vote for SPS was not a vote for Nemtsov alone but also for the others on his party's list. This is as close as we are likely to come to a nationwide vote for Nemtsov personally, however, and in any case the SPS project at a minimum reflects Nemtsov's taking "ownership" of a particular list of candidates and all the compromises this entailed.

Making this study possible is a survey taken of the Russian Federation's population shortly after the December 7, 2003, Duma election designed specifically to study voting patterns. In the field from December 19, 2003, through February 15, 2004, this survey is part of the Russian Election Studies series (referred to here as the 2003–04 RES Survey) and was designed to be nationally representative, with 1,648 adult Russian citizens selected using a multistage area probability sampling strategy and then being interviewed face to face.[22]

The pages that follow thus analyze patterns among people who told interviewers they had voted for Nemtsov's SPS in the 2003 Duma election, including an analysis of what systematically distinguished SPS voters from all other election participants.[23] This

---

20 This figure comes from the 2003–04 Russian Election Studies (RES) Survey organized by Timothy Colton, Henry Hale, and Michael McFaul, described later in this section.
21 For a useful summary of Russian election results over the years, see: "Russia Votes," http://www.russiavotes.org/duma/duma_elections_93-03.php (as of 21 December 2015).
22 This survey was carried out in Russia by the highly qualified and academically oriented Demoscope group.
23 That is, the dependent variable is a simple dummy (binary) variable coded 1 if someone said they voted for SPS and 0 otherwise, with people who said

builds on an earlier study by the author that examined the correlates of voting for all the main parties in the 2003 Duma election using these same survey but that did not focus on SPS and so used a different statistical model with a different set of variables that did not include all of the ones considered here.[24] When focusing a regression analysis specifically on SPS, however, one must take into account that only 30 of the 1,648 respondents in the sample reported having voted for it, generating an estimate that 2.8 per cent of the population voted for Nemtsov's party in 2003 (this reflects a slight underreporting for non-winning parties that is typical for post-election surveys and that is unlikely to impact the analysis much).[25] This matters for methodology because when outcomes are so rare in a dataset, estimates of statistical significance can be biased. For this reason, the results from an ordinary logit regression model (designed specifically for studying binary outcomes) are reported first, then they are double-checked using a "rare events logit" model specifically designed to correct for this bias but that does not lend itself as readily to clear graphic presentation.[26]

---

they did not vote being dropped from the analysis. 1,160 of the 1,648 respondents claimed to have voted.

24   Hale, *Why Not Parties in Russia: Democracy, Federalism, and the State*, 111–113. Specifically, it used a multinomial logit model, which is inefficient for studying any one single party.

25   Here and elsewhere when estimates of the share of the Russian population holding certain dispositions are reported, figures are calculated using weights to correct for certain imbalances that tend to occur in the sample design, such as the greater likelihood of finding women at home when the interviewer comes by.

26   For more about the rare events logit model as used here, with a package for the statistical software Stata, see: Michael Tomz, Gary King, and Langche Zeng, "RELOGIT: Rare Events Logistic Regression, Version 1.1," (Cambridge, MA: Harvard University, 1 October 1999), http://gking.harvard.edu/ (as of 1 May 2016); Gary King and Langche Zeng, "Logistic Regression in Rare Events Data," (Department of Government, Harvard University, 1999) http://GKing.Harvard.Edu (as of 1 May 2016); Gary King and Langche Zeng, "Estimating Absolute, Relative, and Attributable Risks in Case-Control Studies," (Department of Government, Harvard University, 1999), http://GKing.Harvard.Edu (as of 1 May 2016);.

Who Were Nemtsov's Voters in 2003?

At the outset, it is useful to examine how the Russian population evaluated Nemtsov as a leader in 2003-04. Figure 1 reports the share of people who replied "yes" or "probably yes" when asked whether Nemtsov was "an intelligent and knowledgeable person," was "a strong leader," was "an honest and trustworthy person," and "really cares about people like you," comparing these result to those when people were asked about close Putin associate Boris Gryzlov, who at the time was the formal leader of Putin's United Russia Party that was competing against SPS in the 2003 parliamentary election. As can be seen, Nemtsov scored relatively high marks on intelligence, with over a majority attributing this quality to him. But he fared much worse on other aspects of leadership, in particular being widely viewed as dishonest and unsympathetic to ordinary people's concerns. As can be seen, even someone widely regarded as a Putin lackey, Gryzlov, bested Nemtsov on each of these qualities across the whole Russian population. This particular survey did not ask about Putin, but the same respondents were asked about Putin a few months later and perhaps needless to say, his ratings on each item were overwhelmingly positive.[27]

---

27   That is, 1,496 of the same respondents from the 2003-04 RES Survey were reinterviewed between April 4 and May 11, 2004 as part of the same project; this is referred to as the 2004 RES Survey.

Figure 1. Percent Seeing Different Leadership Qualities in Nemtsov and Gryzlov, December 2003-February 2004

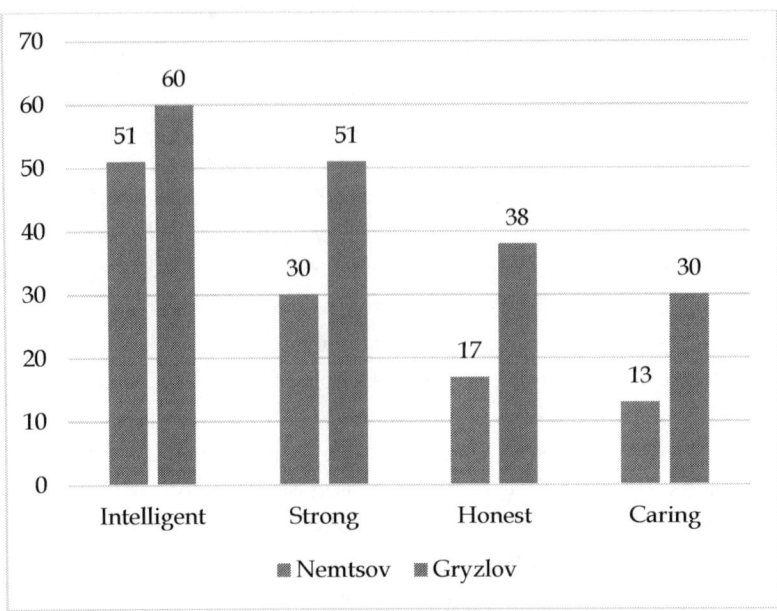

Even though not many voters rated Nemtsov positively on all four items, it is clear that many who did think well of him chose not to vote for his party in 2003. So who in the end were his voters? Figures 2, 3, 4, and 5 look only at those who said they voted for SPS and breaks them down among a variety of characteristics that have often been found to separate candidates from one another in elections.[28] Starting with the demographic breakdown presented in Fig-

---

28   E.g., Timothy J Colton, *Transitional Citizens: Voters and What Influences Them in the New Russia* (Cambridge, Mass.: Harvard University Press, 2000); Timothy J. Colton and Henry E. Hale, "The Putin Vote: Presidential Electorates in a Hybrid Regime," *Slavic Review* 68, no. 3 (2009): 473–503; Timothy J. Colton and Michael McFaul, *Popular Choice and Managed Democracy* (Washington, DC: Brookings Institution Press, 2003); Richard Rose, William Mishler, and Neil Munro, *Russia Transformed: Developing Popular Support for a New Regime* (Cambridge; New York: Cambridge University Press, 2006); Ian McAllister and Stephen White, "'It's the Economy, Comrade!' Parties and Voters in the

ure 2, we observe that a majority of Nemtsov's voters in this election were from the top quintile of population centers (that is, Russia's biggest cities[29]), possessed a higher education degree, were women, and claimed Russian[30] ethnicity. Not all of these are surprising, of course; for example, the vast majority of Russia's population consists of Russians. Thus it may be more meaningful to observe how SPS voters differed from the overall pool of Russian voters, and here we see SPS voters most clearly standing out clearly for being from large urban areas and for having higher education. While only 48 per cent of Nemtsov's electorate were age 39 or under, this was still a far larger share of youth than was in the voting population as a whole (30 per cent). As for geography, SPS drew quite lightly from Russia's southern[31] and eastern[32] populations than did other parties taken together.

2007 Russian Duma Election," *Europe-Asia Studies* 60, no. 6 (August 1, 2008): 931–57, doi:10.1080/09668130802180959.
29 Specifically, in this survey, this included the cities of Moscow, St. Petersburg, Nizhniy Novgorod, Kazan, and Cheliabinsk.
30 That is, they were asked to identify themselves by nationality and answered "russkii" or "russkaia."
31 Defined as south of the 54th parallel.
32 Defined as in Siberia or east of Siberia.

Figure 2. Demographic Breakdown (%) of SPS Voters Compared with All Voters

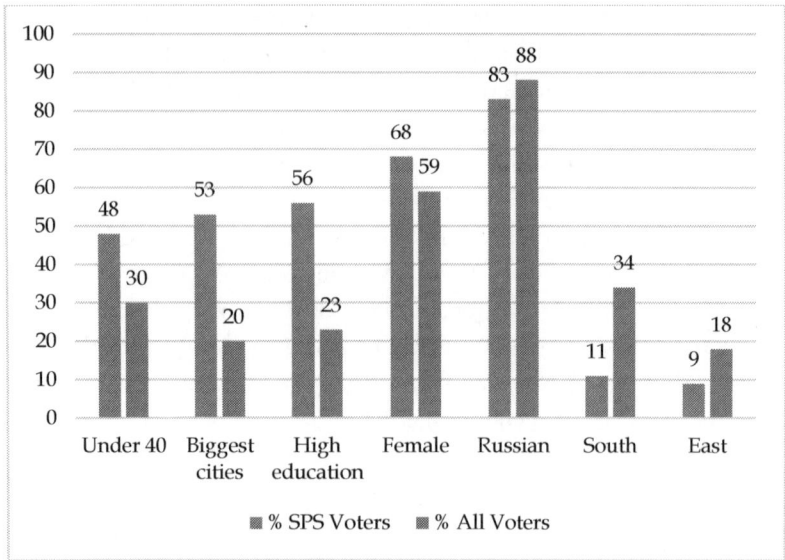

Turning now to other features of Nemtsov's electorate as summarized in Figures 3–5, only two comprise a majority of SPS voters: self-identification as "youth" (62 per cent of SPS voters) and support for continuing and deepening market-oriented economic reforms (83 per cent of SPS voters).[33] The youth result is interesting: This survey question gave respondents a list of 14 different social categories and asked them "to which of the suggested groups you feel particularly close," allowing them to choose more than one. The categories reported in Figure 4 included "the younger generation," "the middle class," "small enterprises," and "big entrepreneurs." The fact that more youth-identified people wound up in the SPS

---

33 This question asked respondents "There are various opinions about the market reforms that are being carried out in our country. What do you think, is it necessary to return to the socialist economy, to leave everything essentially as it is now, or to continue and deepen market reforms?" The answers they could choose from were: "It is necessary to return to the socialist economy"; "It is necessary to leave everything essentially as it is now"; and "it is necessary to continue and deepen market reforms." The variable in the analysis below codes respondents as 1 if they selected the latter response, 0 otherwise.

electorate than people who were actually under 40 suggests that Nemtsov was not simply attracting people on the basis of their age, but on the basis of an identification with the energy and promise of a rising generation. Indeed, it is noteworthy that SPS relied on this category of people far more heavily than did the combined set of other parties. While market supporters make up a majority of the electorate as a whole and not just a majority of SPS supporters, Nemtsov's voters consisted much more uniformly of pro-marketeers than did the electorate as a whole.

Figure 3. Share of SPS Voters by Material Condition Compared with All Voters

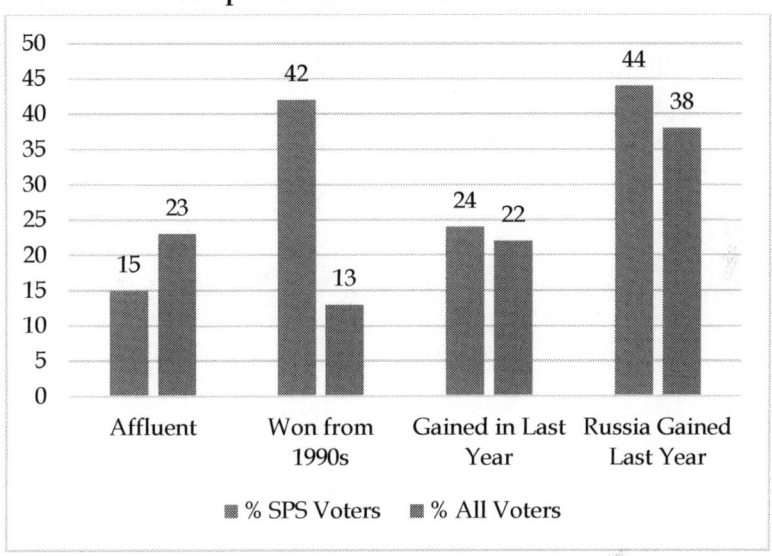

Figure 4. Share of SPS Voters by Identification with Certain Social Groups Compared with All Voters

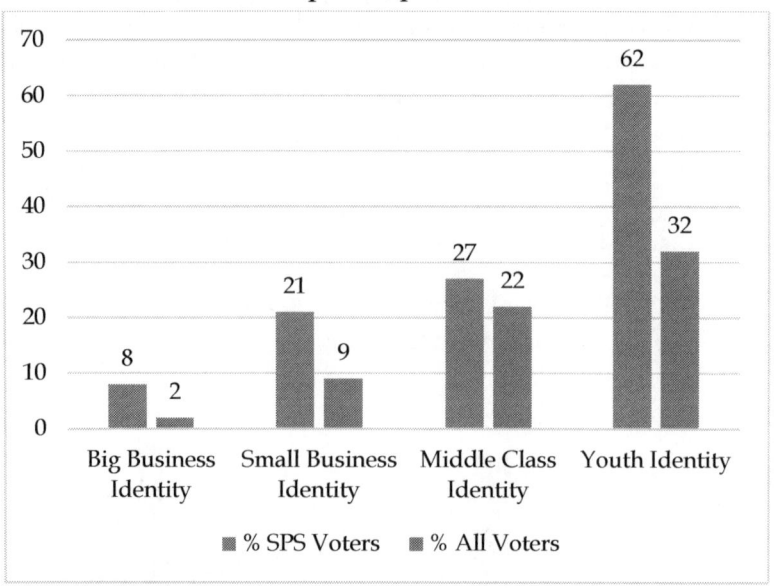

Figure 5. Share of SPS Voters by Issue Positions Compared with All Voters

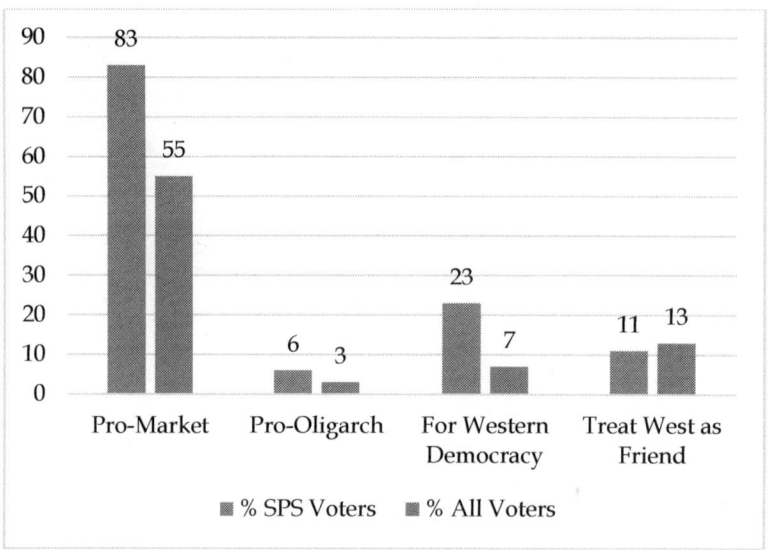

None of the other categories of people considered here made up a majority of SPS voters, but we do find several that wound up disproportionately in Nemtsov's camp in the 2003 election. The most pronounced of these is the set of people who declared that they had benefited more than they had lost from the reforms of the 1990s.[34] While such people comprised 42 per cent of those casting a ballot for the Union of Right Forces, they were only 13 per cent of the electorate as a whole. It also may be noteworthy that while only 23 per cent of Nemtsov backers in this election expressed support for Western-style democracy, this was the choice of only 7 per cent of all voters.[35] SPS voters also appear to have consisted more of people identifying with small business (21 per cent) than the nationwide electorate (9 per cent). SPS did not stand out much from Russia's whole set of voters in terms of affluence,[36] whether their families' economic positions had improved over the past year,[37] whether

---

34 Specifically, the question was "In general, did you win or lose as a result of the reforms carried out in the country beginning in 1992?" Answers given were: won, mostly won, mostly lost, and lost, with volunteered responses of "won some and lost some" also coded. The variable in the analysis below codes respondents as 1 if they selected either of the first two answers, 0 otherwise.

35 Respondents were posed the question, "What kind of political system, in your opinion, would be most appropriate for Russia?" The answers they could choose from were: "the Soviet system we had in our country before perestroika"; "the Soviet system, but in a different, more democratic form"; "the political system that exists today"; and "democracy of the Western type." The variable in the analysis below codes respondents as 1 if they selected the latter response, 0 otherwise.

36 Respondents were asked "which of the following statements best describes your family's financial situation," with the options being: (1) "you don't have enough money even for food"; (2) "you have enough money only for the most necessary things"; (3) "you have enough money for daily expenses, but even the purchase of clothes is difficult for you"; (4) "the purchase of expensive goods is not especially difficult for you, but a car, dacha, or apartment is still unaffordable"; and (5) "At the present time you don't have to deny yourself anything." In the present analysis, people are coded as "affluent" if they answered either (4) or (5), 0 otherwise.

37 Respondents were asked "How has your family's material situation changed over this past twelve months" and given the options (1) improved a lot; (2) improved a little; (3) remained unchanged; (4) worsened a little; (5) worsened a lot. For the statistical analysis below, the values were reversed (with higher

they thought Russia's economy as a whole had improved over the past year,[38] whether they identified with big business, what they thought should be done with the oligarchs,[39] and whether the West should be treated as a friend.[40]

Correlates of the 2003 Vote for Nemtsov's SPS

While the preceding section has painted a certain profile of Nemtsov's electorate in the 2003 Duma election, more rigor is required before we can make meaningful judgments as to which factors systematically won him votes. This rigor is provided by the logit regression analysis described above, a technique designed to identify patterns in the data and assess the degree of confidence with which we can conclude that two variables are related. In this case, we want to know which of all the factors discussed above tended to make someone more likely to cast a vote for Nemtsov's

---

numbers representing the greatest gain) and the mean substituted for the 9 respondents who did not give an answer.

38 Respondents were asked "What do you think, over the past twelve months has the economy of Russia..." and given the options: (1) gotten much better; (2) gotten somewhat better; (3) stayed the same; (4) gotten somewhat worse; (5) gotten much worse. For the statistical analysis below, the values were reversed (with higher numbers representing the most improvement) and the mean substituted for the 142 respondents who did not give an answer.

39 The specific question was "There has been a lot of talk recently about the results of privatization in Russia and especially of what to do with the so-called oligarchs and other rich persons who became wealthy as a result of the privatization of the 1990s. What in general is your point of view on this problem and of what needs to be done about the oligarchs?" The options presented were: "Let the oligarchs keep everything they have"; "Let the oligarchs keep their property but force them to pay taxes"; "Take away everything the oligarchs got as a result of privatization"; and "Take away everything the oligarchs got as a result of privatization and throw them in prison." In the analysis that follows, a respondent is coded as having a "pro-oligarch" position (a value of 1) if he or she gave the first answer, 0 otherwise.

40 The question posed was "There are various opinions about what relations should be like between Russia and the West. What do you think of how Russia should relate to the West?" The answers given were: "as to an enemy"; "as to a rival"; "as to an ally"; and "as to a friend." In the analysis that follows, respondents giving the last answer are coded 1 as being pro-Western, with all others coded 0.

Union of Right Forces, and we would also like to know the magnitude of each factor's impact. Since we know that demographic variables often influence voting patterns both directly and indirectly (through other variables), we calculate our estimates of basic demographic variables like age and gender by themselves (controlling only for each other) and then we estimate the impact of the other variables in an equation that contains all variables, including the demographic ones as controls.[41] The results are reported in graphic form rather than a table full of numbers for ease of interpretation.[42] To check for possible bias resulting from the rarity of voting for SPS in the dataset, as noted above, a rare event logit analysis is also conducted and its results noted in the few cases where its results differ from the standard logit results; a standard logit statistical model nevertheless forms the foundation of this study due to its ease of graphic presentation and the fact that the results do not differ much from the rare events logit analysis.

Figure 6 reports the findings from the standard logit regression analysis of demographic factors. For each factor listed on the left-hand side of the figure (the Y axis), the dot represents the estimate as to how much a one-unit change in that factor increases the probability of voting for Nemtsov's SPS. Such estimates are called marginal effects. The lines on either side of the dot span the margin of error, or the range of values in which we estimate with 95-per cent confidence that the true value lies. Perhaps the most important consideration here is whether the value of zero (an estimate that the factor has no effect on voting for SPS) falls within the 95-per cent confidence interval. If zero falls within this interval, then we consider the factor not to impact voting for SPS because we cannot rule out the possibility of zero effect with at least 95-per cent confidence, a strict but widely used standard for statistical analyses (that is, we say it is not statistically significant). Thus the most important findings will be those that are statistically significant, where the entire

---

[41] A similar approach is used in, for example, Colton, *Transitional Citizens*; Warren E Miller and J. Merrill Shanks, *The New American Voter* (Cambridge, Mass.: Harvard University Press, 1996).
[42] The tables of regression output, though, are available from the author upon request.

range spanned by the dot and its "whiskers" falls either to the right or the left of zero, which is depicted by a vertical line in the graph.

In the case of Figure 6, therefore, we see that only two demographic variables are clearly significantly correlated with voting for Nemtsov's SPS: community size and education. Age comes very close, however, and would pass a 94-per cent significance test; moreover, the rare events logit analysis finds that it in fact passes the 95-per cent significance test, thus it will be considered significant in what follows. Thus turning first to age, the graph tells us when people become ten years older, they become 5.7 per cent less likely to cast a vote for SPS, on average. SPS is confirmed, therefore, to mobilize younger voters more than older ones. As for the size of the population in the city or town where one lives, we find that moving from a lower quintile to the next higher quintile makes one on average 1.4 per cent more likely to vote for SPS, an effect that sounds a little more impressive if worded as follows: moving from the smallest sort of community to the largest makes one about 6 per cent more likely to back Nemtsov's Union of Right Forces. And moving up a notch on the educational scale[43] makes a person 1.2 per cent more likely to fill out one's ballot for Nemtsov's party.

---

43   The points on the scale are (1) no education or elementary education only; (2) incomplete secondary education; (3) secondary education; (4) secondary specialized education; (5) incomplete higher education; and (6) higher education.

Figure 6. Effects on Probability of Vote for Nemtsov's SPS 2003 Demographic Factors, 95% Confidence Intervals

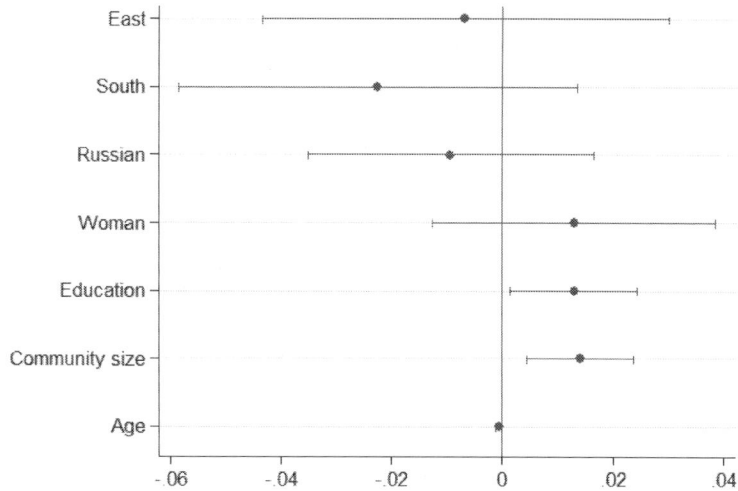

Figure 7 shifts the focus to factors directly related to the economy. The strongest finding here is that, as Nemtsov had hoped in 2003, people who believed that they had personally won more than they had lost from the reforms he had overseen in the 1990s did reward him politically.[44] The problems for Nemtsov, however, were twofold. First, winners were only about 3 per cent more likely to vote for SPS than were others, and second, Figure 3 above shows that only a small share of Russia's voters placed themselves in the category of economic reform winners. While the regular logit analysis reported in Figure 7 indicates that people who believed Russia's economy had been on the rise over the preceding year were slightly more likely to vote for SPS, the rare events check finds that in fact this apparent effect is insignificant. People who believed that their own situation or Russia's economy were improving over the past twelve months, therefore, do not appear to have rewarded

---

44 This is also broadly in line with Joshua A. Tucker, *Regional Economic Voting: Russia, Poland, Hungary, Slovakia, and the Czech Republic, 1990–1999*, 1 edition (Cambridge ; New York: Cambridge University Press, 2006).

Nemtsov. While SPS was sometimes portrayed by its opponents as the party of the super-rich, this analysis finds that the affluent were no more likely to vote for it than for other parties.

Figure 7.   Effects on Probability of Vote for Nemtsov's SPS 2003 Economic Factors, 95% Confidence Intervals

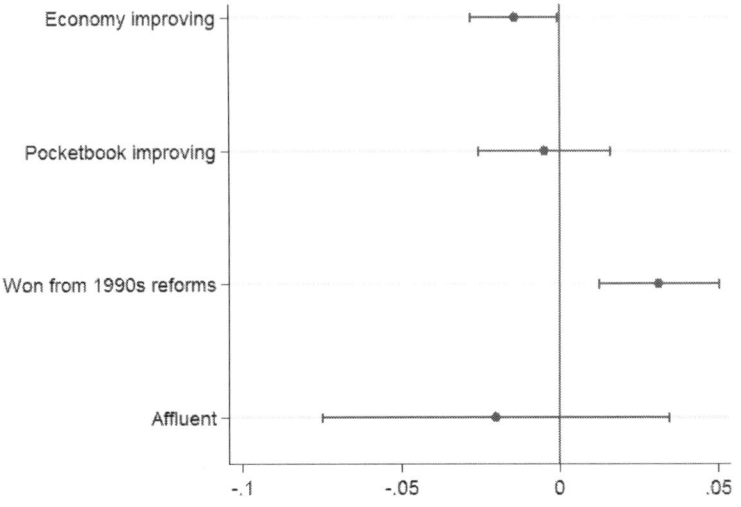

Nemtsov often championed the middle class and small business in his political rhetoric, but the statistical analysis reported in Figure 8 shows that people who self-identified with the middle class were no more likely to vote for him than anyone else and that the same was true of people who felt close to the small business community. At the same time, however, his critics did not appear to be correct that people identifying with Russia's big business elite tended to be SPS supporters. Where Nemtsov did appear to have strong appeal on an identity basis, however, was among people who considered themselves part of the young generation. While the ordinary logit results in Figure 8 indicate that this result barely fails to pass the 95-per cent confidence standard (clocking in at 94-per cent confidence), the rare events logit check concludes that this relationship is in fact significant even at the very strict 99-per cent level. Importantly, this result holds while *controlling* for actual age, indicating that what may have mattered most was an identification with youthfulness that was not necessarily dependent on one's actual years and that Nemtsov himself displayed up until the very end at age 55.

Figure 8. **Effects on Probability of Vote for Nemtsov's SPS 2003 Social Identity Factors, 95% Confidence Intervals**

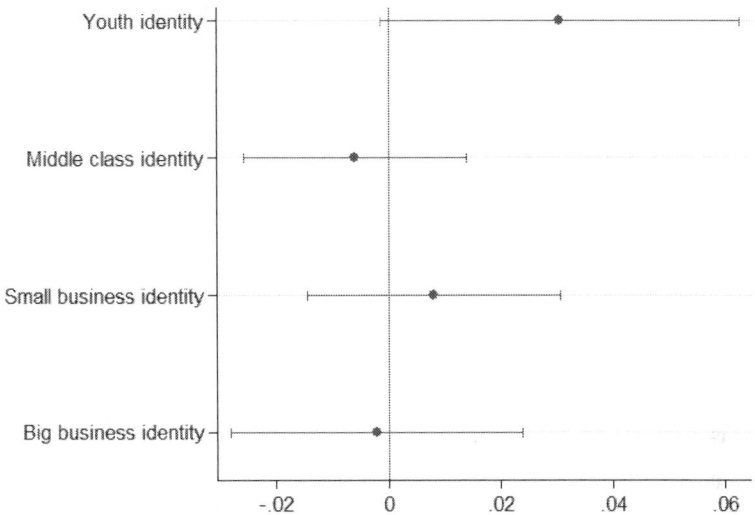

While Nemtsov was very outspoken in his political views, Figure 9 indicates that these were not significant generators of votes for SPS in 2003. People who believed that Russia should treat the West as a friend were no more likely to vote for his party than others. The same is true of people who supported continuing and deepening market reform. Consistent with findings presented above, the statistical analysis also finds that people who were most sympathetic to the oligarchs, thinking they should be essentially left alone by the state and not forced to pay more taxes or be jailed, did not stand out as Union of Right Forces supporters. The only issue position on which Nemtsov is found here to win support is his open advocacy of Western-style democracy: People supportive of this form of government are found to be about 2.5 per cent more likely to have cast a ballot for SPS. The rare events check for possible bias finds that this result actually does not quite meet the 95-per cent confidence standard, but still reports that it is quite close and would pass a 93-per cent confidence requirement.

Figure 9. Effects on Probability of Vote for Nemtsov's SPS 2003 Issue Positions, 95% Confidence Intervals

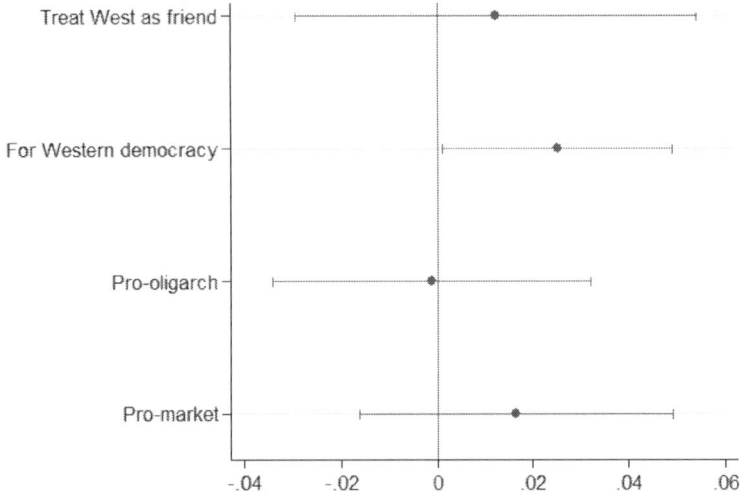

Implications and Conclusion

Overall, this analysis of voting patterns in the one national election where Nemtsov led a political force onto the ballot, the Duma election of 2003, disconfirms some common wisdom about this politician at the same time that it confirms other widely help suppositions. It generally weighs against arguments that Nemtsov was the candidate of the super-wealthy or those who favored the big business that flourished under his watch as first deputy prime minister. His supporters also did not stand out significantly from others for their pro-market agenda or a clear Western foreign policy orientation, positions that are sometimes thought to underlie Nemtsov's (albeit narrow) appeal. Nor were Nemtsov and his team given credit in the elections for positive economic performance during 2002–03; people who saw economic improvement either for themselves or for the country as a whole did not favor SPS more or less than other parties on average. The analysis strongly supports, however, the notions that Nemtsov had a certain generational appeal to the young at heart, that he was rewarded by those who thought they had benefited personally from his reforms, that his supporters tended to be highly educated and concentrated in major urban centers, and that he stood out among voters for supporting Western-style democracy in Russia.

This broad pattern of findings does shed new light on why Nemtsov and others of like mind failed to establish a firm pro-Western liberal foothold at the start of the Putin era, unable to resist political marginalization as the Kremlin's power juggernaut matured. For one thing, the traits found here to reliably generate votes for him were *all* minority traits in the Russia of the 2000s, often quite tiny minority traits. As was reported in Figures 2-5, only small shares of Russia's population thought they had mostly won from the 1990s reforms, supported explicitly Western-style democracy, identified as youth, were actually under 30, had higher education, and lived in the very largest Russian cities. And the "yield" SPS received even on these issues was rather small, with the effects reported above rarely exceeding a change in voting probability of more than 5 per cent, even when the entire range of the variable is considered. At the same time, when we turn to the positions Nemtsov advocated that arguably held the most potential to win votes—especially advocacy of a general market orientation and claiming credit for laying the foundation for the economic improvement Russia was experiencing in the 2000s—we see that these are positions other research has found strongly benefited Putin and his United Russia Party in elections and public opinion more generally.[45]

In other words, while large parts of the population backed a market economic orientation and approved of the direction the

---

[45] Colton and Hale, "The Putin Vote: Presidential Electorates in a Hybrid Regime"; Hale, *Why Not Parties in Russia: Democracy, Federalism, and the State*; McAllister and White, "'It's the Economy, Comrade!' Parties and Voters in the 2007 Russian Duma Election"; Daniel S. Treisman, "Presidential Popularity in a Hybrid Regime: Russia under Yeltsin and Putin," *American Journal of Political Science* 55, no. 3 (July 2011): 590–609.

economy was headed in 2003, these people generally turned to Putin's team rather than Nemtsov's to be their representatives in the state. In effect, Putin stole the pro-Western liberals' electoral thunder on the issues that mattered most, leaving them to win votes primarily on the basis of ideas and positions with much lower electoral potential. Indeed, Putin's co-optation of the market reform issue encouraged many self-professed pro-Western liberals like Anatoly Chubais to back Putin for president repeatedly and ultimately precipitated a major split in SPS, which only added to their marginalization. Indeed, of the small number of people who voted for SPS in December 2003, a remarkable 71 per cent are found to have cast their ballots for Vladimir Putin in the March 2004 presidential race—even though Nemtsov's number two on the SPS ticket, Irina Khakamada, was herself a candidate for president.[46]

All this is consistent with a logic suggesting that Putin's continued dominance is not simply about the repressive environment that some hold responsible for Nemtsov's physical death. It is also about a carefully managed effort to occupy the most politically lucrative political spaces in the country, allowing oppositions to exist and sometimes even get on the ballot for major contests, but primarily when they occupy niches that are not seen to be threatening. While this electoral ghettoization had already largely occurred even before Putin's Kremlin fully controlled Russia's political system and mass media, this control surely helped ensure that this was never reversed under Putin's watch.[47]

By the latter 2000s, however, even such effectively marginalized forces as Nemtsov's appeared to have become too much of a risk for the Kremlin to tolerate, with the latter keeping the former off the most important ballots even when Putin appeared most invincible. Simple repression was increasingly dominating manipulation and co-optation as the central regime strategy against its fiercest political opponents.[48] Whether Nemtsov's 2015 murder is

---

[46] 2004 RES Survey.
[47] Walker and Orttung, "Breaking the News: The Role of State-Run Media."
[48] Gel'man, *Authoritarian Russia*.

part of this ever-escalating sense of risk-aversion, even if the unwanted action of an overeager friend instead of a direct order, may never be known for certain.

Rocking the Sochi Olympic Narrative: Boris Nemtsov and Putin's Sovereignty

Andrey Makarychev and Alexandra Yatsyk

Introduction

The Sochi winter Olympics of 2014 were a momentous element in the ongoing process of Russian identity-making, with political narratives often trumping discussions about sports as such. In the opinion of foreign observers, "these Olympics are about politics as well as sports".[1] Due to its strong political accents the Sochi Games became a linchpin of different practices of governance, on the one hand, and policies of contestation and resistance, on the other.

The voice of Boris Nemtsov, a leader of the anti-Putin movement, who — rather symbolically — was born in Sochi, was one of the loudest among skeptics of the Games' official celebratory narrative. He contested the rationale of the Sochi Olympic project mainly on grounds of corruption charges, mass-scale embezzlement, administrative inefficiency and mismanagement. This is where two research questions we are going to address in this paper unfold: what political strings he pulled by critically addressing a plethora of financial and economic issues, and what academic concepts are needed for understanding the deeply political nature of his anti-corruption campaigning.

For untangling these questions, we intend to analyze Nemtsov's contribution to the Olympic debate not only from the viewpoint of his public activism, but also in terms of some concepts embedded in different political theories. Although Nemtsov himself was a policy practitioner, this paper seeks to inscribe the dis-

---

1 Miriam Lanskoy, Dylan Myles-Primakoff. Sochi's Bitter Medicine, *Foreign Policy*, 31 January 2014, http://foreignpolicy.com/2014/01/31/sochis-bitter-medicine/ (as of 1 September 2017)

course originated from his public campaigning into academic conceptualizations that might shed light on his legacy as seen from a wider perspective of post-Soviet transformations in Russia. More specifically, we deploy Nemtsov's Olympic narrative in a zone of conflictual interactions of *hegemonic and counter-hegemonic discourses*. It appears obvious that, as seen from a political perspective, Nemtsov is strongly grounded in the latter, being one of the most outstanding critics of the Putin regime. Yet what seems to be consensual and almost evident, might turn into a puzzle deserving a subtler academic analysis. Given the blurred boundary between the hegemonic and counter-hegemonic discourses (often reminiscent of a "line in the sand"), we argue that we need a fine-tuned conceptual reference points to substantiate the counter-hegemonic dispositions of Nemtsov's narrative. We find these points in two binaries *of inclusion and exclusion,* and *norms and exceptions.* More specifically, we interpret the counter-hegemonic potential of Nemtsov's narrative as rooted in his intention to challenge two pillars of Putin's concept of sovereignty: a) the ability to define the criteria for inclusion in (and thus exclusion from) Russia as a political community, and b) the rule by exceptions, as opposed to the rule by norms.

Then we show how the two dichotomies can be used for analysis of Nemtsov's Olympic discourse. One way would be to look at them through the prism of an important linkage between *global institutions and authoritarian regimes*, duly articulated by Nemtsov. Another way of using the abovementioned dichotomies is through discussing the uneasy correlation between *soft power and hard power*, as exemplified by Nemtsov's take on linking the Sochi Olympics and the annexation of Crimea in one explanatory framework of analyzing the mechanisms of power under Putin's rule.

Empirically, we base our analysis on two reports co-authored and widely publicized by Boris Nemtsov — "Sochi and the Olympics" (co-authored with Vladimir Milov, 2009) and "The Winter Olympics in Subtropics" (co-authored with Leonid Martyniuk, 2013). To these two texts we add dozens of his interview, available both in written form and video-recorded in the recent six years, in which he elaborated on and further promoted his main arguments. We also include in our empirical base media and Internet materials reflecting Nemtsov's campaign for the mayor of Sochi in 2009, which appears to be an important element in developing his critical attitudes towards the Games and in articulating most of the issues that became topical a few years later.

Nemtsov at the Crossroads of Hegemony and Counter-hegemony

In this section we argue that Boris Nemtsov's engagement with the Sochi Olympic discourse has to be viewed as part of political collisions between hegemonic (i.e. official and Kremlin-generated) and counter-hegemonic / oppositional discourses. Unlike those authors who reduce the political meanings of the Olympics to its potential for boosting "sports nationalism" and demonstrating "national superiority",[2] we venture to explain the political logic of the Sochi Games from the viewpoint of hegemonic and counter-hegemonic discourses clashing with—but also imbricating over—each other, and deploy Boris Nemtsov's narrative in this dichotomous frame. Of course, his contribution to counter-hegemonic strategies was enormous, but a deeper contextualization of his narrative might elucidate and bring up new facets of the interrelationship between hegemony and counter-hegemony.

There are several ways in which the lines between the two are blurred. *First*, the anti-corruption momentum, key for Nemtsov's Olympic scepticism, was to some extent appropriated by the Kremlin that does agree that the problem exists and from time to time launches campaigns for bringing corrupt public servants to trial. In particular, Putin's dismissal of Akhmed Bilalov, the head of "The Resorts of the Northern Caucasus" company,[3] for mismanagement

---

2   For an example of reductionist approaches, see: Vitaly Gorokhov, Natsional'nye identichnosti v global'noi sportivnoi kul'ture: vyzovy Sochi-2014 dlia Olimpiiskoi komandy Rossii, *Zhurnal sotsiologii i sotsial'noi antropologii* 5 (2013): 71–86.
3   Andrey Pertsev, Olimpiada ne povod dlia gordosti, *Gazeta.ru*, 27 June 2013, http://www.gazeta.ru/politics/2013/06/26_a_5394569.shtml (as of 1 September 2017)

of construction works in Sochi, attests to the possible—though always only partial—absorption of anti-corruption discourse by the officialdom.

Second, Nemtsov used to present himself as an experienced regional leader (governor in Nizhny Novgorod and later a member of the legislature in Yaroslavl' oblast) and a federal politician. It is telling, for example, that the cover of the report "Sochi and the Olympiad" presents its co-authors, Boris Nemtsov and Vladimir Milov, as holders of important positions in the Russian government in the past—first vice prime minister (1997-1998) and deputy minister of energy (2002), correspondingly.

As former public servants, they had to find a delicate balance between unveiling the shadow economy of the exorbitantly costly Olympic show, on the one hand, and supporting the idea of the Games in Russia, on the other. Being aware of the dangers of rejecting this idea as such, the two co-authors explicitly affirmed: "We, as many Russians, would like Russia to successfully host these Games. We are in favor of the Olympiad". [4] The main alternative to the initial scenario of the Olympics they proposed is rather technical—the decentralization of the Games, i.e. moving most of competitions away from Sochi to other Russian cities with sports infrastructure much better prepared for hosting winter events, including Moscow, St. Petersburg, Kazan, Yaroslavl, Cheliabinsk, Khanty-Mansiisk, Ufa, Novosibirsk, Saransk, etc.[5]

Third, a paradoxical common ground that Nemstov shared with Putin can be found in the concept of hegemonic masculinity. There are lots of recent works analyzing Putin's regime in gender and biopolitical terms.[6] As Valerie Sperling demonstrates, the same

---

4 Boris Nemtsov and Vladimir Milov, *Sochi i Olimpiada*. Independent expert report of members of "Solidarity" United Democratic Movement (Moscow, 2009), 5, http://www.rusolidarnost.ru/files/Sochi_i_Olimpiada.pdf (as of 1 September 2017)

5 Boris Nemtsov and Vladimir Milov, Sochi i Olimpiada. Independent expert report of members of "Solidarity" United Democratic Movement (Moscow, 2009), 34-35, http://www.rusolidarnost.ru/files/Sochi_i_Olimpiada.pdf (as of 1 September 2017)

6 See, for instance: Anna Bernstein, An Inadvertent Sacrifice: Body Politics and Sovereign Power in the Pussy Riot Affair. *Critical Inquiry*, 40, no.1 (2013): 220–

characteristics are also inherent for Russian counter-discourses, including activist art protest, as exemplified, for instance, by the Pussy Riot group.[7] Yet in contrast to the latter, homophobic exposures and LGBT issues were never high in Nemtsov's critical agenda. He lambasted corruption, ecological degradation and human rights violations from a viewpoint of hegemonic masculinity deeply rooted in a patriarchal society. In 2011 he made some sexist and homophobic remarks toward Evgenia Chirikova, Nadezhda Tolokonnikova, Leonid Parfenov and other liberals as "lesbians, bitches and faggots".[8] His later pronouncements were more balanced: in particular, in his *Livejournal* post in February 2013 he reacted to the infamous amendment to the anti-gay propaganda law by saying that he can't be silent on this "rascals' law".[9]

Internationally, the most visible element of the anti-Sochi protests was the LGBT campaign against the anti-gay propaganda law. "The Winter Olympic Games…are sure to be a site of protests and demonstrations, thanks to myriad issues with human rights, especially Russia's controversial anti-LGBT propaganda law",[10] a Western journalist asserted on the eve of the opening ceremony. Yet Nemtsov's public exposure of his macho life style ("I am a hetero, I love women" [11]) prevented him from embracing strong corporeal

---

241; Helena Goscilo (ed.) *Putin as celebrity and cultural icon* (New York: Routledge, 2013); Peter Rutland, The Pussy Riot affair: gender and national identity in Putin's Russia. *Nationalities Papers*, 42, no.4 (2014): 575–82; Ellen Rutten, "Putin on Panties: Sexing Russia in Late Soviet and Post-Soviet Culture." In Jenny Genis, René Martin, et. al (eds.) *Between West and East: Festschrift for Wim Honselaar* (Amsterdam: Pegasus, 2012), 567–97.

7   Valerie Sperling, Sex, Politics and Putin: Political legitimacy in Russia (NY: Oxford University Press, 2015).

8   "Boris Nemtsov: 'Lesbiyanka, blyad', LGBT, blyad'," *GayRussia*, 21 December 2011, http://www.gayrussia.eu/content/news/russia/3300/ (as of 1 September 2017)

9   Boris Nemtsov, "Eschio odin zakon podletsov," *Livejournal blog*, 1 February 2013, http://b-nemtsov.livejournal.com/168420.html (as of 1 September 2017)

10 Michelle Garcia, "The Long History of Olympic Boycotts, Protests and Demonstrations," 27 January 2014, http://www.advocate.com/sports/2014/01/27/long-history-olympic-boycotts-protests-and-demonstrations (as of 1 September 2017)

11 Boris Nemtsov, "Eschio odin zakon podletsov."

and bodily rhetoric for challenging Putin's regime. In terms of both the sovereign power and Nemtsov's discourse, holding the hegemonic masculine position means insignificancy of such issues as LGBT or feminist claims for emancipation. In his revelatory public campaigning against corruption at the Sochi Olympics he preferred to distance from the LGBT protest, as well as remained indifferent to the international attempts of bringing up another high profile issue – that of Circassian genocide.[12] This demonstrates flexibility of boundaries between the hegemonic and counter-hegemonic discourses, as well as an inner hierarchy constitutive for each of them.

The Inclusion / Exclusion Game

This fuzzy line between hegemony and counter-hegemony may serve a starting point for claiming that Nemtsov's Olympic counter-strategy was double-tracked. On the surface, it was premised on a set of rational and calculable arguments that could have constituted the Habermasian space for public communication with the Kremlin, potentially conducive to a shared understanding of the common good. In this vein, one of his central points was that the exorbitant budget of the Games could be spent with more palpable social effects for each Russian family. This discourse was harmonious with multiple media articles critical of the Sochi project for its opaqueness and the cult of secrecy,[13] but in the meantime avoided excessive symbolic association with cosmopolitan / liberal emancipatory agenda. Nemtsov invested more efforts in strengthening his

---

12   Alexis Zimberg, Christian Caryl, "The Russian Anti-Olympic Protest that Putin Doesn't Want You to Know About," *Foreign Policy*, 19 February 2014, http://foreignpolicy.com/2014/02/19/the-russian-anti-olympic-protest-that-putin-doesnt-want-you-to-know-about/ (as of 1 September 2017)

13   Nikolay Yaremenko, "Strashnye kartinki iz Sochi," *Chastniy Korrespondent*, 10 October 2013, http://www.chaskor.ru/article/strashnye_kartinki_iz_sochi_33788?fb_action_ids=339787069498874&fb_action_types=og.recommends&fb_source=other_multiline&action_object_map=%7B%22339787069498874%22%3A210252419152185%7D&action_type_map=%7B%22339787069498874%22%3A%22og.recommends%22%7D&action_ref_map=%5B%5D (as of 1 September 2017)

reputation as experienced domestic practitioner, rather than in supporting or solidarizing with the types of protest that transcended the cultural boundaries of hegemonic masculinity.

Yet under a closer scrutiny one may discover that Nemtsov's narrative, with its strong emphasis on legal and technical matters, was deeply political in at least two aspects. First, it was aimed at *internationally* de-legitimatizing the regime by means of publicly exposing its corrupt nature. Second, Nemtsov ultimately questioned the *domestic* core of Putin's hegemonic discourse as aimed at defining the rules of belonging to the Russian political community-in-the-making through emotionally articulating the ideas of patriotism and unconditional — if not quasi-religious — loyalty to the state. It is the idea of Russia's domestic heterogeneity and diversity that might explain the search for a "national idea" in 1990s as an instrument for anchoring this community in certain nodal points and thus avoiding its further — and very probable, as many Russian independent analysts deem — decomposition. Endeavors of defining the rules of belonging — and thus the criteria for inclusion in and exclusion from the national community-in-the-making — took different forms, including those based on traditional — ethnic and religious — stabilizers of national identity. Yet obviously, too strong an emphasis on the dominating Orthodoxy and ethnically Russian identity could be divisive and rejected, in particular, by Russian Muslims. With the beginning of Putin's third presidential term, the Kremlin started using different instruments of consolidating national majority on conservative and isolationist principles. This policy included the legal exceptionalization of LGBT people (the anti-gay propaganda law),[14] holders of double citizenship (who since autumn 2014 have to register in this capacity in the Federal Migration Service)[15] and professionals cooperating with foreign partners (the "foreign agents" legislation).[16] Public appeals to strip political dissenters of

---

14 Amendment 6.21 for the Russian Law Book of Administrative Violations, subjects to administrative punishment from 2 to 5 years for 'propaganda of homosexual relations among minors', is effective of June 30, 2013
15 Federal Law of Russian Federation # 142, is effective of 4 June 2014
16 Federal Law of Russian Federation # 121, is effective of 29 June 2012

Russian citizenship—reminiscent of the widely known Soviet practice—are also part of the policy of "purifying" the collective body of the nation by means of marginalizing and ostracizing groups that are believed to misfit the hegemonic vision of "Russianness". The rhetorical labeling of dissenters—including Nemtsov himself—as "the fifth column" and "national traitors" served the same purpose of solidifying the pro-Putin majority against the artificially constructed "internal enemies".

The Putin regime is vitally interested in finding and properly articulating key reference points to be capable of not only consolidating the nation, but also of publicly exposing the distinction between the loyalty to the "common cause" and disloyalty, fidelity and infidelity, with the blackening of the latter. In Etienne Balibar's words, "a collective identity, or the constitution of a relation of belonging ... is the constitution of a bond".[17] The Sochi Olympics was apparently one of those—seemingly non-ideological—mega-projects politically aimed exactly at constructing collective identity and allegiance by means of contriving such a bond. By so doing, this project emotionally invested in both consolidating the political community and differentiating it from the "anti-patriotic" pro-Western opposition, of which Nemtsov was a leading figure.

It is from here that the power of the Kremlin to define criteria of belongingness to the political community of Russia stems. Putin's Sochi project was politically meant to directly attach the inclusion into this community to the patriotic support for the Games as an epitome of Russian grandeur and worldwide respect, regardless of questionable instruments that were employed for this purpose—from enforced evictions to financial wrongdoings. To some extent, Putin's strategy can be understood in the categories of *jouissance*, a Lacanian psychoanalytical concept reinterpreted by Slavoj Zizek as implying normalization through imposed enjoyment and consumption of entertainment as an essential, if not central, part of the spirit of national community that may lose coherence "when

---

17   Etienne Balibar, *Politics and the Other Scene* (London and New York: Verso, 2002), 27

there is no belief in a shared enjoyment, whether shared in a fantasmic past or an idealized future".[18]

This explanatory framework can be helpful for comprehending what is politically counter-hegemonic in Nemtsov's Sochi narrative that seemingly was just another version of multiple anti-corruption investigations and invectives[19], including those integrated in the hegemonic discourse. The kernel of Nemtsov's protestation against the Sochi Olympics was that, speaking about corruption in seemingly financial and economic terms, he in fact touched upon the deeply political issue of *emotionally* constructing the collective Russian Self on the basis of the loyalty to the regime. He contested the key element of Putin's Olympic discourse—the pride on the state, and substituted it with its opposite—the shame for the corrupt ruling class. This contestation exacerbated a deep feeling within the society of a "split into fans of the Olympics and haters of the Olympics... Even close friends fight over it: 'Oh, you like the Olympics—that means you're a traitor'. And vice versa... Critics who accuse the authorities of building a fake export version of Russia in Sochi hurt the feelings of Olympic fans: 'By spitting on Putin, the opposition and the Western media spit on us, at our Olympics' ".[20]

Nemtsov's contestation of the hegemonic discourse only confirmed the original political meanings of the Games as a laboratory for Russian identity-making. Ultimately, it is the sovereign to whom Nemtsov had to address his protest against legalized exceptions and inclusions in the form of prohibition, rejections, bans and denial of rights, thus engaging with an inclusive / exclusive type of relations with the Kremlin.[21]

---

18   Jodi Dean, "Why Zizek for Political Theory?" *International Journal of Zizek Studies*, 1 (1): 22
19   "SOCHI 2014. Encyclopedia of spending," http://sochi.fbk.info/en/ (as of 1 September 2017)
20   Anna Nemtsova, "Patriotism and the Olympics," *Foreign Policy*, 17 February 2014, http://foreignpolicy.com/2014/02/17/patriotism-and-the-olympics/ (as of 1 September 2017)
21   Slawomir Oliwniak, Foucault and Agamben: Law as Inclusive / Exclusive Discourse, *Studies in Logics, Grammar and Rhetoric*, 26, no. 39 (2011), 52

Exceptions versus Norms

In this section we turn to what constitutes, in our opinion, the core of Nemtsov's contestation of a second pillar of Putin's model of sovereign power—the *rule by exceptions*. The political meaning of exception is deeply grounded in the Schmittian understanding of sovereignty as based on political will and the ability to take decisions beyond institutional constraints and commitments. In other words, "the sovereign is by definition endowed with a will so strong that is capable of abolishing any existing system of norms".[22] In political theory this triggered a vivid discussion focused on the Schmittian paradoxical assertion "that to produce law it need not be based on law".[23]

Putin's Olympic project from the outset was conceptually ambiguous, since it embraced two interrelated perspectives. First, this mega-event, according to Kremlin's design, was supposed to give a powerful boost to Russian national identity, a collective We-feeling infused with positive narration of the country's "normalcy" and its comeback to a group of world leaders. Second, the Olympic project was meant to legitimize what might be called, along the lines of Carl Schmitt, the state of sovereign exception through extraordinary measures that are not necessarily harmonious with the law. In fact, Putin's normalization could only be achieved by means of the application of extraordinary—and extra-legal—instruments, which constituted the major political issue Nemtsov tried to unveil by questioning the sovereign's "capacity to distinguish between the legal and the illegal, the normal and the exceptional",[24] with declarations of exceptions quickly turning into a normal condition.

In fact, as an opposition leader, Nemtsov had to face "the state of exception" as a set of policy tool the Kremlin regularly applied

---

22   Camil Ungureanu, Derrida on Free Decision: Between Habermas' Discursivism and Schmitt's Decisionism, *The Journal of Political Philosophy*, 16, no. 3 (2008), 322.
23   Antonio Cerella, Religion and political form: Carl Schmitt's genealogy of politics as critique of Juergen Habermas's post-secular discourse, *Review of International Studies*, 38 (2012), 982
24   R.B.J.Walker, After the Globe, Before the World (London and New York: Routledge, 2010), 35.

to constrain the dissent. As a candidate who ran for the post of the Sochi mayor in 2009, Nemtsov and his team were targets of a policy of sovereign exceptions, with courts directly fulfilling Kremlin's orders instead of protecting equal rights for all candidates, and media outlets refusing to publish political commercials of the oppositional candidate. The whole administrative apparatus, in Nemtsov's later words, was mobilized to prevent him from winning the election where he nevertheless finished second with 13,6 per cent of votes, which was one of the best results achieved by the opposition on municipal level during all years of Putin's presidency.

After the 2009 mayoral election, Nemtsov became even more critical of the Olympic project. He started more consistently claiming that its implementation on the basis of multiple exceptions is detrimental for the country. This is how Boris Nemtsov and Vladimir Milov lambasted Putin's policy of sovereign exceptionalism:

> The federal law on hosting the Olympiad de-facto detaches Sochi from the Russian Constitution for a decade. It declares redundant public hearings and promulgation of conclusions of environmental expertise… In connection to the Games the legislation is being changes in order to facilitate the enforced withholding of land and make impossible to contest it in the court. The most precious territories of natural reserves are stripped of their protection by the state. Thus, in 2006 the functional zoning of the Sochi national park was hastily altered to allow the authorities to start constructing Olympic objects in the areas under protection… In 2003 by a decree of the Russian government many reserve lands lost their status and since that time could be leased for building tourist and sports facilities….[25]

The message was clear: with the rampant corruption Russia is way below international normative standards, and the Games therefore can't "normalize" Russia. Nemtsov also argued that it was the direct personification of the Sochi project with Putin that predetermined the blatant passivity of the Accounting Chamber that refused to disclose the extant information on profligacy and mismanagement in construction works and city infrastructure development during the lead-up to the Games.

The state has breached its own economic norms as well. This is how Boris Nemtsov and Leonid Martyniuk depicted this:

---

25   Nemtsov and Milov, *Sochi i Olimpiada*, 26

> The rule operating with regard to private investments has been that 70 per cent of the investments are covered by loans from the Vneshekonombank (a state corporation!) and 30% by private contributions. However, by the end of 2012, the government admitted that practically all the Olympic construction works ... were running at a loss and would never pay for themselves. As Vneshekonombank cautiously put it, "The investors began to view more critically the market risks for realization of the projects. The question of return on investment arose." And they increased the bank loans to 90 per cent.[26]

The co-authors also pointed to the fact that in spite of Russia's earlier promises to the International Olympic Committee (IOC) during the bidding process, there was no parliamentary oversight of the financial management of the Games. Most of the Olympic orders were obtained without competitive tenders by brothers Rotenberg and other members of Putin's inner circle. In environmental protection, he claimed, international norms were disregarded. Another element of the Olympic exceptionalism raised by Nemtsov is the massive use of migrant workforce — about 16,000 of them were semi-legally employed in Sochi, which created a zone of indistinction between legality and its opposite.

Nemtsov was also critical of enhanced security measures practiced by the organizers of the Games. He particularly mentioned a document known as "fan's passport" that all visitors in the Olympic stadia had to obtain from security services in addition to regular tickets.[27] In Nemtsov's view, this is an example of unjustified restrictions that encroached upon citizens' rights and ultimately legalized "the state of exception" not as a temporary deviation from normal everyday rules, but rather as a model of extra-legal governance with a huge potential of self-dissemination in many other spheres and situations. As a political commentator Sergey Medvedev put it, the Sochi project, sanctified as an act of sovereignty and detached from law, morals and budgetary regulations,

---

26   Boris Nemtsov and Leonid Martyniuk, Winter *Olympics in the Sub-Tropics: Corruption and Abuse in Sochi*. Investigative report, 6 December 2013, 6, http://www.interpretermag.com/winter-olympics-in-the-sub-tropics-corruption-and-abuse-in-sochi/ (as of 1 September 2017)

27   Nemtsov and Martyniuk, Winter *Olympics in the Sub-Tropics: Corruption and Abuse in Sochi* , 26

constitutes in Russia a new financial, legal and societal anomaly to be reproduced further on.[28]

Globalization and Autocracy

Yet Nemtsov not only campaigned against two pillars of Putin's sovereignty—its ability to define rules of belonging and rules of exception, but also unveiled the binary structure of the hegemonic discourse: it is co-produced by the Kremlin and the IOC. It is the latter that boosts sovereignty with exceptional arrangements at its core, and thus bears its share of responsibility for consolidation of authoritarian and corrupt practices within Russia.

Both IOC and Putin's regime present themselves as staying beyond politics, yet nevertheless in practice engage in politics in many different ways[29], basically through defining rules of inclusion and exclusion, as well as the content of key messages translated through Olympics. In this light, one of the strongest Nemtsov's statements was a direct accusation of IOC in corrupt liaisons with Moscow[30], which unveiled global sports institutions' penchant for organizing mega-events in non-democratic countries—a tendency that obviously stretches far beyond Russia. Nemtsov's invectives were consonant with harsh international criticism of the IOC for lack of transparency and corruptive scandals[31], which can be matched only by the evidences of corruption within FIFA.

Nemtsov pointed to one of the most controversial—and definitely pivotal—elements of the Kremlin Olympic project—its full

---

28 Sergey Medvedev, Osada Sochi: kak Olimpiada prevraschaetsa v chrezvychainoe polozhenie, *Forbes*, 18 September 2013, http://m.forbes.ru/article.php?id=244779 (as of 1 September 2017)
29 M. Patrick Cottrell, "Not just the Games? Power, protest and politics at the Olympics," *European Journal of International Relations*, 17, no. 4(2010), 744.
30 Boris Nemtsov, "My platim ne tol'ko za Olimpiadu, no i za dvorets Yakunina," *Radio Free Europe*, 3 June 2013, http://www.svoboda.org/content/article/25005247.html (as of 1 September 2017)
31 Jules Boykoff, "A Bid for a Better Olympics," *The New York Times*, 13 August 2014, http://mobile.nytimes.com/2014/08/14/opinion/a-chance-to-reform-the-olympic-movement.html?smid=tw-share&_r=3&referrer= (as of 1 September 2017)

legitimation by the IOC, in spite of the highly problematic practices of human rights violations, environmental deterioration, and corruption. According to IOC regulations, "no kind of demonstration or political, religious or racial propaganda is permitted in the Olympic areas",[32] which lays ground for suppressing actions of civic activism and disagreement of any sort. In all cases of this kind the IOC took the side of the Russian government. Asked about the case of imprisonment of an environmental activist Evgeniy Vitishko in Sochi, an IOC spokesman, Mark Adams, stated that he was guilty of vandalising a house and said the IOC is satisfied with assurances given by Russian authorities: "We received clarification from Sochi that this is, and we think it remains, a non-Olympic case".[33] In the meantime, the IOC has warned the "Pussy Riot" group not to come to the Olympic park for any political demonstration.[34] This obvious similarity between the policies of the Kremlin and the IOC strengthen Nemtsov's argument of a structural liaison between global sports institutions and local practices of autocratic rule.

The importance of highlighting the shadow connections between authoritarian governments and global sport institutions extend far beyond the case of Sochi, and can be projected to the forthcoming FIFA 2018 World Cup. There were multiple accusations in the international media of corruptive linkages between FIFA officials, on the one hand, and the Russian government and its business structures—such as "Gazprom"—on the other. In particular, the documentary film shot by the *Deutsche Welle* on May 2015 and titled

---

32 "IOC President: 'Freedom of expression is a basic human right, and that application of rule 51 is a matter of common sense'," *Olympic.org*, 10 April 2008, http://www.olympic.org/content/news/media-resources/manual-news/1999-2009/2008/04/10/freedom-of-expression-is-a-basic-human-right/ (as of 1 September 2017)

33 "Russian protestors fall silent while Olympic roadshow occupies Sochi," *The Guardian*, 16 February 2014, http://www.theguardian.com/sport/2014/feb/16/russian-protesters-olympic-sochi-gay (as of 1 September 2017)

34 Nick Miller, "Sochi Winter Olympics: IOC warns Pussy Riot over protests," *The Sydney Morning Herald*, 19 February 2014, http://www.smh.com.au/sport/winter-olympics/sochi-winter-olympics-ioc-warns-pussy-riot-over-protests-20140219-3318a.html (as of 1 September 2017)

the "Sold Football" (dir. by Robert Kempe and Jochen Leufgens) makes many of these facts public.[35]

Against this backdrop, FIFA, the organizer of the World Football Cup in Russia in 2018, plays the same role in stabilizing the hegemonic regime in Russia, as IOC did. Thus, the then president of FIFA Sepp Blatter, responding to the appeals of US Senators to strip Russia of the FIFA tournament as a reaction to Kremlin's policy in Ukraine, suggested that his opponents could "stay home".[36]

Nemtsov's invectives against indulgent and gratifying policy of the IOC towards multiple irregularities and direct legal offenses during the implementation of the Sochi project can be helpful for understanding the scandal erupted around FIFA in May 2015. Nemtsov was one of those who predicted that the 2018 World Football Cup could be harmful for the integrity of Russia that, like Greece, might face deplorable repercussions of corrupt economy.[37] Commenting on the probability of revoking the FIFA decision to host the World Cup in Russia, Nemtsov claimed that it is the Kremlin's policy towards Ukraine that can make this option feasible, but in the meantime this can help the country save huge amount of money.[38] Months after Nemtsov's murder it was exactly this argument—Russia's involvement in the military insurgency in eastern Ukraine and the Western economic sanctions—that was discussed as possible reasons to move the FIFA Cup to a different country.

---

35   Andrei Gurkov, "Fil'm telekanala ARD rasskazal, kak Katar i Rossiya podkupali FIFA," *DW* portal, 5 May 2015, http://www.dw.de/фильм-телеканала-ard-рассказал-как-катар-и-россия-подкупали-фифа/a-18429855 (as of 1 September 2017)
36   "Blatter prizval ostat'sa doma politikov, ne dovol'nykh provedeniem ChM-2018 v Rossii," *Gazeta.ru*, 20 April 2015, http://www.gazeta.ru/sport/news/2015/04/20/n_7125437.shtml (as of 1 September 2017)
37   "Nemtsov: Chempionat mira po futbolu—2018 mozhet razvalit' stranu," *Regnum Information Agency*, 24 June 2013, http://www.regnum.ru/news/polit/1675632.html (as of 1 September 2017)
38   "Nemtsov ob ugroze FIFA lishit' Rossiyu prav na provedenie ChM—2018: Zato s'ekonomim 3 trilliona," *Glavred*, 12 August 2014, http://glavred.info/sport/nemcov-ob-ugroze-fifa-lishit-rossiyu-prav-na-provedenie-chm-2018-zato-sekonomim-3-trilliona-287361.html (as of 1 September 2017)

Hard and Soft Powers: the Sochi–Crimea nexus

Another momentous element of Kremlin's hegemonic policies is the annexation of Crimea, an act of external projection of sovereignty. In March 2014 it became another — of a drastically different kind, but paradoxically sharing with the Olympics its function of revealing the "fifth column" and "national traitors" — mega-project masterminded by the Kremlin. It played a role of litmus test for Kremlin's rules of belonging and henceforth the official version of patriotism implying the right of the sovereign to exceptionalize relations with some neighbors and politically treat them differently to other countries.

What was at stake in both cases (in Sochi and Crimea) is the making of collective identity, and the construction of bonds constitutive for relations of belonging to a "collective We". By establishing and imposing its "hierarchy of communal references",[39] the state performed a hegemonic function, yet in the meantime unleashed counter-hegemonic discourses. In this section we dwell upon Nemtsov's disavowal of the widely spread reading of the Sochi Games as a heyday of Russian soft power, which — as it might stem from what he said — was never a top priority goal for Putin.

"Images we'll see of the majestic Caucasus Mountains surrounding Sochi during the Olympics could help to erase some of the painful memories of the recent wars in the Caucasus",[40] a political commentator wrote only a month before the Games. The rosy expectations did not however come true — by annexing Crimea in the immediate aftermath of the closing ceremony in Sochi, Russia only reactualized the "painful memories" and extended them to the whole post-Soviet region. It would be fair to posit that "Russia's response to the Ukrainian crisis and the Olympic Games in Sochi

---

39   Etiene Balibar, *Politics and the Other Scene*, 69.
40   Dominic Basulto, "Hosting the Sochi Olympics is all about soft power," *Russia Direct*, 3 January 2014, http://www.russia-direct.org/opinion/hosting-sochi-olympics-all-about-soft-power (as of 1 September 2017)

are essentially rooted in the same impetus: Putin's geopolitical ambitions".[41]

If the Sochi project legitimized corruption and suppressed civil activism, the annexation of Crimea that immediately followed the Olympics in March 2014 included another key element in the loyalty matrix: legitimation of land grabs and forceful border changes. Boris Nemtsov straightforwardly claimed that the annexation of Crimea was planned during the Olympic Games, which makes it the first case of land appropriation designed during a global mega-event. This questions the widely spread characterization of the Sochi project as an indication of Russia's principled preference for soft power tools, as opposed to military instrument of controlling foreign territories. This is an important argument for deconstructing the popular interpretation of the Sochi Olympic as a zenith of Russia's soft power that was abruptly reversed by the Russia's policy in Ukraine after the EuroMaidan revolution. Nemtsov's reasoning is fully consistent with those commentators in the West who deem that "the Sochi Olympics proved a calculated cover for Vladimir Putin's plans to invade Ukraine".[42]

The economic part of the annexation of Crimea pointed to another similarity with the Sochi project: Nemtsov expected Russian investments in Crimea to be as costly as another Olympics for the Russian budget.[43] Alexei Kudrin confirmed this by estimating that the annexation of Crimea will cost Russia from 150 to 200 billion USD, which includes capital flee and loses caused by economic

---

41   Stefan Haus, "The Putin Games," *Foreign Policy in Focus*, 5 March 2014, http://fpif.org/putin-games/ (as of 1 September 2017)
42   Jens Laurson and George Pieler, "The Ukraine After Sochi: Lessons on Hard Power and Soft Power," *Forbes*, 18 March 2014, http://www.forbes.com/sites/laursonpieler/2014/03/17/the-ukraine-after-sochi-lessons-on-hard-power-and-soft-power/ (as of 1 September 2017)
43   Boris Nemtsov, "Krym oboidiotsa Rossii v eschio odnu Sochinskuyu Olimpiadu," *UkrInform* Information Agency, 17 March 2013, http://www.ukrinform.ua/rus/news/krim_oboydetsya_rossii_v_eshche_odnu_sochinskuyu_olimpiadu___boris_nemtsov_1613959 (as of 1 September 2017)

sanctions.⁴⁴ Nemtsov's prediction that the funds invested into the Olympics won't bring pay-off effects was fully corroborated by the developments after the Olympics. In particular, the Sochi–Crimea nexus was indirectly substantiated by the huge losses that VEB Bank incurred in 2014 due to its funding of the Sochi project and credit risks in Ukraine.⁴⁵

Therefore, Nemtsov was one of those public figures who interpreted the annexation of Crimea as another link in the chain of Kremlin's unlawful policies with strong security repercussions. It is quite illustrative that the vocabulary of the Nemtsov-Milov report was replete with securitization language—they refer to "engineering and transportation collapse", "chronic energy deficit", "irreparable blow to environment", "destruction of the urban milieu in Sochi", "threats of a military conflict" in the near-by South Caucasus, and "risks of growing inter-ethnic tensions" (allegedly due to the probable inflow of migrants).⁴⁶

Exceptionality is what makes Sochi and Crimea comparable to each other: Nemtsov harshly lambasted Putin for signing a decree allowing public servants from Crimea to keep doing business due to "specific situation" ⁴⁷ on the ground, which contravenes Russian legislation. For integrating Crimea into Russia the State Duma passed 21 legal acts in which special measures were in one way or another stipulated, which made experts claim that Crimea might turn in "another Chechnya", a territory where Russian legislation either is invalid or applies with numerous amendments.⁴⁸ Yet the two cases are also comparable in terms of their constitutive roles in

---

44 "Kudrin: Krym budet stoit' Rossii $ 150–200 billions," *Gazeta.ru*, 31 March 2015, http://www.gazeta.ru/business/news/2015/03/31/n_7066205.shtml (as of 1 September 2017)
45 Ivan Gidaspov, "Olympiiskiy antirekord VEBa," *Gazeta.ru*, 30 April 2015, http://www.gazeta.ru/business/2015/04/30/6662573.shtml (as of 1 September 2017)
46 Nemtsov and Milov, *Sochi i Olimpiada*,
47 Boris Nemtsov, "Novaya politicheskaya real'nost," Ekho Moskvy, 16 May 2014, http://www.echo.msk.ru/programs/year2014/1319266-echo/ (as of 1 September 2017)
48 Katerina Shulman, "Poluostrov iskliucheniy," *Kommersant*, 17 March, 2015, http://kommersant.ru/doc/2688488 (as of 1 September 2017)

determining the rules of inclusion and exclusion as mechanisms of identity-making based on the loyalty to the regime and the differentiation between its patriotic supporters and "infidel" opposition.

Conclusion

The debate on Nemtsov's Olympic discourse stretches far beyond the case of Sochi and gains even a greater profile and topicality against the backdrop of the deep crisis in Russia's relations with the West as a result of a series of events that followed the Sochi Olympics. Instead of celebrating Russian soft power potential and demonstrating the end of economic troubles in the country,[49] as pro-Putin loyalists have expected, only a few months after the closure of the Games Russia found itself under severe economic sanctions, with many of its officials on travel ban, the growing domestic economic and financial troubles and de-facto involvement in the military conflict with Ukraine. Perspectives of ameliorating "the image of wild Russia"[50] are again delayed to a far distant future.

Hosting the Sochi Olympics neither prevented Russia from resorting to a hybrid war against Ukraine, nor warranted success of future mega-events in this country: the lead-up to the FIFA 2018 World Cup takes place under the growing economic isolation, with Western businesses gradually leaving Russian markets. The crisis in the entire industry of Russian football—from scandalous arrear payments to the national team coach [51] to the ousting of the head of the Russian Football Union in the immediate aftermath of the international legal investigation against FIFA—is another trouble that Russia faces. These developments only support the *telos* of

---

49 "Sochi Games as a display of soft power," *Aljazeera*, 8 February 2014, http://www.aljazeera.com/news/europe/2014/02/sochi-games-are-display-soft-power-201428193756823316.html (as of 1 September 2017)

50 Victor Cepoi, "The Power of Winter Olympic Games," *Analyzing Europe*, 20 February 2014, http://analyzingeurope.com/the-power-of-winter-olympic-games/ (as of 1 September 2017)

51 See, for instance: Egor Maksimov, "Rossiyskiy futbol'nyi konfuz" *Dozhd'* TV channel, 2 October, 2014, http://tvrain.ru/news/istochnik_dozhdja_fabio_kapello_mozhet_podat_v_otstavku_13_oktjabrja-376114/ (as of 1 September 2017)

Nemtsov's narrative of contesting the basics of Putin's sovereignty—the rule by exceptions sustained by international sports institutions, castigation of disloyalty to the regime, and preference to hard power—as opposed to soft power—instruments.

The rule by exceptions, elevated by Putin at the highest point of his political agenda, corrupts the entire system of relations of power in Russia and undermines its governability. The same goes for sovereign division of the society into numerically dominant loyal majority and statistically much smaller yet politically troublesome groups of dissenters. The crisis of Putinism obliterates the PR effects of the Sochi Olympics and ushers in an isolationist Russia enmeshed in a self-exhausting conflict with the West.

Nemtsov: "Ukraine's Success Gives Russia a Chance!"

Kateryna Smagliy

Some argue that "if Boris Nemtsov were alive, his place would likely be in Ukraine."[1] Following in the footsteps of Mikheil Saakashvili, Natalie Jaresko, Aivaras Abromavicius, Khatia Dekanoidze, Masha Gaidar and other foreigners who took Ukrainian citizenship to help the post-Euromaidan government implement reforms, Nemtsov could have held office in Kyiv and worked on unpopular but necessary market changes. After the Revolution of Dignity, Nemtsov regularly visited Ukraine and supported Ukraine's new leadership. He developed a close friendship with President Petro Poroshenko and Mikheil Saakashvili and could have easily applied his talents in Ukraine. When appointed as Odesa Governor, Saakashvili invited Maria Gaidar, the daughter of former Russian Prime Minister Yegor Gaidar, to serve as adviser for social reforms, demonstrating Ukraine's openness to partners from its northern neighbor.[2]

Never hesitant to introduce tough reform measures in Russia, he could clean up the Augean stables of Ukraine's corrupt monopolies, streamline state subsidies, or lead civil service reform. His excellent knowledge of the many crimes committed by the Kremlin[3] could assist Ukraine's newly-established Information Policy Ministry in fighting Russia's disinformation war. In Kyiv Nemtsov would have live surrounded by many friends and good colleagues.

---

1   Yulia Kurnyshova, "Boris Nemtsov: A Ukrainian Afterward," *Demokratizatsiya. The Journal of Post-Soviet Democratization*, 24, no. 1, Winter 2016: 41.
2   For more on Saakashvili's reforms in Odesa see Kateryna Smagliy, "Reforms in Kyiv on Slow Burn but in Odesa Saakashvili Already Delivers," *Atlantic Council*, July 2015, http://www.atlanticcouncil.org/blogs/ukrainealert/reform-agenda-in-kyiv-on-slow-burn-but-in-odesa-saakashvili-already-delivers (as of 1 September 2017)
3   The texts of Boris Nemsov's investigative reports on corruption in Russia are available at: http://nemtsov.ru/category/doklady/ (as of 1 September 2017)

After all, it was a place where he always "smiled freely and with no particular reason immediately after landing at the Kyiv Boryspil airport."[4]

The tragic murder of Nemtsov has removed the possibility of this path. The most ardent Russian supporter of Ukraine's democratization, he did not live to see the many reform breakthroughs achieved by Ukraine after the Revolution of Dignity: the opening of the National Anti-Corruption Bureau and the launch of the transparent state procurement system ProZorro. He missed the many forums of Ukraine's newly-established political parties devoid of any oligarchic funding and did not get a chance to share the nation's joy on the day when the Ukraine-EU visa liberalization regime finally entered into force.

He also did not live to see some of Ukraine's post-revolutionary developments, which would have left him deeply troubled. He died not knowing that his close friend Pavel Sheremet, who moved to Kyiv after independent journalism was crushed in Belarus and then in Russia, would be killed in a car bomb on 20 July 2016. This brutal murder was just one episode in the broader pattern of harassment and threats against the media and investigative journalists.[5] The number of reports about Ukraine's anti-corruption activists becoming subject to wiretapping, surveillance, searches, smear campaigns, and even death threats has only grown since then.[6] More than 20 reformers left the cabinet in 2016 and in the summer of 2017 Mikheil Saakashvili was stripped of his Ukrainian citizenship. Three years after Poroshenko assumed the presidency, the consensus is that a new Ukraine remains out of reach and a counter-revolution is underway.

---

4 Interview to Gordon, Bulval Gordona, 16, no. 208, 22 April 2009, http://bulvar.com.ua/gazeta/archive/s16_62922/5337.html (as of 1 September 2017)

5 Kateryna Smagliy, "'Make Sure He Has Not Died in Vain!' Pavel Sheremet's Mother Pleads for Ukraine to Keep Fighting," Wilson Center, Kennan Institute, 28 July 2016, https://www.wilsoncenter.org/article/make-sure-he-did-not-die-vain-pavel-sheremets-mother-pleads-for-ukraine-to-keep-fighting (as of 1 September 2017)

6 Halayna Korba, "Harassment of Anti-Corruption Activists", [in Ukrainian], *Novoe vremya*, no. 27, 28 July 2017, http://magazine.nv.ua/article/post/64142-travlya-borcov-s-korrupcyey (as of 1 September 2017)

With his untimely death, Boris never learnt about the mixed results of Ukraine's post-Euromaidan transformations. If he had, would he feel disillusioned, disappointed, defeated? Or still hopeful and unbroken? The answers to these questions remain unknown. But thinking about them is of tremendous importance for Ukraine's democratization and societal values. Having paid a high price to restore its democracy during the Revolution of Dignity and, as Russian poet Andrey Orlov has put it, "In the ranks of the Russian Heavenly Hundred, holding the right-flank is—Boris Nemtsov." Ukraine's political leaders and civil society should always remember their moral to those heroes, who sacrificed their lives in standing up for Ukraine's right to protect its freedom and democracy.

After the Orange revolution, when many Ukrainian citizens and foreign observers became discouraged by the Yushchenko-Tymoshenko government, Nemtsov kept urging them not to lose drive: "The road to success is always difficult and dramatic. Every revolution passes through stages. The people initially love their revolutionary leaders and wait for the miracle to come… When the second, more prosaic period starts … this should not be seen as a tragedy."[7] Despite the many mistakes made by Ukraine's leaders on the bumpy road to democracy, Nemtsov kept praising Ukraine as "the only democratic country in the post-Soviet space," which "crossed the distance Russia would be crossing for one hundred years."[8] He never tired of repeating that Ukraine was a symbol of hope. For him, it was "the strong argument, the lighthouse, and the guiding star."[9]

Nemtsov was one of the few Russian politicians to sound the alarm of the Kremlin's war crimes in the Donbas and human rights

---

7   "The brown revolution is more threatening to us than the Orange", *GZT.ru*, 20 November 2005, http://nemtsov.ru/old/index6ec7.html?id=704599 (as of 1 September 2017)

8   "Boris Nemtsov: Yuschchenko povtoryaet put' El'tsina", *Segodnya*, 5 July 2007, http://www.segodnya.ua/life/interview/boric-nemtsov-jushchenko-povt orjaet-put-eltsina.html (as of 1 September 2017)

9   Boris Nemtsov's interview to Gordon, *Bulval Gordona*, 16, no. 208, 22 April 2009, http://bulvar.com.ua/gazeta/archive/s16_62922/5337.html (as of 1 September 2017)

abuses in Crimea. Yet his pro-Ukrainian rhetoric and his actions in support of Ukraine were meant to serve only one long-term goal — to reawaken Russian society. He fought hard to consolidate Russian liberals against the many wrongdoings of the Kremlin and bring more citizens into the civic opposition. Thus, regardless of many tempting professional or political opportunities in Ukraine, Nemtsov *could* never and *would* never have left his native country. The fight for Russian democracy and freedom was his ultimate calling and it is to his own country that he stayed committed. For Nemtsov, those were the goals worth any sacrifices, even his life.

Several days after Nemtsov's murder, Poroshenko pledged that Boris would always be remembered as "a great friend of Ukraine and Russian patriot." With his "sincere and respectful attitude toward Ukraine" as well as stamina to "fight for his own country's freedom," Nemstov was a "bridge" between the two countries.[10] On March 3, 2015, Ukraine's president posthumously awarded Nemtsov with the Order for Freedom, reminding that Euromaidan's slogan *For freedom ours and yours!* became Boris Nemtsov's life credo.[11]

The analysis that follows is an attempt to study the many extraordinary deeds and tireless efforts undertaken by Boris Nemtsov in support of Ukraine. Hopefully, this study will open a conversation on Nemtsov's role in Ukraine's two democratic revolutions and pave the way to the wider public acknowledgement and commemoration of his efforts.

Nemtsov and the 2004 Orange Revolution

Nemtsov's involvement with Ukraine was a result of his political partnership with Viktor Yushchenko. The Russian media claimed

---

[10] " Poroshenko: Nemtsov promised to present evidence of Russian military presence in Donbas," [in Ukrainian] *Hromadske TV*, 28 February 2015, https://www.youtube.com/watch?v=EDHR5qBG8J4 (as of 1 September 2017)

[11] "Petro Poroshenko awarded Boris Nemtsov with the Order for Freedom," 3 March 2015, Official web-site of the President of Ukraine, http://www.president.gov.ua/news/petro-poroshenko-nagorodiv-borisa-nyemcova-ordenom-svobodi-34856 (as of 1 September 2017)

that the two developed close professional ties in 1997–1998, when Nemtsov served as first deputy prime minister of Russia and Viktor Yushchenko as governor of the National Bank of Ukraine (NBU).[12] However, according to Oleg Rybachuk, the former chief of NBU's foreign relations department, as NBU governor Yushchenko only dealt with high ranking officials at the Central Bank of Russia, not the prime minister's office.[13] The two charismatic politicians began cooperating only in 2002, when both started developing political opposition to incumbent presidents.

As a result of the 2002 parliamentary elections, Yushchenko became the leader of the biggest faction in the Verkhovna Rada. His political bloc "Our Ukraine" received 23,6 per cent and with its 119 deputies became the biggest parliamentary faction. On October 23, 2002 Yushchenko unofficially visited Moscow to meet with leaders of the Russian liberal party the Union of Right Forces, established by Sergei Kirienko, Boris Nemtsov, and Irina Khakamada. Two weeks later Nemtsov arrived in Kyiv to sign a partnership manifesto between the Union of Right Forces and "Our Ukraine."[14] The leaders agreed to hold regular talks on policy issues and ground their partnership on the principle "Together into Europe without pushing each other aside."

When the Orange Revolution erupted as a result of rigged presidential elections, Nemtsov came to Kyiv and addressed the protesters together with Yushchenko and Yulia Tymoshenko. He was the only Russian public figure to unequivocally support Yushchenko even though the political situation in Kyiv was quite unstable and unforeseeable. Speaking at the Maidan on November 22, 2004, Nemtsov cheered the protesters with many colorful jokes and,

---

12 Aleksei Levchenko, "Nemtsova gonyat s Ukrainy," Газета.ru, 3 June 2005, http://nokia-rss.gazeta.ru/politics/2005/06/03_a_295661.shtml (as of 1 September 2017)
13 Author's interview with Oleg Rybachuk, 6 September 2017, Kyiv.
14 "Nasha Ukraïna" ta Soyuz pravikh sil Rosiï pidpisali manifest pro spil'ni diï," Khreshchatyk, 14 November 2002, http://www.kreschatic.kiev.ua/ua/3703/art/8760.html (as of 1 September 2017)

referring to President Putin's years with the KGB and Viktor Yanukovych's two convictions, compared their alliance to "the union of chekists and recidivists."[15]

Boris was inside the Verkhovna Rada chamber on the historic day of November 23, 2004, when Yushchenko took oath as Ukraine's president ahead of the Central Election Commission's ruling annulling the rigged election results. Nemtsov watched this moment of "history-in-the-making" from the Rada balcony together with foreign diplomats and journalists. Standing next to Nemtsov,[16] one could sense that he was completely taken away by the energy of Maidan. Nemtsov was joyful, energized but also envious: Ukraine's opposition safeguarded democracy and curbed the rising tide of authoritarianism. This success gave Russia a chance to achieve the same goal. Years later Nemtsov would confirm that he joined the Orange Maidan out of "purely pro-Russian" motives: "I thought that if Ukraine succeeds with fair and free elections—and the Maidan fought exactly for that—it would give Russia a chance to hold fair elections and gain freedom."[17]

Yushchenko's Adviser: a Mixed Record

Boris Nemtsov visited Kyiv again on 23 January 2015 to participate in the inaugural ceremony of President Yushchenko. This time he was accompanied by Anatolii Chubais, the then co-leader of the Union of the Right Forces party. At the ceremony, Nemtsov stood next to Tymoshenko and Petro Poroshenko, exchanging pleasantries and cheering the crowds at Kreshchatyk and Independence Square.[18]

Two weeks later the president appointed Nemtsov his freelance adviser to attract Russian investments and improve Ukraine's

---

15 "Yushchenko and Netsov on Maidan," 22 November 2014, https://www.youtube.com/watch?v=pSf7vIeW_Wc (as of 1 September 2017)
16 In 2003–2008 the author served as a Political Assistant/Verkhovna Rada liason officer at the U.S. Embassy in Kyiv.
17 Interview with Boris Nemtsov, 4 March 2013, http://echo.msk.ru/programs/razbor_poleta/1024154-echo/ (as of 1 September 2017)
18 "Nemtsov and Chubais at the Orange Maidan," 23 January 2005, https://www.youtube.com/watch?v=xItPkD6Ay3k (as of 1 September 2017)

investment climate. Not much is known about Nemtsov's activities or accomplishments as Yushchenko's adviser. With a benefit of hindsight, one could argue that the title provided no real authority or practical mechanisms to speed up economic reforms. The position was merely a token of respect paid by Yushchenko to Nemtsov for his courageous decision to openly side with him at the Maidan, yet it brought no political dividends for him either in Ukraine or Russia. The traces of Yushchenko's mysterious poisoning on the eve of the Orange Revolution led to the Kremlin,[19] and thus by accepting this advisory post Nemtsov explicitly challenged Vladimir Putin and showed his defiance to his administration.

Some Russian analysts saw the possibility of Nemtsov serving as an intermediary between Yushchenko and Putin on such contentious issues as the Russian Black Sea Fleet in Sevastopol.[20] However, that was not how Nemtsov understood his role. Nemtsov's goal was to present Ukraine as a success story of democracy and encourage medium-sized businesses — the backbone of Russia's middle class — to demand political change at home. When asked how he planned to attract Russian investment into Ukraine, Nemtsov argued that Russia's deteriorating political situation, insecure economic environment, and absence of legal mechanisms to protect private property would prompt Russian businessmen to invest in Ukraine: "I can admit that too many friends of mine look at Ukraine with interest and many of them even think of moving there, if situation in Russia gets worse."[21]

Nemtsov's optimism about the inflow of Russian capital into Ukraine proved to be unfounded. No one — neither in the East, nor in the West — rushed to invest capital in Ukraine's unreformed market and corrupt economy. Nemtsov's advisory role soon became

---

19 "Berezovsky is confident that traces of Yushchenko's poisoning lead to Putin," [in Ukrainian], *Lega.News*, 20 October 2009, http://news.liga.net/ua/news/politics/468686-berezovskiy-vpevneniy-shcho-sl-di-otru-nnya-yushchenka-vedut-do-put-na.htm?no_mobile_version=yes (as of 1 September 2017)

20 Anatolii Belyaev, "Naznachenie Borisa Nemtsova: minusov bol'she, chem plyusov," RIA Novosti, 6 June 2008, https://ria.ru/analytics/20050217/32466438.html (as of 1 September 2017)

21 Interview with Boris Nemtsov, *Ekho Moskvy*, 14 February 2005, http://echo.msk.ru/programs/beseda/34577/?=top (as of 1 September 2017)

subjected to criticism, as even his contacts in the financial sector—at that time his daughter Zhanna Nemtsova was vice president of Mercury Capital Trust in Moscow—could not help bolster Russian investment in Ukraine.[22] But how realistic was it to expect that Nemtsov could deliver on higher investments? As Nemstova rightly pointed out, "Investments cannot be attracted by advisers, but by the presidents, who are responsible for creating the right investment climate and designing interesting programs and business deals to foreign companies. With no executive powers of his own, Boris Nemtsov could only stay within the limits of his advisory authority. He could offer recommendations, but decisions were for the president to take."[23]

Nemtsov certainly over-exaggerated the attractiveness of Ukraine's market and overestimated the quality of its investment climate. One could argue that he would do Ukraine more good, had he not praised the country and its leaders excessively, but stressed the importance of vigorous anti-corruption and judicial reforms as the only way to boost foreign investments. Political dissident and human rights activists Semen Gluzman argued that Nemtsov was "too kind to Ukraine," and "lacked objectivity."

Boris Nemtsov was relieved of his advisory duties on 9 October 2006. In one of his later interviews he acknowledged that at a certain moment Yushchenko only expected him to criticize Prime Minister Tymoshenko. Nemtsov genuinely believed that Tymoshenko's populist rhetoric was damaging Ukraine's economy and in many ways supported the idea of dismissing her cabinet. As a result, Tymoshenko's allies in parliament gave 250 votes in support of a resolution tabled by MP Oleg Tyagnybok, recommending Pres-

---

22 Andre Mommen, "Boris Nemtsov, 1959–2015. The Rise and Fall of a Provincial Democrat," *Democratizatsiya, The Journal of Post-Soviet Democratization*, 24, no. 1:26.
23 Author's interview with Zhanna Nemtsova, 7 September 2017.

ident Yushchenko strip Nemtsov of advisory powers for "interfering with Ukraine's internal affairs."[24] The president initially refused, but then did dismiss Nemtsov after decorating him with the Order of Yaroslav the Wise on the fifteenth anniversary of Ukraine's independence.[25]

Boris pursued good intentions when he criticized Tymoshenko's actions as prime minister. He certainly aimed to protect Ukraine's economy from her destructive populism, but his disparaging public comments only poured oil on fire and widened the gap between the two Orange leaders. The conflict between Tymoshenko and Yushchenko, which lasted four out of five years of Yushchenko's presidency, certainly derailed the much needed economic, judicial, and anti-corruption transformations in Ukraine and led to disillusionment with Orange leaders with a subsequent victory of revanchist forces in the 2006 parliamentary and 2009 presidential elections.

Nemtsov's political experience should have taught him that deep-seated divisions and lack of unity among the opposition leaders could seriously damage their ability to implement reforms, lead to the loss of popularity, and result in a much more complicated return to power. As Yushchenko's adviser, Nemtsov should have encouraged Yushchenko and Tymoshenko to act together and not waste their time on internal bickering. In his later interviews Nemtsov acknowledged his disillusionment in both of them: "Ukrainians have traveled a very hard road, but failed to cross it until the end. Too many problems up there. I am deeply disappointed in Yushchenko and Tymoshenko…because they missed their incredible opportunities. They did nothing."[26]

---

24   Aleksei Levchenko, "Nemtsova gonyat s Ukrainy," *Gazeta.ru*, 3 June 2005, http://nokia-rss.gazeta.ru/politics/2005/06/03_a_295661.shtml (as of 1 September 2017)
25   "Solana i Nemtsov poluchat orden Yaroslava Mudrogo," *Commentarii.UA*, 21 August 2006, https://comments.ua/politics/82486-Solana-Nemtsov-poluchat-orden.html (as of 1 September 2017)
26   Interview with Boris Nemtsov, *Ekho Moskvy*, 4 March 2013, http://echo.msk.ru/programs/razbor_poleta/1024154-echo/ (as of 1 September 2017)

Still, he continued to respect Yushchenko and often compared him to Boris Yeltsin: "They both wanted democracy and freedom of speech, they came to power on the wave of democracy—one at the Maidan, the other [speaking] on a tank. They were superheroes, but both failed to meet people's expectations and soon lost trust and popularity...The difference is there, however: Yeltsin's dream of a free and democratic Russia has been crushed by Putin, whereas Yushchenko's dream if a free and democratic Ukraine has been fulfilled...As a result of the Orange Revolution, the country is democratic. And for many years, if not forever, this will be seen as Yushchenko's accomplishment."[27]

Euromaidan, Crimea, and Donbas

During the 2009 presidential election in Ukraine, Nemtsov supported neither Tymoshenko nor Yanukovych and saw no difference between the two. An experienced politician, Boris understood that having received millions from Ukraine's oligarchs to cover their electoral campaign expenditures, Tymoshenko and Yanukovych only increased their dependency on clans and that this vulnerability would only hinder their anti-corruption efforts.[28]

Immediately after the presidential election, Nemtsov did not rush to ridicule Yanukovych and was very cautious to comment on his policies. Nemtsov broke silence after Yanukovych decided to imprison Tymoshenko for the allegedly fraudulent gas agreement signed between Naftogaz and Gasprom in January 2009. Nemtsov draw parallels between Tymoshenko and Mikhail Khodorkovsky, arguing that both were political prisoners and that Tymoshenko's sentence was not a result of her gas deal with Putin, but of her posing a real threat to Yanukovych.

---

27   "Boris Nemtsov: "Yushchenko Walks in Yeltsin's Footsteps," *Segondya*, 5 July 2007, http://www.segodnya.ua/interview/boric-nemtsov-jushchenko-povt orjaet-put-eltsina.html (as of 1 September 2017)

28   Alesya Batsmanm, "Boris Nemtsov: 'Ya ne veryu, chto Yanukovich i Timoshenko sposobny borot'sya s korruptsiei'," *Zerkalo Nedeli*, 12 February 2010, https://zn.ua/politics/boris_nemtsov_ya_ne_veryu,_chto_yanukovic h_i_timoshenko_sposobny_borotsya_s_korruptsiey.html (as of 1 September 2017)

Interestingly, Nemtsov did not reach out to the new opposition leaders like Arseniy Yatsenyuk or Oleg Tyagnybok to support Ukraine's fight against the Yanukovych regime. This time he aimed to awaken Ukraine's civil society. Nemtsov was confident that Ukraine's opposition would not be able to topple the Yanukovych regime without large-scale citizen involvement at the grassroots level. In a live TV address from Moscow, Nemtsov spoke directly to the millions of Ukrainian viewers: "It won't depend on Yanukovych, but on Ukraine's civil society. If people continue sitting at their kitchen tables, drinking, eating, and occasionally joking about Donetsk guys seizing power, they will let "Putinism" flourish in its full beauty…I had a feeling that you [Ukrainians] were not ready to be slaughtered like a flock of sheep."[29]

When Yanukovych failed to sign the Ukraine-EU association agreement, leading to the start of Ukraine's Euromaidan revolution on the night of November 21, 2013 Nemtsov was the first to organize a rally in solidarity with the Ukrainian opposition in front of the Ukrainian Embassy in Moscow. The demonstration was very peaceful, but police detained 11 people, Nemtsov including, and tore down their "Ukraine, we are with you!" banner.[30]

Ten days later Nemtsov attempted to join the protesters in Kyiv, but he was stopped at the border. Ukraine's security services detained him upon arrival to the Boryspil airport and did not let him enter. No official explanation followed, but on his Facebook page Boris wrote that Yanukovych was annoyed by the December 2 "Ukraine, we are with you!" protest in Moscow and was afraid of him speaking at the Euromaidan.[31]

In Russia, Nemtsov spoke highly of the Euromaidan revolution and underscored that it was not merely Yanukovych's, but also

---

29 "Nemtsov uveren, chto 'putinizatsiya' stanet katastrofoi dlya Ukrainy," *Zerkalo Nedeli*, 4 February 2011, https://zn.ua/politics/nemtsov_uveren,_chto_putinizatsiya_stanet_katastrofoy_dlya_ukrainy.html (as of 1 September 2017)

30 "V Moskve zaderzhali storonnikov Evromaidana," *Mirror Weekly*, 2 December 2013, https://zn.ua/world/v-moskve-zaderzhali-storonnikov-evromaydana-134118_.html (as of 1 September 2017)

31 Boris Nemtsov, FP post by 13 December 2013, https://www.facebook.com/boris.nemtsov/posts/561387787264159 (as of 1 September 2017)

Putin's, nightmare. When asked whether a similar protest could spontaneously occur in Russia, he used colorful metaphors in support of his sharp assessments: "The Kremlin residents, I am sure, wake up in a cold sweat every night, vividly imagining the burning car tires and Molotov cocktails...The honest answer is yes. This is possible in Russia...The [*Ukrainian–K.S.*] authorities systematically and methodically wore people's patience thin. They listened to nobody. They talked to nobody. They made no compromises. They've got the result. But ask yourself: is Putin's clan any different from the Donetsk clan? Only by the level of financial resources and by the number of security forces. Our people are patient, but this won't help. They will strip the threads and get the Maidan."[32]

Nemtsov's fight against Russia's illegal annexation of Crimea and the war in eastern Ukraine was the pinnacle of his political activities in support of Ukraine's pro-European choice. The annexation of Crimea immediately followed the Sochi Olympics in March 2014 — the Russian mega-event that was harshly criticized by Nemtsov for corruption and mismanagement.[33] Nemtsov claimed that the annexation of Crimea was not a spontaneous, but a well-planned decision — it happened during the Sochi Olympics Games — the global mega-event — to divert the international community's attention away from Putin's orders to invade Ukraine.[34]

Nemtsov harshly lambasted Putin for annexing Crimea, but his position was also fluid. In one of his interviews he failed to make an unequivocal promise to honor international norms and return the peninsula to Ukraine. Speaking at Radio Liberty, Nemtsov of-

---

[32] Nemtsov schitaet vozmozhnym povtorenie ukrainskogo Evromaidana v Rossii", *Korrespondent.net*, January 27, 2014, http://korrespondent.net/ukraine/politics/3297663-nemtsov-schytaet-vozmozhnym-povtorenye-ukraynskoho-evromaidana-v-rossyy (as of 1 September 2017)

[33] Boris Nemtsov and Leonid Martyniuk, *Winter Olympics in the Sub-Tropics: Corruption and Abuse in Sochi. Investigative report*, 6 December 2013, http://www.putin-itogi.ru/cp/wp-content/uploads/2013/05/Report_ENG_SOCHI-2014_preview.pdf (as of 1 September 2017)

[34] Andrey Makarychev, Alexandra Yatsyk, "Rocking the Sochi Olympics Narrative: Boris Nentsov and Putin's Sovereignty," *Democratizatsiya. The Journal of Post-Soviet Democratization*, 24 (1) Winter 2016: 89–104.

fered the following solution to the problem: "I am a responsible person. Our position should be based on people's opinion formed by Crimean residents...There are 2.5 million people in Crimea and their destiny cannot be decided by a stroke of a feather...If it turns out that life standards in Ukraine are better than in Crimea, it would be realistic to talk about its return to Ukraine. But if Ukraine's economy remains as weak as it is today, there will be nothing to talk about. You cannot force people into poverty, they will start protesting."[35] In another interview he stressed that Crimea's annexation was an outcome of Ukraine's failed social and economic policies and indirectly put partial blame for what happened on Ukraine itself: "For the last 23 years the [Ukrainian authorities] only talked about reforms and did nothing. The country was governed by populists—rampant corruption, incredibly high taxes, impossible state expenditures on the pension system, and state bureaucracy..."[36]

Boris Nemtsov re-doubled his efforts at consolidating the opposition to Putin's aggressive policies toward Ukraine after the start of the military occupation of the Donbas. The Kremlin has repeatedly denied sending Russian troops or weapons into eastern Ukraine to support pro-Russian separatists and thus Nemtsov focused his activities on collecting the evidence to the opposite. He was also one of the key organizers of the anti-war demonstrations opposing Russian military intervention in Ukraine. The anti-war rallies were held on 2 March, 15 March, and 21 September 2014. The *Marsh Mira* (rally for peace), held on 15 March, was attended by thousands of protesters, who carried Russian and Ukrainian flags and chanted "No to war!" and "Stop lying!" Smaller rallies also took place in Yekaterinburg and Barnaul. The media estimated that

---

[35] "Herzen would not forgive us," Boris Nemtsov's interview to Ilya Azar, *Meduza*, 21 November 2014, https://meduza.io/feature/2014/11/21/gertsen-nam-by-ne-prostil (as of 1 September 2017)

[36] Vladimir Sokolov, Interview with Boris Nemtsov: "Putin is afraid of responsibility for the war in Ukraine", *Radio Liberty*, 25 November 2014, http://www.svoboda.org/content/transcript/26709410.html (as of 1 September 2017)

crowds were anywhere between 20,000–50,000[37] — the largest opposition protest since Putin's inauguration to a third presidential term in May 2012. Per Andrei Piontkovsky's assessments, "Nemtsov played the key role in organizing the pro-Ukraine rallies all around Russia and 90 per cent of their success is owed to his efforts. Nemtsov was uniquely skilled to charm people and help the most ardent opponents to find a common language. This quality was extremely important when it came to uniting the Russian opposition in support of Ukraine."[38]

On February 16, 2015, Nemtsov submitted a request to the Moscow mayor's office to hold the big anti-crisis march *Vesna* (spring) scheduled for March 1, 2014. The organizers planned for 100,000 participants. In his last interview to Ekho Moskvy just hours before his murder on Bolshoy Moskovoretsky Bridge near the Kremlin, Nemtsov in an interview argued that protesters' key demand was for the authorities to stop supporting the Donbas "rebels" militarily. The protesters also planned to carry banners in support of the Ukrainian pilot Nadia Savchenko, who was illegally arrested and taken to Russia, demanding her immediate release.[39]

In addition to his pro-Ukraine activities inside Russia, Nemtsov worked hard to mobilize the support of international leaders. In 2013–2014 he made regular visits to the United States, where he met Republican Senator John McCain and independent Senator Joe Lieberman to discuss human rights abuses in Russia and its aggressive policies toward Ukraine.[40] Speaking regularly at international conferences and meeting various European politicians, he presented the results of his investigations on Russia's military presence in the Donbas.

---

37 "Ukraine Crisis: Thousands March in Moscow Anti-War Rally," *BBC*, 22 September 2014 http://www.bbc.com/news/world-europe-29300213 (as of 1 September 2017); "Thousands March Against War In Moscow, St. Petersburg," *RFE/RL*, 21 September 2014, https://www.rferl.org/a/russia-antiwar-marches-ukraine/26597971.html (as of 1 September 2017)
38 Author's interview with Andrei Piontkovskyi, 27 August 2017.
39 Boris Nemtsov's Last Interview; https://www.youtube.com/watch?v=hZYzSnFRM28 (as of 1 September 2017)
40 Senator McCain on Twitter: https://twitter.com/senjohnmccain/status/344948028081319936?lang=ru (as of 1 September 2017)

Nemtsov was also reaching out to the Russian servicemen. In his many interviews, he urged them not to take part in Putin's war against Ukraine, reminding they pledged to protect their country from the enemies, not to fight with neighboring Slavic Ukrainian people. "The war with Ukraine is a crime," — he once wrote on his Facebook page, — "This war serves no one but Russia's enemies. This is not your war. This is not our war. This is Putin's war for his power and money."[41]

Nemtsov's regular meetings with the military veterans' organizations in Russia and investigative activities of his team helped to shed light on the Kremlin's actions in the Donbas and Russia's military presence there. Nemtsov started collecting information for the "Putin. The War" [42] report in early 2015. After his murder, Nemtsov's aides completed this work and presented it on May 12, 2015. The 66-page document detailed the death of Russian soldiers in the key battle for Ilovaisk and the battle for Debaltseve — two small towns in the Donetsk region. The report also documented sightings of Russian military hardware provided to the rebels in eastern Ukraine and spotted there, such as T-73B3 tanks and a Pantsir-S1 anti-aircraft missile launcher. Even after Nemtsov's death, his work continued helping Ukraine and serving as compelling evidence for the US and EU-imposed sanctions against Russia.

Remembering Boris Nemtsov

Nemtsov played a significant role in Ukraine's two democratic revolutions and post-Euromaidan transformations. But why did Ukraine matter? Why did he care?

He believed that a successful European and democratic Ukraine would set in motion the process of democratic change in

---

[41] "Nemtsov prizval rossiiskikh soldat ne uchastvovat' v voine Putina protiv Ukrainy," *Mirror Weekly*, 29 August 2014, https://zn.ua/WORLD/nemcov-prizval-rossiyskih-soldat-ne-uchastvovat-v-voyne-putina-protiv-ukrainy-151842_.html (as of 1 September 2017)

[42] "*Putin. The War. An Independent Report*," *Open Russia Foundation*, https://openrussia.org/post/view/4803/ (as of 1 September 2017)

Russia. For Boris and like-minded Russian activists, Ukraine's success could inevitably strengthen Russia's civil society and consolidate its fight for a democratic Russia, respectful its own citizens and its neighbors. It would provide a strong argument against Putin's kleptocracy and unite Russian liberals against totalitarianism and criminality.

Those who murdered Nemtsov thought that by silencing him they would succeed in silencing the Russian opposition. They miscalculated. The memory of Boris Nemtsov goes on and his leadership continues to inspire millions of people inside and outside Russia. The Kremlin puts enormous pressure on the opposition, besmirches activists, and silences the independent media. The authorities do everything to make people forget Nemtsov: they remove an improvised memorial near the Kremlin where Nemtsov was gunned down, they take away the flowers, candles and posters from the site, they detain activists who protect the memorial, and organized tenders to reconstruct the bridge during 2018 and 2019 only to block access to some parts of the bridge.[43]

On 7 September 2017, when activists placed a plaque honoring Boris on the Moscow apartment block where he lived, the Moscow authorities found the move illegal and reminded that per Russian law a memorial plaque for any citizen can only be installed only 10 years after his or her death.[44] Five days later, on 12 September, the plaque was torn down by a radical organization SERB. Similarly, in Yaroslavl, the local authorities threatened to remove the Nemtsov plaque on the grounds that it was installed without the consent of city officials.[45]

---

43 "Makeshift Nemtsov Memorial On Bridge Near Kremlin Removed Again," *Radio Free EUrope/Radio Liberty*, 2 March 2017, https://www.rferl.org/a/nemtsov-memorial-removed-again-russia/28343721.html (as of 1 September 2017)

44 "Moscow Officials Seek Removal of Nemtsov Plaque, " *The Moscow Times*, 8 September 2017, https://themoscowtimes.com/news/moscow-officials-seek-removal-of-nemtsov-plaque-58882 (as of 1 September 2017)

45 "Yaroslavl's mayor threatens to remove plaque dedicated to Boris Nemtsov," *Meduza*, 29 February 2016, https://meduza.io/en/news/2016/02/29/yaroslavl-s-mayor-threatens-to-remove-plaque-dedicated-to-boris-nemtsov (as of 1 September 2017)

In 2015 US Senator Marco Rubio introduced legislation to rename the stretch of Wisconsin Avenue in front of the Russian Embassy in Washington into "Boris Nemtsov Plaza" in order to "to permanently remind Putin's regime and the Russian people that these dissidents' voices live on, and that defenders of liberty will not be silenced."[46] Kyiv mayor Vitaliy Klitschko also pledged to rename the Povitroflotskyi Avenue in Kyiv—the location of the Russian Embassy—into the Boris Nemtsov Avenue. "[Nemtsov] really cared about our country and wanted it to be democratic,"[47]—said Klitschko to the press and promised that Ukraine would "never forget" Boris. However, Klitschko's promise remains unfulfilled until present day.

Ukraine's civil society has taken steps to keep the memory of Nemtsov alive. On 9 October 2017, when Boris Nemtsov would have turned 58 years old, the network of civil society organizations and parliamentarians held a press conference to remind the Kyiv municipal authorities about the need to have a street named after Nemtsov in Kyiv, to erect a monument to honor Boris and hold regular forums in Ukraine between Russian and Ukrainian civil societies. The Boris Nemtsov Foundation and the Open Russia movement has already launched the Boris Nemtsov Forum in Berlin. This platform brings together representatives of the expert and business community, politicians and civil society leaders, both in Russia and the West, who are interested in developing a European future for Russia. However, the road to an improved Russia-EU dialogue cannot bypass Ukraine.

The promotion of public knowledge about Nemtsov's admiration of Ukraine's fight for democracy would only strengthen the

---

46   Vladimir V. Kara-Murza, "How to Make Sure the Kremlin Remembers Boris Nemtsov," *The Washington Post*, 15 March 2016, https://www.washingtonpost.com/opinions/how-to-make-sure-the-kremlin-remembers-boris-nemtsov/2017/03/15/407b817a-080c-11e7-93dc-00f9bdd74ed1_story.html?utm_term=.7f8150ca6484 (as of 1 September 2017)

47   "Kyiv May Name One of the Streets After Klychko, " *Interfax*, 16 June 2015, http://interfax.com.ua/news/general/272393.html (as of 1 September 2017); Aleksandr Gorbachev, "Klitschko: Kiev May Name Street After Boris Nemtsov", *Newsweek*, 16 June 2015, http://www.newsweek.com/klitschko-kiev-may-name-street-after-boris-nemtsov-343642 (as of 1 September 2017).

values upon which the new Ukraine is being built. A respectful attitude toward his legacy would lay the groundwork for an enduring partnership between Ukraine's and Russia's civil societies—something that Boris Nemtsov would have strongly encouraged and supported. The remembrance of his life and death in Russia and Ukraine may help activists accomplish what politicians have failed to achieve—to build mutual understanding, respect, and lasting peace.

Appendix

Table 1. Regional democracy (Petrov-Titkov composite score for 1991–2001) and imperial-era literacy, 1897 census Note: Regions are sorted based on highest-to-lowest democracy scores.

Region	Democracy, 1991–01	Literacy	Female Literacy
St. Petersburg	45	62.6	51.5
Sverdlovskaya	43	19.2	10.8
Karelia	41	25.3	10
Perm	41	19.2	10.8
Nizhniy Novgorod	40	22	11.1
Arkhangelsk	37	23.3	11.7
Irkutsk	37	15.2	7.6
Novosibirsk	37	10.4	4.3
Samara	37	22.1	14.1
Yaroslavl	37	36.2	24
Chelyabinsk	34	20.4	11.4
Volgograd	34	23.8	13.6
Krasnoyarsk	33	13.6	6.7
Sakhalin	33	26.8	12.5
Udmurtia	33	16	7.5
Leningradskaya	32	55.1	43.8
Vologda	32	19.1	6.7
Chuvashiya	31	17.9	11.1
Kostroma	31	24	12.3
Buryatiya	30	13.4	3.8
Moscow (City)	30	56.3	42.3
Murmansk	30	23.3	11.7
Novgorod	30	23	10.7
Tyumen	30	11.3	5
Ivanovo	29	27	13.4
Kaluga	29	19.4	8.6

Kamchatka	29	24.7	8.2
Khakassiya	29	13.6	6.7
Kirov	29	16	7.5
Moscow (Obl.)	29	40.2	25.5
Omsk	29	10.4	4.3
Tomsk	29	10.4	4.3
Vladimir	29	27	13.4
Altai (Rep.)	28	10.4	4.3
Astrakhan	28	15.5	8.1
Belgorod	28	16.3	6.6
Bryansk	28	17.6	7.3
Kemerovo	28	10.4	4.3
Mariy El	28	16	7.5
Tver	28	24.5	11.9
Komi	27	23.3	11.7
Lipetsk	27	16.6	6.9
Pskov	27	14.6	7.2
Ryazan	27	20.3	8.2
Smolensk	27	17.3	7.1
Amur	26	24.8	11.9
Krasnodar	26	16.8	6.6
Magadan	26	24.8	11.9
Orenburg	26	20.4	11.4
Saratov	26	23.8	13.6
Tambov	26	16.6	6.9
Tula	26	20.7	8.9
Altay (Kray)	25	10.4	4.3
Chita	25	13.4	3.8
Khabarovskiy	25	24.8	11.9
Penza	25	14.7	6.3
Stavropol	25	14.4	6.2
Voronezh	25	16.3	6.4
Dagestan	24	9.2	2.5

Karachaevo-Cherkessiya	24	16.8	6.6
Kurgan	24	11.3	5
Rostov	24	22.4	9.8
Jewish	23	24.8	11.9
Primorskiy	23	24.7	8.2
Tatarstan	23	17.9	11.1
Adygeya	22	16.8	6.6
Ulyanovsk	22	15.6	6.6
Kursk	21	16.3	6.6
Mordovia	21	14.7	6.3
Orel	21	17.6	7.3
Sakha	21	4.1	1.7
North Ossetia	19	12.7	6
Bashkortostan	18	16.7	11.7
Chukotka	17	24.7	8.2
Kabardino-Balkariya	17	12.7	6
Ingushetiya	15	12.7	6
Kalmykiya	14	15.5	8.1

Index

A

American Enterprise Institute 41
Arzamas 16, 44
Authoritarianism 41, 49, 50, 54, 55, 57, 135, 136

B

Basaev, Shamil 28
Belykh, Nikita 13
Bolotnaya Square 21

C

Chechnya 13, 27, 28, 38, 62, 100, 116, 186
Chubais, Anatoly 13, 30, 85, 111, 112, 119, 123, 127, 128, 129, 132, 133, 134, 137, 146, 147, 166, 194
Communist Party of the Soviet Union 74, 94
Corporatism 41, 49, 50, 51, 53, 58

D

Developmentalism 50
Dubrovka Theatre 28

F

FIFA 2018 World Cup 182, 187

G

Gaidar, Maria 85, 115, 118, 119, 131, 132, 133, 134, 137, 189
Gingrich, Newt 47, 122

Gorbachev, Mikhail 31, 71, 75, 85, 91, 92, 94, 109, 112, 122, 205

H

Hegemony and counter-hegemony 171
Huntington, Samuel 41, 50, 59, 87

I

Illiberal democracy 50
Inclusion / exclusion 39, 105, 170, 175, 176, 181, 187
International Olympic Committee 180
International Republican Institute 55

J

Juppe, Alain 47

K

Kadyrov, Ramzan 24, 27, 28, 29, 140
Kasparov, Garry 39, 135, 136
Khakamada, Irina 13, 85, 133, 134, 135, 137, 146, 166, 193
Kirienko, Sergey 13, 146, 193
Klitschko, Vitaliy 205

L

LGBT 173, 175
Lieberman, Joe 140, 202
Litvinenko, Alexander 24

Lobachevsky State University 78, 80
Los Alamos 34, 35, 36, 37

M

Magnitsky Act 21, 25
Maidan 38, 193, 194, 195, 198, 200
Major, John 47, 122
Makaryevskaya Trade Fair 78
Maskhadov, Aslan 28
McCain, John 140, 202, 215
Milov, Vladimir 139, 170, 172, 179, 186
Minsk agreements 40
Moncloa Pact 90

N

National Endowment for Democracy 41, 55, 140
Navalny, Aleksei 21, 138, 148
Nizhegorodskaya Oblast 9
Nomenklatura 87, 92
Novodvorskaya, Valeria 39

P

Pluralism 53, 91, 92
Politkovskaya, Anna 27
Poroshenko, Petro 139, 189, 190, 192, 194
Putin, Vladimir 9, 10, 15, 16, 19, 20, 22, 24, 26, 28, 30, 31, 38, 39, 40, 43, 47, 48, 56, 59, 62, 81, 83, 86, 91, 109, 112, 118, 125, 132, 133, 134, 135, 136, 137, 138, 139, 140, 141, 143, 144, 145, 146, 147, 151, 152, 165, 166, 169, 170, 171, 172, 173, 174, 175, 176, 177, 178, 179, 180, 181, 184, 185, 186, 187, 188, 194, 195, 198, 200, 201, 203, 204, 205

S

Saakashvili, Mikhail 38, 140, 189, 190
Sachs, Jeffrey 46
Sarov 34, 35, 78
Sheremet, Pavel 190
Sochi Olympics 24, 170, 174, 176, 177, 184, 185, 187, 188, 200
Strauss, Robert 46

T

Tatarstan 62, 103, 104, 105, 106, 121, 209
Thatcher, Margaret 47, 122
Totalitarianism 53
Tyagnybok, Oleg 196, 199
Tymoshenko, Yulia 38, 191, 193, 194, 196, 197, 198

U

U.S. Agency for International Development 55
United Russia 81, 151, 165

V

Verkhovna Rada 38, 193, 194

W

Woodrow Wilson International Center for Scholars 42, 45

Y

Yavlinsky, Grigory 19, 99, 115, 123, 131, 132, 133, 134, 136
Yeltsin, Boris 14, 16, 30, 44, 47, 49, 61, 88, 91, 92, 95, 96, 98, 100, 107, 109, 111, 112, 113, 115, 116, 117, 118, 122, 123, 124, 125, 126, 127, 128, 129,

130, 132, 133, 141, 142, 145, 146, 165, 198
Yushchenko, Viktor 38, 135, 138, 191, 192, 193, 194, 195, 196, 197, 198

Z

Zakaria, Fareed 43, 50, 58

Notes on Contributors

Alexandra Yatsyk is Researcher at Uppsala Institute for Russian and Eurasian Studies, Sweden.

Alla Kassianova is Senior Research Associate, Stanford University.

Andrey Makarychev is Visiting Professor at the Johan Skytte Institute of Political Studies, University of Tartu, Estonia.

David J. Kramer is senior director for human rights and democracy at the McCain Institute for International Leadership in Washington, DC, USA.

Dmitry Mitin is assistant Professor at the School of Public and International Affairs, North Carolina State University, USA

Kateryna Smagliy is Director of the Kennan Institute in Kyiv, Ukraine.

Henry E. Hale is Professor of Political Science and International Affairs at The George Washington University, Washington, DC, USA.

Miguel Vázquez Liñán is associate professor of journalism at Seville University, Spain.

Sharon Werning Rivera is Associate Professor of Government at Hamilton College, USA.

Stefan Meister is based at The German Council on Foreign Relations (DGAP), Germany.

Tomila Lankina is Associate Professor in the Department of International Relations at the London School of Economics and Political Science, UK.

Vladimir Gel'man is Finland Distinguished Professor (FiDiPro) at the University of Helsinki and Professor at the Department of Political Science and Sociology at the European University in Saint-Petersburg, Russia.

Vladimir V. Kara-Murza is the coordinator of the Open Russia movement and the deputy leader of the People's Freedom Party. He was a longtime friend and colleague of Boris Nemtsov.

Yulia Kurnyshova is currently program manager at Pact, Inc. (Kyiv) and analyst at Foreign Policy Council "Ukrainian Prism".

Zhanna Nemtsova is a journalist for the Deutsche Welle's Russian Service at Bonn, founder of the Boris Nemtsov Foundation for Freedom, and co-founder of the Boris Nemtsov Center for the Study of Russia at Charles University in Prague.

Until his death in 2017, **Andre Mommen** was Professor of Political Science at the University of Amsterdam, the Netherlands.

Until his death in 2015, **Howard J. Wiarda** was the Dean Rusk Professor of International Relations at the School of Public and International Affairs (SPIA), University of Georgia, USA, and a Senior Scholar at the Center for Strategic and International Studies (CSIS), Washington, D.C. He wrote this contribution about Nemtsov shortly before he passed away.

SOVIET AND POST-SOVIET POLITICS AND SOCIETY

Edited by Dr. Andreas Umland

ISSN 1614-3515

1 Андреас Умланд (ред.)
   Воплощение Европейской
   конвенции по правам человека в
   России
   Философские, юридические и
   эмпирические исследования
   ISBN 3-89821-387-0

2 Christian Wipperfürth
   Russland – ein vertrauenswürdiger
   Partner?
   Grundlagen, Hintergründe und Praxis
   gegenwärtiger russischer Außenpolitik
   Mit einem Vorwort von Heinz Timmermann
   ISBN 3-89821-401-X

3 Manja Hussner
   Die Übernahme internationalen Rechts
   in die russische und deutsche
   Rechtsordnung
   Eine vergleichende Analyse zur
   Völkerrechtsfreundlichkeit der Verfassungen
   der Russländischen Föderation und der
   Bundesrepublik Deutschland
   Mit einem Vorwort von Rainer Arnold
   ISBN 3-89821-438-9

4 Matthew Tejada
   Bulgaria's Democratic Consolidation
   and the Kozloduy Nuclear Power Plant
   (KNPP)
   The Unattainability of Closure
   With a foreword by Richard J. Crampton
   ISBN 3-89821-439-7

5 Марк Григорьевич Меерович
   Квадратные метры, определяющие
   сознание
   Государственная жилищная политика в
   СССР. 1921 – 1941 гг
   ISBN 3-89821-474-5

6 Andrei P. Tsygankov, Pavel
   A.Tsygankov (Eds.)
   New Directions in Russian
   International Studies
   ISBN 3-89821-422-2

7 Марк Григорьевич Меерович
   Как власть народ к труду приучала
   Жилище в СССР – средство управления
   людьми. 1917 – 1941 гг.
   С предисловием Елены Осокиной
   ISBN 3-89821-495-8

8 David J. Galbreath
   Nation-Building and Minority Politics
   in Post-Socialist States
   Interests, Influence and Identities in Estonia
   and Latvia
   With a foreword by David J. Smith
   ISBN 3-89821-467-2

9 Алексей Юрьевич Безугольный
   Народы Кавказа в Вооруженных
   силах СССР в годы Великой
   Отечественной войны 1941-1945 гг.
   С предисловием Николая Бугая
   ISBN 3-89821-475-3

10 Вячеслав Лихачев и Владимир
   Прибыловский (ред.)
   Русское Национальное Единство,
   1990-2000. В 2-х томах
   ISBN 3-89821-523-7

11 Николай Бугай (ред.)
   Народы стран Балтии в условиях
   сталинизма (1940-е – 1950-е годы)
   Документированная история
   ISBN 3-89821-525-3

12 Ingmar Bredies (Hrsg.)
   Zur Anatomie der Orange Revolution
   in der Ukraine
   Wechsel des Elitenregimes oder Triumph des
   Parlamentarismus?
   ISBN 3-89821-524-5

13 Anastasia V. Mitrofanova
   The Politicization of Russian
   Orthodoxy
   Actors and Ideas
   With a foreword by William C. Gay
   ISBN 3-89821-481-8

14 Nathan D. Larson
    Alexander Solzhenitsyn and the
    Russo-Jewish Question
    ISBN 3-89821-483-4

15 Guido Houben
    Kulturpolitik und Ethnizität
    Staatliche Kunstförderung im Russland der
    neunziger Jahre
    Mit einem Vorwort von Gert Weisskirchen
    ISBN 3-89821-542-3

16 Leonid Luks
    Der russische „Sonderweg"?
    Aufsätze zur neuesten Geschichte Russlands
    im europäischen Kontext
    ISBN 3-89821-496-6

17 Евгений Мороз
    История «Мёртвой воды» – от
    страшной сказки к большой
    политике
    Политическое неоязычество в
    постсоветской России
    ISBN 3-89821-551-2

18 Александр Верховский и Галина
    Кожевникова (ред.)
    Этническая и религиозная
    интолерантность в российских СМИ
    Результаты мониторинга 2001-2004 гг.
    ISBN 3-89821-569-5

19 Christian Ganzer
    Sowjetisches Erbe und ukrainische
    Nation
    Das Museum der Geschichte des Zaporoger
    Kosakentums auf der Insel Chortycja
    Mit einem Vorwort von Frank Golczewski
    ISBN 3-89821-504-0

20 Эльза-Баир Гучинова
    Помнить нельзя забыть
    Антропология депортационной травмы
    калмыков
    С предисловием Кэролайн Хамфри
    ISBN 3-89821-506-7

21 Юлия Лидерман
    Мотивы «проверки» и «испытания»
    в постсоветской культуре
    Советское прошлое в российском
    кинематографе 1990-х годов
    С предисловием Евгения Марголита
    ISBN 3-89821-511-3

22 Tanya Lokshina, Ray Thomas, Mary
    Mayer (Eds.)
    The Imposition of a Fake Political
    Settlement in the Northern Caucasus
    The 2003 Chechen Presidential Election
    ISBN 3-89821-436-2

23 Timothy McCajor Hall, Rosie Read
    (Eds.)
    Changes in the Heart of Europe
    Recent Ethnographies of Czechs, Slovaks,
    Roma, and Sorbs
    With an afterword by Zdeněk Salzmann
    ISBN 3-89821-606-3

24 Christian Autengruber
    Die politischen Parteien in Bulgarien
    und Rumänien
    Eine vergleichende Analyse seit Beginn der
    90er Jahre
    Mit einem Vorwort von Dorothée de Nève
    ISBN 3-89821-476-1

25 Annette Freyberg-Inan with Radu
    Cristescu
    The Ghosts in Our Classrooms, or:
    John Dewey Meets Ceauşescu
    The Promise and the Failures of Civic
    Education in Romania
    ISBN 3-89821-416-8

26 John B. Dunlop
    The 2002 Dubrovka and 2004 Beslan
    Hostage Crises
    A Critique of Russian Counter-Terrorism
    With a foreword by Donald N. Jensen
    ISBN 3-89821-608-X

27 Peter Koller
    Das touristische Potenzial von
    Kam''janec–Podil's'kyj
    Eine fremdenverkehrsgeographische
    Untersuchung der Zukunftsperspektiven und
    Maßnahmenplanung zur
    Destinationsentwicklung des „ukrainischen
    Rothenburg"
    Mit einem Vorwort von Kristiane Klemm
    ISBN 3-89821-640-3

28 Françoise Daucé, Elisabeth Sieca-
    Kozlowski (Eds.)
    Dedovshchina in the Post-Soviet
    Military
    Hazing of Russian Army Conscripts in a
    Comparative Perspective
    With a foreword by Dale Herspring
    ISBN 3-89821-616-0

29 *Florian Strasser*
Zivilgesellschaftliche Einflüsse auf die Orange Revolution
Die gewaltlose Massenbewegung und die ukrainische Wahlkrise 2004
Mit einem Vorwort von Egbert Jahn
ISBN 3-89821-648-9

30 *Rebecca S. Katz*
The Georgian Regime Crisis of 2003-2004
A Case Study in Post-Soviet Media Representation of Politics, Crime and Corruption
ISBN 3-89821-413-3

31 *Vladimir Kantor*
Willkür oder Freiheit
Beiträge zur russischen Geschichtsphilosophie
Ediert von Dagmar Herrmann sowie mit einem Vorwort versehen von Leonid Luks
ISBN 3-89821-589-X

32 *Laura A. Victoir*
The Russian Land Estate Today
A Case Study of Cultural Politics in Post-Soviet Russia
With a foreword by Priscilla Roosevelt
ISBN 3-89821-426-5

33 *Ivan Katchanovski*
Cleft Countries
Regional Political Divisions and Cultures in Post-Soviet Ukraine and Moldova
With a foreword by Francis Fukuyama
ISBN 3-89821-558-X

34 *Florian Mühlfried*
Postsowjetische Feiern
Das Georgische Bankett im Wandel
Mit einem Vorwort von Kevin Tuite
ISBN 3-89821-601-2

35 *Roger Griffin, Werner Loh, Andreas Umland (Eds.)*
Fascism Past and Present, West and East
An International Debate on Concepts and Cases in the Comparative Study of the Extreme Right
With an afterword by Walter Laqueur
ISBN 3-89821-674-8

36 *Sebastian Schlegel*
Der „Weiße Archipel"
Sowjetische Atomstädte 1945-1991
Mit einem Geleitwort von Thomas Bohn
ISBN 3-89821-679-9

37 *Vyacheslav Likhachev*
Political Anti-Semitism in Post-Soviet Russia
Actors and Ideas in 1991-2003
Edited and translated from Russian by Eugene Veklerov
ISBN 3-89821-529-6

38 *Josette Baer (Ed.)*
Preparing Liberty in Central Europe
Political Texts from the Spring of Nations 1848 to the Spring of Prague 1968
With a foreword by Zdeněk V. David
ISBN 3-89821-546-6

39 *Михаил Лукьянов*
Российский консерватизм и реформа, 1907-1914
С предисловием Марка Д. Стейнберга
ISBN 3-89821-503-2

40 *Nicola Melloni*
Market Without Economy
The 1998 Russian Financial Crisis
With a foreword by Eiji Furukawa
ISBN 3-89821-407-9

41 *Dmitrij Chmelnizki*
Die Architektur Stalins
Bd. 1: Studien zu Ideologie und Stil
Bd. 2: Bilddokumentation
Mit einem Vorwort von Bruno Flierl
ISBN 3-89821-515-6

42 *Katja Yafimava*
Post-Soviet Russian-Belarussian Relationships
The Role of Gas Transit Pipelines
With a foreword by Jonathan P. Stern
ISBN 3-89821-655-1

43 *Boris Chavkin*
Verflechtungen der deutschen und russischen Zeitgeschichte
Aufsätze und Archivfunde zu den Beziehungen Deutschlands und der Sowjetunion von 1917 bis 1991
Ediert von Markus Edlinger sowie mit einem Vorwort versehen von Leonid Luks
ISBN 3-89821-756-6

44 *Anastasija Grynenko in Zusammenarbeit mit Claudia Dathe*
    Die Terminologie des Gerichtswesens der Ukraine und Deutschlands im Vergleich
    Eine übersetzungswissenschaftliche Analyse juristischer Fachbegriffe im Deutschen, Ukrainischen und Russischen
    Mit einem Vorwort von Ulrich Hartmann
    ISBN 3-89821-691-8

45 *Anton Burkov*
    The Impact of the European Convention on Human Rights on Russian Law
    Legislation and Application in 1996-2006
    With a foreword by Françoise Hampson
    ISBN 978-3-89821-639-5

46 *Stina Torjesen, Indra Overland (Eds.)*
    International Election Observers in Post-Soviet Azerbaijan
    Geopolitical Pawns or Agents of Change?
    ISBN 978-3-89821-743-9

47 *Taras Kuzio*
    Ukraine – Crimea – Russia
    Triangle of Conflict
    ISBN 978-3-89821-761-3

48 *Claudia Šabić*
    "Ich erinnere mich nicht, aber L'viv!"
    Zur Funktion kultureller Faktoren für die Institutionalisierung und Entwicklung einer ukrainischen Region
    Mit einem Vorwort von Melanie Tatur
    ISBN 978-3-89821-752-1

49 *Marlies Bilz*
    Tatarstan in der Transformation
    Nationaler Diskurs und Politische Praxis 1988-1994
    Mit einem Vorwort von Frank Golczewski
    ISBN 978-3-89821-722-4

50 *Марлен Ларюэль (ред.)*
    Современные интерпретации русского национализма
    ISBN 978-3-89821-795-8

51 *Sonja Schüler*
    Die ethnische Dimension der Armut
    Roma im postsozialistischen Rumänien
    Mit einem Vorwort von Anton Sterbling
    ISBN 978-3-89821-776-7

52 *Галина Кожевникова*
    Радикальный национализм в России и противодействие ему
    Сборник докладов Центра «Сова» за 2004-2007 гг.
    С предисловием Александра Верховского
    ISBN 978-3-89821-721-7

53 *Галина Кожевникова и Владимир Прибыловский*
    Российская власть в биографиях I
    Высшие должностные лица РФ в 2004 г.
    ISBN 978-3-89821-796-5

54 *Галина Кожевникова и Владимир Прибыловский*
    Российская власть в биографиях II
    Члены Правительства РФ в 2004 г.
    ISBN 978-3-89821-797-2

55 *Галина Кожевникова и Владимир Прибыловский*
    Российская власть в биографиях III
    Руководители федеральных служб и агентств РФ в 2004 г.
    ISBN 978-3-89821-798-9

56 *Ileana Petroniu*
    Privatisierung in Transformationsökonomien
    Determinanten der Restrukturierungs-Bereitschaft am Beispiel Polens, Rumäniens und der Ukraine
    Mit einem Vorwort von Rainer W. Schäfer
    ISBN 978-3-89821-790-3

57 *Christian Wipperfürth*
    Russland und seine GUS-Nachbarn
    Hintergründe, aktuelle Entwicklungen und Konflikte in einer ressourcenreichen Region
    ISBN 978-3-89821-801-6

58 *Togzhan Kassenova*
    From Antagonism to Partnership
    The Uneasy Path of the U.S.-Russian Cooperative Threat Reduction
    With a foreword by Christoph Bluth
    ISBN 978-3-89821-707-1

59 *Alexander Höllwerth*
    Das sakrale eurasische Imperium des Aleksandr Dugin
    Eine Diskursanalyse zum postsowjetischen russischen Rechtsextremismus
    Mit einem Vorwort von Dirk Uffelmann
    ISBN 978-3-89821-813-9

60 Олег Рябов
«Россия-Матушка»
Национализм, гендер и война в России XX века
С предисловием Елены Гощило
ISBN 978-3-89821-487-2

61 Ivan Maistrenko
Borot'bism
A Chapter in the History of the Ukrainian Revolution
With a new introduction by Chris Ford
Translated by George S. N. Luckyj with the assistance of Ivan L. Rudnytsky
ISBN 978-3-89821-697-5

62 Maryna Romanets
Anamorphosic Texts and Reconfigured Visions
Improvised Traditions in Contemporary Ukrainian and Irish Literature
ISBN 978-3-89821-576-3

63 Paul D'Anieri and Taras Kuzio (Eds.)
Aspects of the Orange Revolution I
Democratization and Elections in Post-Communist Ukraine
ISBN 978-3-89821-698-2

64 Bohdan Harasymiw in collaboration with Oleh S. Ilnytzkyj (Eds.)
Aspects of the Orange Revolution II
Information and Manipulation Strategies in the 2004 Ukrainian Presidential Elections
ISBN 978-3-89821-699-9

65 Ingmar Bredies, Andreas Umland and Valentin Yakushik (Eds.)
Aspects of the Orange Revolution III
The Context and Dynamics of the 2004 Ukrainian Presidential Elections
ISBN 978-3-89821-803-0

66 Ingmar Bredies, Andreas Umland and Valentin Yakushik (Eds.)
Aspects of the Orange Revolution IV
Foreign Assistance and Civic Action in the 2004 Ukrainian Presidential Elections
ISBN 978-3-89821-808-5

67 Ingmar Bredies, Andreas Umland and Valentin Yakushik (Eds.)
Aspects of the Orange Revolution V
Institutional Observation Reports on the 2004 Ukrainian Presidential Elections
ISBN 978-3-89821-809-2

68 Taras Kuzio (Ed.)
Aspects of the Orange Revolution VI
Post-Communist Democratic Revolutions in Comparative Perspective
ISBN 978-3-89821-820-7

69 Tim Bohse
Autoritarismus statt Selbstverwaltung
Die Transformation der kommunalen Politik in der Stadt Kaliningrad 1990-2005
Mit einem Geleitwort von Stefan Troebst
ISBN 978-3-89821-782-8

70 David Rupp
Die Rußländische Föderation und die russischsprachige Minderheit in Lettland
Eine Fallstudie zur Anwaltspolitik Moskaus gegenüber den russophonen Minderheiten im „Nahen Ausland" von 1991 bis 2002
Mit einem Vorwort von Helmut Wagner
ISBN 978-3-89821-778-1

71 Taras Kuzio
Theoretical and Comparative Perspectives on Nationalism
New Directions in Cross-Cultural and Post-Communist Studies
With a foreword by Paul Robert Magocsi
ISBN 978-3-89821-815-3

72 Christine Teichmann
Die Hochschultransformation im heutigen Osteuropa
Kontinuität und Wandel bei der Entwicklung des postkommunistischen Universitätswesens
Mit einem Vorwort von Oskar Anweiler
ISBN 978-3-89821-842-9

73 Julia Kusznir
Der politische Einfluss von Wirtschaftseliten in russischen Regionen
Eine Analyse am Beispiel der Erdöl- und Erdgasindustrie, 1992-2005
Mit einem Vorwort von Wolfgang Eichwede
ISBN 978-3-89821-821-4

74 Alena Vysotskaya
Russland, Belarus und die EU-Osterweiterung
Zur Minderheitenfrage und zum Problem der Freizügigkeit des Personenverkehrs
Mit einem Vorwort von Katlijn Malfliet
ISBN 978-3-89821-822-1

75 Heiko Pleines (Hrsg.)
    Corporate Governance in post-
    sozialistischen Volkswirtschaften
    ISBN 978-3-89821-766-8

76 Stefan Ihrig
    Wer sind die Moldawier?
    Rumänismus versus Moldowanismus in
    Historiographie und Schulbüchern der
    Republik Moldova, 1991-2006
    Mit einem Vorwort von Holm Sundhaussen
    ISBN 978-3-89821-466-7

77 Galina Kozhevnikova in collaboration
    with Alexander Verkhovsky and
    Eugene Veklerov
    Ultra-Nationalism and Hate Crimes in
    Contemporary Russia
    The 2004-2006 Annual Reports of Moscow's
    SOVA Center
    With a foreword by Stephen D. Shenfield
    ISBN 978-3-89821-868-9

78 Florian Küchler
    The Role of the European Union in
    Moldova's Transnistria Conflict
    With a foreword by Christopher Hill
    ISBN 978-3-89821-850-4

79 Bernd Rechel
    The Long Way Back to Europe
    Minority Protection in Bulgaria
    With a foreword by Richard Crampton
    ISBN 978-3-89821-863-4

80 Peter W. Rodgers
    Nation, Region and History in Post-
    Communist Transitions
    Identity Politics in Ukraine, 1991-2006
    With a foreword by Vera Tolz
    ISBN 978-3-89821-903-7

81 Stephanie Solywoda
    The Life and Work of
    Semen L. Frank
    A Study of Russian Religious Philosophy
    With a foreword by Philip Walters
    ISBN 978-3-89821-457-5

82 Vera Sokolova
    Cultural Politics of Ethnicity
    Discourses on Roma in Communist
    Czechoslovakia
    ISBN 978-3-89821-864-1

83 Natalya Shevchik Ketenci
    Kazakhstani Enterprises in Transition
    The Role of Historical Regional Development
    in Kazakhstan's Post-Soviet Economic
    Transformation
    ISBN 978-3-89821-831-3

84 Martin Malek, Anna Schor-
    Tschudnowskaja (Hrsg.)
    Europa im Tschetschenienkrieg
    Zwischen politischer Ohnmacht und
    Gleichgültigkeit
    Mit einem Vorwort von Lipchan Basajewa
    ISBN 978-3-89821-676-0

85 Stefan Meister
    Das postsowjetische Universitätswesen
    zwischen nationalem und
    internationalem Wandel
    Die Entwicklung der regionalen Hochschule
    in Russland als Gradmesser der
    Systemtransformation
    Mit einem Vorwort von Joan DeBardeleben
    ISBN 978-3-89821-891-7

86 Konstantin Sheiko in collaboration
    with Stephen Brown
    Nationalist Imaginings of the
    Russian Past
    Anatolii Fomenko and the Rise of Alternative
    History in Post-Communist Russia
    With a foreword by Donald Ostrowski
    ISBN 978-3-89821-915-0

87 Sabine Jenni
    Wie stark ist das „Einige Russland"?
    Zur Parteibindung der Eliten und zum
    Wahlerfolg der Machtpartei
    im Dezember 2007
    Mit einem Vorwort von Klaus Armingeon
    ISBN 978-3-89821-961-7

88 Thomas Borén
    Meeting-Places of Transformation
    Urban Identity, Spatial Representations and
    Local Politics in Post-Soviet St Petersburg
    ISBN 978-3-89821-739-2

89 Aygul Ashirova
    Stalinismus und Stalin-Kult in
    Zentralasien
    Turkmenistan 1924-1953
    Mit einem Vorwort von Leonid Luks
    ISBN 978-3-89821-987-7

90 Leonid Luks
    Freiheit oder imperiale Größe?
    Essays zu einem russischen Dilemma
    ISBN 978-3-8382-0011-8

91 Christopher Gilley
    The 'Change of Signposts' in the
    Ukrainian Emigration
    A Contribution to the History of
    Sovietophilism in the 1920s
    With a foreword by Frank Golczewski
    ISBN 978-3-89821-965-5

92 Philipp Casula, Jeronim Perovic
    (Eds.)
    Identities and Politics
    During the Putin Presidency
    The Discursive Foundations of Russia's
    Stability
    With a foreword by Heiko Haumann
    ISBN 978-3-8382-0015-6

93 Marcel Viëtor
    Europa und die Frage
    nach seinen Grenzen im Osten
    Zur Konstruktion 'europäischer Identität' in
    Geschichte und Gegenwart
    Mit einem Vorwort von Albrecht Lehmann
    ISBN 978-3-8382-0045-3

94 Ben Hellman, Andrei Rogachevskii
    Filming the Unfilmable
    Casper Wrede's 'One Day in the Life
    of Ivan Denisovich'
    Second, Revised and Expanded Edition
    ISBN 978-3-8382-0044-6

95 Eva Fuchslocher
    Vaterland, Sprache, Glaube
    Orthodoxie und Nationenbildung
    am Beispiel Georgiens
    Mit einem Vorwort von Christina von Braun
    ISBN 978-3-89821-884-9

96 Vladimir Kantor
    Das Westlertum und der Weg
    Russlands
    Zur Entwicklung der russischen Literatur und
    Philosophie
    Ediert von Dagmar Herrmann
    Mit einem Beitrag von Nikolaus Lobkowicz
    ISBN 978-3-8382-0102-3

97 Kamran Musayev
    Die postsowjetische Transformation
    im Baltikum und Südkaukasus
    Eine vergleichende Untersuchung der
    politischen Entwicklung Lettlands und
    Aserbaidschans 1985-2009
    Mit einem Vorwort von Leonid Luks
    Ediert von Sandro Henschel
    ISBN 978-3-8382-0103-0

98 Tatiana Zhurzhenko
    Borderlands into Bordered Lands
    Geopolitics of Identity in Post-Soviet Ukraine
    With a foreword by Dieter Segert
    ISBN 978-3-8382-0042-2

99 Кирилл Галушко, Лидия Смола
    (ред.)
    Пределы падения – варианты
    украинского будущего
    Аналитико-прогностические исследования
    ISBN 978-3-8382-0148-1

100 Michael Minkenberg (ed.)
    Historical Legacies and the Radical
    Right in Post-Cold War Central and
    Eastern Europe
    With an afterword by Sabrina P. Ramet
    ISBN 978-3-8382-0124-5

101 David-Emil Wickström
    Rocking St. Petersburg
    Transcultural Flows and Identity Politics in
    the St. Petersburg Popular Music Scene
    With a foreword by Yngvar B. Steinholt
    Second, Revised and Expanded Edition
    ISBN 978-3-8382-0100-9

102 Eva Zabka
    Eine neue „Zeit der Wirren"?
    Der spät- und postsowjetische Systemwandel
    1985-2000 im Spiegel russischer
    gesellschaftspolitischer Diskurse
    Mit einem Vorwort von Margareta Mommsen
    ISBN 978-3-8382-0161-0

103 Ulrike Ziemer
    Ethnic Belonging, Gender and
    Cultural Practices
    Youth Identitites in Contemporary Russia
    With a foreword by Anoop Nayak
    ISBN 978-3-8382-0152-8

104 Ksenia Chepikova
‚Einiges Russland' - eine zweite KPdSU?
Aspekte der Identitätskonstruktion einer postsowjetischen „Partei der Macht"
Mit einem Vorwort von Torsten Oppelland
ISBN 978-3-8382-0311-9

105 Леонид Люкс
Западничество или евразийство? Демократия или идеократия?
Сборник статей об исторических дилеммах России
С предисловием Владимира Кантора
ISBN 978-3-8382-0211-2

106 Anna Dost
Das russische Verfassungsrecht auf dem Weg zum Föderalismus und zurück
Zum Konflikt von Rechtsnormen und -wirklichkeit in der Russländischen Föderation von 1991 bis 2009
Mit einem Vorwort von Alexander Blankenagel
ISBN 978-3-8382-0292-1

107 Philipp Herzog
Sozialistische Völkerfreundschaft, nationaler Widerstand oder harmloser Zeitvertreib?
Zur politischen Funktion der Volkskunst im sowjetischen Estland
Mit einem Vorwort von Andreas Kappeler
ISBN 978-3-8382-0216-7

108 Marlène Laruelle (ed.)
Russian Nationalism, Foreign Policy, and Identity Debates in Putin's Russia
New Ideological Patterns after the Orange Revolution
ISBN 978-3-8382-0325-6

109 Michail Logvinov
Russlands Kampf gegen den internationalen Terrorismus
Eine kritische Bestandsaufnahme des Bekämpfungsansatzes
Mit einem Geleitwort von Hans-Henning Schröder
und einem Vorwort von Eckhard Jesse
ISBN 978-3-8382-0329-4

110 John B. Dunlop
The Moscow Bombings of September 1999
Examinations of Russian Terrorist Attacks at the Onset of Vladimir Putin's Rule
Second, Revised and Expanded Edition
ISBN 978-3-8382-0388-1

111 Андрей А. Ковалёв
Свидетельство из-за кулис российской политики I
Можно ли делать добро из зла?
(Воспоминания и размышления о последних советских и первых послесоветских годах)
With a foreword by Peter Reddaway
ISBN 978-3-8382-0302-7

112 Андрей А. Ковалёв
Свидетельство из-за кулис российской политики II
Угроза для себя и окружающих
(Наблюдения и предостережения относительно происходящего после 2000 г.)
ISBN 978-3-8382-0303-4

113 Bernd Kappenberg
Zeichen setzen für Europa
Der Gebrauch europäischer lateinischer Sonderzeichen in der deutschen Öffentlichkeit
Mit einem Vorwort von Peter Schlobinski
ISBN 978-3-89821-749-1

114 Ivo Mijnssen
The Quest for an Ideal Youth in Putin's Russia I
Back to Our Future! History, Modernity, and Patriotism according to Nashi, 2005-2013
With a foreword by Jeronim Perović
Second, Revised and Expanded Edition
ISBN 978-3-8382-0368-3

115 Jussi Lassila
The Quest for an Ideal Youth in Putin's Russia II
The Search for Distinctive Conformism in the Political Communication of Nashi, 2005-2009
With a foreword by Kirill Postoutenko
Second, Revised and Expanded Edition
ISBN 978-3-8382-0415-4

116 Valerio Trabandt
Neue Nachbarn, gute Nachbarschaft?
Die EU als internationaler Akteur am Beispiel ihrer Demokratieförderung in Belarus und der Ukraine 2004-2009
Mit einem Vorwort von Jutta Joachim
ISBN 978-3-8382-0437-6

117 **Fabian Pfeiffer**
Estlands Außen- und Sicherheitspolitik I
Der estnische Atlantizismus nach der
wiedererlangten Unabhängigkeit 1991-2004
Mit einem Vorwort von Helmut Hubel
ISBN 978-3-8382-0127-6

118 **Jana Podßuweit**
Estlands Außen- und Sicherheitspolitik II
Handlungsoptionen eines Kleinstaates im
Rahmen seiner EU-Mitgliedschaft (2004-2008)
Mit einem Vorwort von Helmut Hubel
ISBN 978-3-8382-0440-6

119 **Karin Pointner**
Estlands Außen- und Sicherheitspolitik III
Eine gedächtnispolitische Analyse estnischer
Entwicklungskooperation 2006-2010
Mit einem Vorwort von Karin Liebhart
ISBN 978-3-8382-0435-2

120 **Ruslana Vovk**
Die Offenheit der ukrainischen
Verfassung für das Völkerrecht und
die europäische Integration
Mit einem Vorwort von Alexander
Blankenagel
ISBN 978-3-8382-0481-9

121 **Mykhaylo Banakh**
Die Relevanz der Zivilgesellschaft
bei den postkommunistischen
Transformationsprozessen in mittel-
und osteuropäischen Ländern
Das Beispiel der spät- und postsowjetischen
Ukraine 1986-2009
Mit einem Vorwort von Gerhard Simon
ISBN 978-3-8382-0499-4

122 **Michael Moser**
Language Policy and the Discourse on
Languages in Ukraine under President
Viktor Yanukovych (25 February
2010–28 October 2012)
ISBN 978-3-8382-0497-0 (Paperback edition)
ISBN 978-3-8382-0507-6 (Hardcover edition)

123 **Nicole Krome**
Russischer Netzwerkkapitalismus
Restrukturierungsprozesse in der
Russischen Föderation am Beispiel des
Luftfahrtunternehmens "Aviastar"
Mit einem Vorwort von Petra Stykow
ISBN 978-3-8382-0534-2

124 **David R. Marples**
'Our Glorious Past'
Lukashenka's Belarus and
the Great Patriotic War
ISBN 978-3-8382-0574-8 (Paperback edition)
ISBN 978-3-8382-0675-2 (Hardcover edition)

125 **Ulf Walther**
Russlands "neuer Adel"
Die Macht des Geheimdienstes von
Gorbatschow bis Putin
Mit einem Vorwort von Hans-Georg Wieck
ISBN 978-3-8382-0584-7

126 **Simon Geissbühler (Hrsg.)**
Kiew – Revolution 3.0
Der Euromaidan 2013/14 und die
Zukunftsperspektiven der Ukraine
ISBN 978-3-8382-0581-6 (Paperback edition)
ISBN 978-3-8382-0681-3 (Hardcover edition)

127 **Andrey Makarychev**
Russia and the EU
in a Multipolar World
Discourses, Identities, Norms
With a foreword by Klaus Segbers
ISBN 978-3-8382-0629-5

128 **Roland Scharff**
Kasachstan als postsowjetischer
Wohlfahrtsstaat
Die Transformation des sozialen
Schutzsystems
Mit einem Vorwort von Joachim Ahrens
ISBN 978-3-8382-0622-6

129 **Katja Grupp**
Bild Lücke Deutschland
Kaliningrader Studierende sprechen über
Deutschland
Mit einem Vorwort von Martin Schulz
ISBN 978-3-8382-0552-6

130 **Konstantin Sheiko, Stephen Brown**
History as Therapy
Alternative History and Nationalist
Imaginings in Russia, 1991-2014
ISBN 978-3-8382-0665-3

131 **Elisa Kriza**
Alexander Solzhenitsyn: Cold War
Icon, Gulag Author, Russian
Nationalist?
A Study of the Western Reception of his
Literary Writings, Historical Interpretations,
and Political Ideas
With a foreword by Andrei Rogatchevski
ISBN 978-3-8382-0589-2 (Paperback edition)
ISBN 978-3-8382-0690-5 (Hardcover edition)

132 Serghei Golunov
    The Elephant in the Room
    Corruption and Cheating in Russian
    Universities
    ISBN 978-3-8382-0570-0

133 Manja Hussner, Rainer Arnold (Hgg.)
    Verfassungsgerichtsbarkeit in
    Zentralasien I
    Sammlung von Verfassungstexten
    ISBN 978-3-8382-0595-3

134 Nikolay Mitrokhin
    Die "Russische Partei"
    Die Bewegung der russischen Nationalisten in
    der UdSSR 1953-1985
    Aus dem Russischen übertragen von einem
    Übersetzerteam unter der Leitung von Larisa Schippel
    ISBN 978-3-8382-0024-8

135 Manja Hussner, Rainer Arnold (Hgg.)
    Verfassungsgerichtsbarkeit in
    Zentralasien II
    Sammlung von Verfassungstexten
    ISBN 978-3-8382-0597-7

136 Manfred Zeller
    Das sowjetische Fieber
    Fußballfans im poststalinistischen
    Vielvölkerreich
    Mit einem Vorwort von Nikolaus Katzer
    ISBN 978-3-8382-0757-5

137 Kristin Schreiter
    Stellung und Entwicklungspotential
    zivilgesellschaftlicher Gruppen in
    Russland
    Menschenrechtsorganisationen im Vergleich
    ISBN 978-3-8382-0673-8

138 David R. Marples, Frederick V. Mills
    (eds.)
    Ukraine's Euromaidan
    Analyses of a Civil Revolution
    ISBN 978-3-8382-0660-8

139 Bernd Kappenberg
    Setting Signs for Europe
    Why Diacritics Matter for
    European Integration
    With a foreword by Peter Schlobinski
    ISBN 978-3-8382-0663-9

140 René Lenz
    Internationalisierung, Kooperation
    und Transfer
    Externe bildungspolitische Akteure in der
    Russischen Föderation
    Mit einem Vorwort von Frank Ettrich
    ISBN 978-3-8382-0751-3

141 Juri Plusnin, Yana Zausaeva, Natalia
    Zhidkevich, Artemy Pozanenko
    Wandering Workers
    Mores, Behavior, Way of Life, and Political
    Status of Domestic Russian Labor Migrants
    Translated by Julia Kazantseva
    ISBN 978-3-8382-0653-0

142 David J. Smith (eds.)
    Latvia – A Work in Progress?
    100 Years of State- and Nation-Building
    ISBN 978-3-8382-0648-6

143 Инна Чувычкина (ред.)
    Экспортные нефте- и газопроводы
    на постсоветском пространстве
    Анализ трубопроводной политики в свете
    теории международных отношений
    ISBN 978-3-8382-0822-0

144 Johann Zajaczkowski
    Russland – eine pragmatische
    Großmacht?
    Eine rollentheoretische Untersuchung
    russischer Außenpolitik am Beispiel der
    Zusammenarbeit mit den USA nach 9/11 und
    des Georgienkrieges von 2008
    Mit einem Vorwort von Siegfried Schieder
    ISBN 978-3-8382-0837-4

145 Boris Popivanov
    Changing Images of the Left in
    Bulgaria
    The Challenge of Post-Communism in the
    Early 21st Century
    ISBN 978-3-8382-0667-7

146 Lenka Krátká
    A History of the Czechoslovak Ocean
    Shipping Company 1948-1989
    How a Small, Landlocked Country Ran
    Maritime Business During the Cold War
    ISBN 978-3-8382-0666-0

147 Alexander Sergunin
    Explaining Russian Foreign Policy
    Behavior
    Theory and Practice
    ISBN 978-3-8382-0752-0

148 Darya Malyutina
     Migrant Friendships in a Super-Diverse City
     Russian-Speakers and their Social Relationships in London in the 21st Century
     With a foreword by Claire Dwyer
     ISBN 978-3-8382-0652-3

149 Alexander Sergunin, Valery Konyshev
     Russia in the Arctic
     Hard or Soft Power?
     ISBN 978-3-8382-0753-7

150 John J. Maresca
     Helsinki Revisited
     A Key U.S. Negotiator's Memoirs on the Development of the CSCE into the OSCE
     With a foreword by Hafiz Pashayev
     ISBN 978-3-8382-0852-7

151 Jardar Østbø
     The New Third Rome
     Readings of a Russian Nationalist Myth
     With a foreword by Pål Kolstø
     ISBN 978-3-8382-0870-1

152 Simon Kordonsky
     Socio-Economic Foundations of the Russian Post-Soviet Regime
     The Resource-Based Economy and Estate-Based Social Structure of Contemporary Russia
     With a foreword by Svetlana Barsukova
     ISBN 978-3-8382-0775-9

153 Duncan Leitch
     Assisting Reform in Post-Communist Ukraine 2000–2012
     The Illusions of Donors and the Disillusion of Beneficiaries
     With a foreword by Kataryna Wolczuk
     ISBN 978-3-8382-0844-2

154 Abel Polese
     Limits of a Post-Soviet State
     How Informality Replaces, Renegotiates, and Reshapes Governance in Contemporary Ukraine
     With a foreword by Colin Williams
     ISBN 978-3-8382-0845-9

155 Mikhail Suslov (ed.)
     Digital Orthodoxy in the Post-Soviet World
     The Russian Orthodox Church and Web 2.0
     With a foreword by Father Cyril Hovorun
     ISBN 978-3-8382-0871-8

156 Leonid Luks
     Zwei „Sonderwege"? Russisch-deutsche Parallelen und Kontraste (1917-2014)
     Vergleichende Essays
     ISBN 978-3-8382-0823-7

157 Vladimir V. Karacharovskiy, Ovsey I. Shkaratan, Gordey A. Yastrebov
     Towards a New Russian Work Culture
     Can Western Companies and Expatriates Change Russian Society?
     With a foreword by Elena N. Danilova
     Translated by Julia Kazantseva
     ISBN 978-3-8382-0902-9

158 Edmund Griffiths
     Aleksandr Prokhanov and Post-Soviet Esotericism
     ISBN 978-3-8382-0903-6

159 Timm Beichelt, Susann Worschech (eds.)
     Transnational Ukraine?
     Networks and Ties that Influence(d) Contemporary Ukraine
     ISBN 978-3-8382-0944-9

160 Mieste Hotopp-Riecke
     Die Tataren der Krim zwischen Assimilation und Selbstbehauptung
     Der Aufbau des krimtatarischen Bildungswesens nach Deportation und Heimkehr (1990-2005)
     Mit einem Vorwort von Swetlana Czerwonnaja
     ISBN 978-3-89821-940-2

161 Olga Bertelsen (ed.)
     Revolution and War in Contemporary Ukraine
     The Challenge of Change
     ISBN 978-3-8382-1016-2

162 Natalya Ryabinska
     Ukraine's Post-Communist Mass Media
     Between Capture and Commercialization
     With a foreword by Marta Dyczok
     ISBN 978-3-8382-1011-7

163 Alexandra Cotofana,
James M. Nyce (eds.)
Religion and Magic in Socialist and
Post-Socialist Contexts I
Historic and Ethnographic Case Studies of
Orthodoxy, Heterodoxy, and Alternative
Spirituality
With a foreword by Patrick L. Michelson
ISBN 978-3-8382-0989-0

164 Nozima Akhrarkhodjaeva
The Instrumentalisation of Mass
Media in Electoral Authoritarian
Regimes
Evidence from Russia's Presidential Election
Campaigns of 2000 and 2008
ISBN 978-3-8382-1013-1

165 Yulia Krasheninnikova
Informal Healthcare in Contemporary
Russia
Sociographic Essays on the Post-Soviet
Infrastructure for Alternative Healing
Practices
ISBN 978-3-8382-0970-8

166 Peter Kaiser
Das Schachbrett der Macht
Die Handlungsspielräume eines sowjetischen
Funktionärs unter Stalin am Beispiel des
Generalsekretärs des Komsomol
Aleksandr Kosarev (1929-1938)
Mit einem Vorwort von Dietmar Neutatz
ISBN 978-3-8382-1052-0

167 Oksana Kim
The Effects and Implications of
Kazakhstan's Adoption of
International Financial Reporting
Standards
A Resource Dependence Perspective
With a foreword by Svetlana Vlady
ISBN 978-3-8382-0987-6

168 Anna Sanina
Patriotic Education in
Contemporary Russia
Sociological Studies in the Making of the
Post-Soviet Citizen
With a foreword by Anna Oldfield
ISBN 978-3-8382-0993-7

169 Rudolf Wolters
Spezialist in Sibirien
Faksimile der 1933 erschienenen
ersten Ausgabe
Mit einem Vorwort von Dmitrij Chmelnizki
ISBN 978-3-8382-0515-1

170 Michal Vít,
Magdalena M. Baran (eds.)
Transregional versus National
Perspectives on Contemporary Central
European History
Studies on the Building of Nation-States and
Their Cooperation in the 20th and 21st Century
With a foreword by Petr Vágner
ISBN 978-3-8382-1015-5

171 Philip Gamaghelyan
Conflict Resolution Beyond the
International Relations Paradigm
Evolving Designs as a Transformative
Practice in Nagorno-Karabakh and Syria
With a foreword by Susan Allen
ISBN 978-3-8382-1057-5

172 Maria Shagina
Joining a Prestigious Club
Cooperation with Europarties and Its Impact
on Party Development in Georgia, Moldova,
and Ukraine 2004–2015
With a foreword by Kataryna Wolczuk
ISBN 978-3-8382-1084-1

173 Alexandra Cotofana,
James M. Nyce (eds.)
Religion and Magic in Socialist and
Post-Socialist Contexts II
Baltic, Eastern European, and Post-USSR
Case Studies
With a foreword by Anita Stasulane
ISBN 978-3-8382-0990-6

174 Barbara Kunz
Kind Words, Cruise Missiles, and
Everything in Between
The Use of Power Resources in U.S. Policies
towards Poland, Ukraine, and Belarus
1989–2008
With a foreword by William Hill
ISBN 978-3-8382-1065-0

175 Eduard Klein
Bildungskorruption in Russland und
der Ukraine
Eine komparative Analyse der Performanz
staatlicher Antikorruptionsmaßnahmen im
Hochschulsektor am Beispiel universitärer
Aufnahmeprüfungen
Mit einem Vorwort von Heiko Pleines
ISBN 978-3-8382-0995-1

177 Anton Oleinik
Building Ukraine from Within
A Sociological, Institutional, and Economic
Analysis of a Nation-State in the Making
ISBN 978-3-8382-1150-3

178 *Peter Rollberg,*
Marlene Laruelle (eds.)
Mass Media in the Post-Soviet World
Market Forces, State Actors, and Political
Manipulation in the Informational
Environment after Communism
ISBN 978-3-8382-1116-9

179 *Mikhail Minakov*
Development and Dystopia
Studies in post-Soviet Ukraine and Eastern
Europe
With a foreword by Alexander Etkind
ISBN 978-3-8382-1112-1

180 *Aijan Sharshenova*
The European Union's Democracy Promotion in Central Asia
A Study of Political Interests, Influence, and
Development in Kazakhstan and Kyrgyzstan
in 2007–2013
With a foreword by Gordon Crawford
ISBN 978-3-8382-1151-0

181 *Andrey Makarychev,*
Alexandra Yatsyk (eds.)
Boris Nemtsov and Russian Politics
Power and Resistance
With a foreword by Zhanna Nemtsova
ISBN 978-3-8382-1122-0

***ibidem**.eu*

Zeitfracht Medien GmbH
Ferdinand-Jühlke-Straße 7,
99095 - DE, Erfurt
produktsicherheit@zeitfracht.de